CW00553181

Mental Health (Care and Treatment) (Scotland) Act 2003

2003 asp 13

CONTENTS

CHAPTER 3

COMPULSORY TREATMENT ORDERS: CARE PLAN

CHAPTER 4

REVIEW OF ORDERS

Mandatory reviews by responsible medical officer

Revocation of order by responsible medical officer or Commission

Further steps to be taken where order not revoked

Extension of order by responsible medical officer

Extension and variation of order: application by responsible medical officer

Variation of order: application by responsible medical officer

Recorded matters: reference to Tribunal by responsible medical officer

Reference to Tribunal by Commission

Applications by patient etc.

PART 9

COMPULSION ORDERS

CHAPTER 1

DUTIES FOLLOWING MAKING OF ORDER

CHAPTER 2

REVIEW OF COMPULSION ORDERS

Mandatory reviews by responsible medical officer

Revocation of order by responsible medical officer or Commission

Further steps to be taken where order not revoked

Extension of order following first review

Extension of order following further review

Extension and variation of order

Variation of order

PART 10

COMPULSION ORDERS AND RESTRICTION ORDERS

CHAPTER 1

PRELIMINARY

CHAPTER 2

REVIEW OF ORDERS

Annual review of orders

Consequences of annual review

Responsible medical officer's duty to keep orders under review

Reference to Tribunal by Scottish Ministers

Scottish Ministers' duty to keep orders under review

Application by patient etc.

Proceedings before Tribunal

Effect of modification or revocation of orders

Meaning of "modify"

PART 17

PATIENT REPRESENTATION ETC.

CHAPTER 1

NAMED PERSON

CHAPTER 2

ADVOCACY ETC.

Advocacy

Information

Access to medical practitioner

CHAPTER 3

DETENTION IN CONDITIONS OF EXCESSIVE SECURITY

State hospitals

Other hospitals

Enforcement: civil proceedings

Interpretation of Chapter

PART 18

MISCELLANEOUS

Code of practice

Advance statements

Education

Parental relations

PART 19

ENTRY, REMOVAL AND DETENTION POWERS

PART 20

ABSCONDING

Absconding

Effect of unauthorised absence

Patients from other jurisdictions

Absconding by certain other patients

PART 21

OFFENCES

PART 22

APPEALS

PART 23

GENERAL

Mental Health (Care and Treatment) (Scotland) Act 2003

2003 asp 13

The Bill for this Act of the Scottish Parliament was passed by the Parliament on 20th March 2003 and received Royal Assent on 25th April 2003

An Act of the Scottish Parliament to restate and amend the law relating to mentally disordered persons; and for connected purposes.

PART 1

INTRODUCTORY

1   Principles for discharging certain functions

(1)   Subsections (2) to (4) below apply whenever a person who does not fall within subsection (7) below is discharging a function by virtue of this Act in relation to a patient who has attained the age of 18 years.

(2)   In discharging the function the person shall, subject to subsection (9) below, have regard to the matters mentioned in subsection (3) below in so far as they are relevant to the function being discharged.

(3)   The matters referred to in subsection (2) above are—

    (a)   the present and past wishes and feelings of the patient which are relevant to the discharge of the function;

    (b)   the views of—

        (i)   the patient's named person;

        (ii)   any carer of the patient;

        (iii) any guardian of the patient; and

        (iv)   any welfare attorney of the patient,

    which are relevant to the discharge of the function;

    (c)   the importance of the patient participating as fully as possible in the discharge of the function;

    (d)   the importance of providing such information and support to the patient as is necessary to enable the patient to participate in accordance with paragraph (c) above;

      (e) the range of options available in the patient's case;

      (f) the importance of providing the maximum benefit to the patient;

      (g) the need to ensure that, unless it can be shown that it is justified in the circumstances, the patient is not treated in a way that is less favourable than the way in which a person who is not a patient might be treated in a comparable situation;

      (h) the patient's abilities, background and characteristics, including, without prejudice to that generality, the patient's age, sex, sexual orientation, religious persuasion, racial origin, cultural and linguistic background and membership of any ethnic group.

(4)   After having regard to—

      (a) the matters mentioned in subsection (3) above;

      (b) if subsections (5) and (6) below apply, the matters mentioned there; and

      (c) such other matters as are relevant in the circumstances,

the person shall discharge the function in the manner that appears to the person to be the manner that involves the minimum restriction on the freedom of the patient that is necessary in the circumstances.

(5)   Whenever a person who does not fall within subsection (7) below is discharging a function by virtue of this Act (other than the making of a decision about medical treatment) in relation to a patient, the person shall have regard, in so far as it is reasonable and practicable to do so, to—

      (a) the needs and circumstances of any carer of the patient which are relevant to the discharge of the function and of which the person is aware; and

      (b) the importance of providing such information to any carer of the patient as might assist the carer to care for the patient.

(6)   Whenever a person who does not fall within subsection (7) below is discharging a function by virtue of this Act in relation to a person who is, or has been, subject to—

      (a) detention in hospital authorised by a certificate granted under section 36(1) of this Act (any such certificate being referred to in this Act as an "emergency detention certificate");

      (b) detention in hospital authorised by a certificate granted under section 44(1) of this Act (any such certificate being referred to in this Act as a "short-term detention certificate");

      (c) an order made under section 64(4)(a) of this Act (any such order being referred to in this Act as a "compulsory treatment order"); or

      (d) an order made under section 57A(2) of the 1995 Act (any such order being referred to in this Act as a "compulsion order"),

the person who is discharging the function shall have regard to the importance of the provision of appropriate services to the person who is, or has been, subject to the certificate or order concerned (including, without prejudice to that generality, the provision of continuing care when the person is no longer subject to the certificate or order).

(7)   A person falls within this subsection if the person is discharging the function by virtue of being—

    (a) the patient;

    (b) the patient's named person;

    (c) the patient's primary carer;

    (d) a person providing independent advocacy services to the patient under section 259 of this Act;

    (e) the patient's legal representative;

    (f) a curator *ad litem* appointed by the Tribunal in respect of the patient;

    (g) a guardian of the patient; or

    (h) a welfare attorney of the patient.

(8) In subsection (3)(a) above, the reference to wishes and feelings of the patient is a reference to those wishes and feelings in so far as they can be ascertained by any means of communication, whether human or by mechanical aid (whether of an interpretative nature or otherwise), appropriate to the patient.

(9) The person need not have regard to the views of a person mentioned in subsection (3)(b) above in so far as it is unreasonable or impracticable to do so.

(10) In subsection (3)(d) above, the reference to information is to information in the form that is mostly likely to be understood by the patient.

(11) In this section, a reference to "discharging", in relation to a power, includes a reference to exercising the power by taking no action; and "discharge" shall be construed accordingly.

2   Welfare of the child

(1) This section applies whenever a person who does not fall within section 1(7) of this Act is discharging a function, by virtue of this Act, to which subsection (2) or (3) below applies in relation to a patient who is under the age of 18 years.

(2) This subsection applies to any duty which may be discharged in more than one manner.

(3) This subsection applies to any power.

(4) The person shall discharge the function in the manner that appears to the person to be the manner that best secures the welfare of the patient.

(5) In determining the manner of discharging the function that best secures the welfare of the patient, the person shall have regard to—

    (a) the matters mentioned in section 1(3) of this Act;

    (b) the matters mentioned in section 1(5) and (6) of this Act (where those subsections apply); and

    (c) the importance of the function being discharged in the manner that appears to the person to be the manner that involves the minimum restriction on the freedom of the patient that is necessary in the circumstances.

(6) Subsections (8) to (10) of section 1 of this Act shall apply for the purpose of subsection (5)(a) above as they apply in relation to subsection (3) of that section.

(7) In this section, a reference to "discharging", in relation to a power, includes a reference to exercising the power by taking no action; and "discharge" shall be construed accordingly.

3   **Equal opportunities**

(1)   Subsection (2) below applies whenever a person mentioned in subsection (3) below is discharging a function by virtue of this Act.

(2)   The person shall discharge the function in a manner that encourages equal opportunities and in particular the observance of the equal opportunity requirements.

(3)   The persons referred to in subsection (1) above are—

      (a)   the Scottish Ministers;

      (b)   the Commission;

      (c)   a local authority;

      (d)   a Health Board;

      (e)   a Special Health Board;

      (f)   a National Health Service trust;

      (g)   the managers of a hospital;

      (h)   a mental health officer;

      (i)   a patient's responsible medical officer;

      (j)   a medical practitioner; and

      (k)   a nurse.

(4)   In this section "equal opportunities" and "equal opportunity requirements" have the same meanings as in Section L2 of Part II of Schedule 5 to the Scotland Act 1998 (c.46).

PART 2

THE MENTAL WELFARE COMMISSION FOR SCOTLAND

Continued existence of Commission

4   **The Mental Welfare Commission for Scotland**

(1)   There shall continue to be a body corporate known as the Mental Welfare Commission for Scotland (in this Act referred to as "the Commission").

(2)   The Commission shall discharge such functions as are conferred on it by virtue of—

      (a)   this Act;

      (b)   the Adults with Incapacity (Scotland) Act 2000 (asp 4); and

      (c)   any other enactment.

(3)   Schedule 1 to this Act (which makes provision as respects the Commission) shall have effect.

General duties

5   **Duty to monitor operation of Act and promote best practice**

The Commission shall—

      (a)   monitor the operation of this Act; and

    (b) promote best practice in relation to the operation of this Act (including, without prejudice to that generality, the observance of Part 1 of this Act).

6   Reporting on operation of Act

The Commission shall bring to the attention of the Scottish Ministers such matters concerning the operation of this Act as the Commission considers ought to be brought to their attention.

Particular functions

7   Duty to bring matters generally to attention of Scottish Ministers and others

The Commission shall bring to the attention of—

    (a) the Scottish Ministers;

    (b) a local authority;

    (c) a Health Board;

    (d) a Special Health Board;

    (e) a National Health Service trust;

    (f) the Scottish Commission for the Regulation of Care; or

    (g) such other person, or group of persons, as it considers appropriate,

any matter of general interest or concern as respects the welfare of any persons who have a mental disorder which is a matter that the Commission considers ought to be brought to their attention.

8   Duty to bring specific matters to attention of Scottish Ministers and others etc.

(1)   If it appears to the Commission that a relevant person has, or may have, powers or duties, the exercise or performance of which might prevent or remedy or assist in preventing or remedying, as respects a person who has a mental disorder, any of the circumstances mentioned in subsection (2) below, the Commission shall—

    (a) bring the facts of the person's case to the attention of the relevant person; and

    (b) if it considers it appropriate to do so, make recommendations as respects the case to the relevant person.

(2)   Those circumstances are—

    (a) the circumstances mentioned in section 11(2)(a), (d), (e) or (f) of this Act;

    (b) that—

        (i) the patient is detained in hospital and the detention is authorised by virtue of this Act or the 1995 Act; and

        (ii) there may be some impropriety in relation to that detention.

(3)   For the purposes of subsection (1) above, "relevant person" means—

    (a) the Scottish Ministers;

    (b) the Public Guardian;

    (c) a local authority;

(d) a Health Board;

(e) a Special Health Board;

(f) a National Health Service trust;

(g) a mental health officer;

(h) a responsible medical officer;

(i) the managers of a registered care service;

(j) the managers of—

    (i) a prison; or

    (ii) a young offenders institution;

(k) the Scottish Commission for the Regulation of Care;

(l) a police force; or

(m) such other person, or group of persons, as the Commission considers appropriate.

(4) In subsection (3)(i) above, "registered care service" means a care service registered under Part 1 of the Regulation of Care (Scotland) Act 2001 (asp 8).

9   Duty to give advice

(1) The Commission shall give advice to any person mentioned in subsection (2) below on any matter arising out of this Act which has been referred to the Commission, with its agreement, by that person.

(2) Those persons are—

(a) the Scottish Ministers;

(b) a local authority;

(c) a Health Board;

(d) a Special Health Board;

(e) the Scottish Commission for the Regulation of Care; or

(f) the Scottish Public Services Ombudsman.

10   Publishing information, guidance etc.

(1) Subject to subsection (2) below, the Commission may publish information or guidance about any matter relevant to its functions and, without prejudice to that generality, may publish information or guidance as respects—

(a) its conclusions in relation to—

    (i) an investigation under section 11(1) of this Act; or

    (ii) an inquiry under section 12(1) of this Act;

(b) its conclusions in relation to any action taken (or not taken) in relation to such conclusions; or

(c) matters which it considers arise or come to light (or have arisen or come to light) in the course of—

    (i) such investigations or inquiries; or

        (ii)   visits under section 13(1) or (3) of this Act.

(2)   The Commission may, with the agreement of a person mentioned in subsection (2) of section 9 of this Act, publish advice which it gives under subsection (1) of that section to that person.

11   Investigations

(1)   If it appears to the Commission that any of the circumstances mentioned in subsection (2) below apply in respect of a patient, the Commission may—

    (a)   carry out such investigation as it considers appropriate into the patient's case; and

    (b)   make such recommendations as it considers appropriate as respects the case.

(2)   Those circumstances are—

    (a)   that the patient may be unlawfully detained in hospital;

    (b)   that the patient is detained in hospital and the detention is authorised by virtue of—

        (i)   this Act; or

        (ii)   the 1995 Act;

    (c)   that the patient, though not detained in hospital, is subject to—

        (i)   a compulsory treatment order;

        (ii)   an interim compulsory treatment order;

        (iii) an emergency detention certificate;

        (iv) a short-term detention certificate;

        (v)   a compulsion order;

        (vi) an interim compulsion order;

        (vii) an assessment order;

        (viii)a treatment order;

        (ix) a hospital direction; or

        (x)   a transfer for treatment direction;

    (d)   that the patient may be, or may have been, subject, or exposed, to—

        (i)   ill-treatment;

        (ii)   neglect; or

        (iii) some other deficiency in care or treatment;

    (e)   that, because of the mental disorder, the patient's property—

        (i)   may be suffering, or may have suffered, loss or damage; or

        (ii)   may be, or may have been, at risk of suffering loss or damage;

    (f)   that the patient may be—

        (i)   living alone or without care; and

        (ii)   unable to look after himself or his property or financial affairs.

12   Investigations: further provision

(1)   The Commission may, if it considers it appropriate to do so, cause an inquiry to be held for the purpose of carrying out an investigation, under section 11(1) of this Act, into any case.

(2)   The Commission—

     (a)   may appoint such person (or persons) as it considers appropriate to chair or to conduct any such inquiry and to report to it on the findings of any such inquiry; and

     (b)   may pay to a person appointed by it under paragraph (a) above such—

         (i)   remuneration; and

         (ii)   expenses,

     as it may, with the consent of the Scottish Ministers, determine.

(3)   A person appointed to chair any such inquiry—

     (a)   may, by notice, require any person to attend and give evidence at a time and place set out in the notice; and

     (b)   may administer oaths and examine witnesses on oath and may accept, in place of evidence on oath by a person, evidence on affirmation or a statement in writing by the person.

(4)   A person required, by virtue of notice under subsection (3)(a) above, to attend and give evidence for the purposes of an inquiry under subsection (1) above—

     (a)   shall not be obliged to attend and give evidence as required in the notice unless the necessary expenses of attendance are paid or tendered to the person; and

     (b)   shall not be obliged at the inquiry to answer a question which the person would be entitled to decline to answer, on the ground of privilege or confidentiality, if the question were asked in the course of proceedings in a court.

(5)   Proceedings in an inquiry under this section shall have the privilege of proceedings in a court.

(6)   The Commission shall pay to a person required by notice under subsection (3)(a) above to attend for the purposes of an inquiry under subsection (1) above such expenses as it considers appropriate.

(7)   A person—

     (a)   who is required to attend for the purposes of an inquiry by virtue of notice under subsection (3)(a) above; and

     (b)   who refuses or wilfully neglects to attend or, subject to subsection (4)(b) above, to give evidence,

     shall be guilty of an offence and liable, on summary conviction, to a fine not exceeding level 3 on the standard scale.

13   Visits in relation to patients

(1)   The Commission shall secure that a person authorised by it visits, as often as the Commission considers it appropriate to do so, such patients who fall within the categories mentioned in subsection (2) below as it considers appropriate.

(2)   Those categories are—

    (a)   patients who are detained in hospital and whose detention is authorised by virtue of—

        (i)   this Act; or

        (ii)   the 1995 Act;

    (b)   patients who, though not detained in hospital, are subject to—

        (i)   a compulsory treatment order;

        (ii)   an interim compulsory treatment order;

        (iii) an emergency detention certificate;

        (iv)   a short-term detention certificate;

        (v)   a compulsion order;

        (vi)   an interim compulsion order;

        (vii) an assessment order;

        (viii) a treatment order;

        (ix)   a hospital direction; or

        (x)   a transfer for treatment direction;

    (c)   patients who are subject to—

        (i)   an intervention order of which the Commission has been notified under section 53(10)(b) of the Adults with Incapacity (Scotland) Act 2000 (asp 4); or

        (ii)   a guardianship order of which the Commission has been notified under section 58(7)(d) of that Act;

    (d)   patients in respect of whom a person is a guardian by virtue of sub-paragraph (4), (5), (6) or (7) of paragraph 1 of schedule 4 to the Adults with Incapacity (Scotland) Act 2000 (asp 4); and

    (e)   patients who have granted, in accordance with section 16 of that Act, a welfare power of attorney, a copy of which has been sent to the Commission under section 19(2)(c) of that Act.

(3)   If it appears to the Commission that patients—

    (a)   may be resident, or may be receiving medical treatment, in premises mentioned in subsection (4) below; or

    (b)   may use facilities provided in such premises,

a person authorised by the Commission may visit such premises for either of the purposes mentioned in subsection (5) below.

(4)   Those premises are—

    (a)   a health service hospital (as defined in section 108(1) of the National Health Service (Scotland) Act 1978 (c.29));

    (b)   premises in which—

        (i)   an independent health care service is provided;

> > (ii)   a care home service is provided; or
>
> > (iii)   a secure accommodation service is provided;
>
> (c)   premises provided by a local authority for the purpose of their duty under section 26 of this Act;
>
> (d)   a prison; and
>
> (e)   a young offenders institution.

(5)   The purposes are—

> (a)   to inspect such premises or the facilities available in such premises; and
>
> (b)   to provide an opportunity for any patients who may be present in the premises at the time when the visit takes place to meet representatives of the Commission and to discuss with such representatives any concerns that such patients may have.

(6)   A visit under subsection (1) or (3) above may be made with or without prior notification.

(7)   A person proposing to conduct a visit under subsection (1) or (3) above shall, if requested to do so, produce an authenticated document showing that the Commission has given the requisite authority for the visit.

(8)   In—

> (a)   subsection (4)(b)(ii) above, "care home service" has the meaning given to that expression by section 2(3) of the Regulation of Care (Scotland) Act 2001 (asp 8); and
>
> (b)   subsection (4)(b)(iii) above, "secure accommodation service" has the meaning given to that expression by section 2(9) of that Act.

14   Interviews

(1)   A person authorised to do so by the Commission (an "authorised person") may, in connection with the discharge by the Commission of any of its functions under this Act or the Adults with Incapacity (Scotland) Act 2000 (asp 4)—

> (a)   interview—
>
> > (i)   any patient; or
>
> > (ii)   any other person that the authorised person considers it appropriate to interview; and
>
> (b)   require any such interview to be conducted in private.

(2)   Without prejudice to the generality of subsection (1) above—

> (a)   an authorised person conducting a visit under subsection (1) of section 13 of this Act shall afford an opportunity, on request, during the visit, to—
>
> > (i)   the patient who is the subject of the visit; and
>
> > (ii)   other patients whose presence in the premises where the visit takes place is known to the authorised person,
>
> to be interviewed in private by the authorised person; and

    (b)   an authorised person conducting a visit under subsection (3) of that section shall afford an opportunity, on request, during the visit, to patients whose presence in the premises that are being visited is known to the authorised person, to be so interviewed.

(3)   An authorised person proposing to interview a person under subsection (1) or (2) above shall, if requested to do so, produce an authenticated document showing that the Commission has given the requisite authority for the purposes of this section.

15   Medical examination

(1)   A person authorised by the Commission (an "authorised person") may, in connection with the discharge by the Commission of any of its functions under—

    (a)   this Act; or

    (b)   the Adults with Incapacity (Scotland) Act 2000 (asp 4),

carry out in private a medical examination of a patient.

(2)   An authorised person shall be—

    (a)   a medical commissioner; or

    (b)   a member of staff of the Commission who has such qualifications and experience, and has undertaken such training, as may be prescribed by regulations.

(3)   An authorised person proposing to exercise the power conferred by subsection (1) above shall, if requested to do so, produce an authenticated document showing that the Commission has given the requisite authority for the purposes of this section.

16   Inspection etc. of records

(1)   A person authorised by the Commission (an "authorised person") may, in connection with the discharge by the Commission of any of its functions under—

    (a)   this Act; or

    (b)   the Adults with Incapacity (Scotland) Act 2000 (asp 4),

require any person holding medical or other records of a patient to produce them for inspection by the authorised person.

(2)   An authorised person shall be—

    (a)   a member of the Commission; or

    (b)   a member of the staff of the Commission.

(3)   An authorised person proposing to exercise the power conferred by subsection (1) above shall, if requested to do so, produce an authenticated document showing that the authorised person is a member of the Commission or, as the case may be, a member of staff of the Commission.

17   Duties of Scottish Ministers, local authorities and others as respects Commission

(1)   The persons mentioned in subsection (2) below shall afford the Commission, or a person authorised by the Commission, all facilities necessary to enable the Commission, or that person, to discharge the Commission's, or (as the case may be) that person's, functions under this Act.

(2)   Those persons are—

    (a)   the Scottish Ministers;

    (b)   a local authority;

    (c)   a Health Board;

    (d)   a Special Health Board;

    (e)   a National Health Service trust;

    (f)   a police force;

    (g)   the managers of a registered care service;

    (h)   the managers of—

        (i)   a prison; or

        (ii)   a young offenders institution;

    (i)   the Scottish Commission for the Regulation of Care;

    (j)   the Scottish Public Services Ombudsman; and

    (k)   such other persons as may be prescribed by regulations.

(3)   In subsection (2)(g) above, "registered care service" has the meaning given by section 8(4) of this Act.

18   Annual report

(1)   The Commission shall, as soon as practicable after the end of each financial year of the Commission, submit to the Scottish Ministers, a report on the discharge of its functions during that year.

(2)   The Scottish Ministers shall lay before the Scottish Parliament a copy of each report submitted to them under subsection (1) above.

(3)   The financial year of the Commission is the period of 12 months ending with 31st March.

19   Statistical information

The Commission shall, in accordance with directions given to it by the Scottish Ministers, provide the Ministers with, and publish, statistical or other information relating to the discharge of its functions.

20   Protection from actions of defamation

(1)   For the purposes of the law of defamation, any statement made in pursuance of any of sections 6, 7 to 10 and 18(1) of this Act by the Commission, or any of its employees, shall be privileged unless such statement is shown to be made with malice.

(2)   In this section—

    "statement" has the same meaning as in the Defamation Act 1996 (c. 31); and

    "employees" shall be construed in accordance with paragraph 7 of schedule 1 to this Act.

PART 3

THE MENTAL HEALTH TRIBUNAL FOR SCOTLAND

21   The Mental Health Tribunal for Scotland

(1)   There shall be a tribunal to be known as the Mental Health Tribunal for Scotland (in this Act referred to as "the Tribunal").

(2)   The Tribunal shall discharge such functions as are conferred on it by virtue of this Act.

(3)   Regulations may make such provision in connection with the Tribunal as the Scottish Ministers consider appropriate.

(4)   Schedule 2 to this Act (which makes provision as respects the Tribunal and its proceedings) shall have effect.

PART 4

HEALTH BOARD AND LOCAL AUTHORITY FUNCTIONS

CHAPTER 1

HEALTH BOARD DUTIES

Approved medical practitioners

22   Approved medical practitioners

(1)   Subject to subsection (3) below, the persons mentioned in subsection (2) below shall each compile and maintain a list of medical practitioners who—

    (a)   have such qualifications and experience, and have undertaken such training, as may be specified in directions given by the Scottish Ministers; and

    (b)   are approved for the purposes of this paragraph by the Board concerned as having special experience in the diagnosis and treatment of mental disorder.

(2)   Those persons are—

    (a)   a Health Board; and

    (b)   the State Hospitals Board for Scotland.

(3)   A list compiled by a Health Board under subsection (1) above shall be compiled for its area.

(4)   A medical practitioner included for the time being in any list maintained under subsection (1) above is referred to in this Act as an "approved medical practitioner".

Services and accommodation: particular cases

23   Provision of services and accommodation for certain patients under 18

(1)   A Health Board shall provide for any child or young person who—

    (a)   is detained in hospital under Part 5 or 6 of this Act; or

    (b)   has been admitted to hospital, whether voluntarily or not, for the purposes of receiving treatment for a mental disorder,

14   *Mental Health (Care and Treatment) (Scotland) Act 2003 (asp 13)*
Part 4—Health Board and local authority functions
Chapter 2—Local authority functions

such services and accommodation as are sufficient for the particular needs of that child or young person.

(2)   In this section, "child or young person" means a person under the age of 18 years.

24   Provision of services and accommodation for certain mothers with post-natal depression

(1)   A Health Board shall provide for any woman who—

    (a) is the mother or adoptive mother of a child less than one year old;

    (b) cares for the child;

    (c) is not likely to endanger the health or welfare of the child; and

    (d) has been admitted to hospital, whether voluntarily or not, for the purposes of receiving treatment for post-natal depression,

such services and accommodation as are necessary to ensure that the woman is able, if she wishes, to care for the child in hospital.

(2)   Each Health Board shall collaborate with other Health Boards to whatever extent is necessary to fulfil its duty under subsection (1) above.

<h2 align="center">CHAPTER 2</h2>

LOCAL AUTHORITY FUNCTIONS

Provision of services

25   Care and support services etc.

(1)   A local authority—

    (a) shall—

        (i) provide, for persons who are not in hospital and who have or have had a mental disorder, services which provide care and support; or

        (ii) secure the provision of such services for such persons; and

    (b) may—

        (i) provide such services for persons who are in hospital and who have or have had a mental disorder; or

        (ii) secure the provision of such services for such persons.

(2)   Services provided by virtue of subsection (1) above shall be designed to—

    (a) minimise the effect of the mental disorder on such persons; and

    (b) give such persons the opportunity to lead lives which are as normal as possible.

(3)   In subsection (1) above, "care and support"—

    (a) includes, without prejudice to the generality of that expression—

        (i) residential accommodation; and

Mental Health (Care and Treatment) (Scotland) Act 2003 (asp 13) 15
Part 4—Health Board and local authority functions
Chapter 2—Local authority functions

   (ii)   personal care and personal support (each of those expressions having the meaning given by section 2(28) of the Regulation of Care (Scotland) Act 2001 (asp 8)); but

   (b)   does not include nursing care.

(4)   In section 59(1) of the Social Work (Scotland) Act 1968 (c.49) (duty of local authorities as respects provision and maintenance of residential or other establishments), for the words "or under" there shall be substituted "sections 25 and 26 of the Mental Health (Care and Treatment) (Scotland) Act 2003 (asp 13) or".

26   Services designed to promote well-being and social development

(1)   A local authority—

   (a)   shall—

      (i)   provide, for persons who are not in hospital and who have or have had a mental disorder, services which are designed to promote the well-being and social development of those persons; or

      (ii)   secure the provision of such services for such persons; and

   (b)   may—

      (i)   provide such services for persons who are in hospital and who have or have had a mental disorder; or

      (ii)   secure the provision of such services for such persons.

(2)   Services provided by virtue of subsection (1) above shall include, without prejudice to the generality of that subsection, services which provide—

   (a)   social, cultural and recreational activities;

   (b)   training for such of those persons as are over school age; and

   (c)   assistance for such of those persons as are over school age in obtaining and in undertaking employment.

(3)   Subsection (1) above is without prejudice to the operation of—

   (a)   section 1 of the Education (Scotland) Act 1980 (c.44) (duties and powers of education authorities in relation to the provision of social, cultural and recreative activities and vocational and industrial training); and

   (b)   section 1 of the Further and Higher Education (Scotland) Act 1992 (c.37) (duty of Scottish Ministers in relation to the provision of further education).

(4)   In subsection (2)(b) and (c) above, "school age" has the same meaning as in section 31 of the Education (Scotland) Act 1980 (c.44).

27   Assistance with travel

A local authority—

   (a)   shall—

16   *Mental Health (Care and Treatment) (Scotland) Act 2003 (asp 13)*
Part 4—Health Board and local authority functions
Chapter 2—Local authority functions

(i) provide, for persons who are not in hospital and who have or have had a mental disorder, such facilities for, or assistance in, travelling as the authority may consider necessary to enable those persons to attend or participate in any of the services mentioned in sections 25 and 26 of this Act; or

(ii) secure the provision of such facilities or assistance for such persons; and

(b) may—

(i) provide such facilities or assistance for persons who are in hospital and who have or have had a mental disorder; or

(ii) secure the provision of such facilities or assistance for such persons.

Charging for services

28   Services under sections 25 to 27: charging

(1) In section 87 of the Social Work (Scotland) Act 1968 (c.49) (charges that may be made for certain services)—

(a) in subsection (1), for the words from "section 7" to "Act 1984" there shall be substituted "section 25 (care and support services for persons who have or have had a mental disorder), 26 (services designed to promote well-being and social development of such persons) or 27 (assistance with travel in connection with such services) of the Mental Health (Care and Treatment) (Scotland) Act 2003 (asp 13)";

(b) in paragraph (a) of subsection (1A), for the words "section 7 or 8 of the said Act of 1984" there shall be substituted "section 25, 26 or 27 of the Mental Health (Care and Treatment) (Scotland) Act 2003 (asp 13)"; and

(c) in each of subsections (2), (3) and (4), for the words "section 7 of the said Act of 1984" there shall be substituted the words "section 25 of the Mental Health (Care and Treatment) (Scotland) Act 2003 (asp 13)".

(2) In—

(a) section 2 of the Community Care and Health (Scotland) Act 2002 (asp 5) (meaning of "accommodation" for purpose of certain enactments), for the words from "section 7" to "in relation to" there shall be substituted "section 25 of the 2003 Act (provision of care and support services etc. for"; and

(b) section 22(1) of that Act (interpretation)—

(i) the definition of "the 1984 Act" shall be repealed;

(ii) after the definition of "the 1995 Act", there shall be inserted—

""the 2003 Act" means the Mental Health (Care and Treatment) (Scotland) Act 2003 (asp 13);"; and

(iii) for paragraph (b) of the definition of "social care" there shall be substituted—

Mental Health (Care and Treatment) (Scotland) Act 2003 (asp 13)   17
Part 4—Health Board and local authority functions
Chapter 2—Local authority functions

      "(b) under section 25 (care and support services for persons who have or have had a mental disorder), 26 (services designed to promote well-being and social development of such persons) or 27 (assistance with travel in connection with such services) of the 2003 Act"; and

    (iv) in that definition, for the word "either" there shall be substituted "any".

Relationship with general duties

29 Relationship between duties under sections 25 to 27 and duties under Social Work (Scotland) Act 1968 and Children (Scotland) Act 1995

(1) The duties of a local authority under sections 25 to 27 of this Act are without prejudice to the duties imposed on them by the enactments mentioned in subsection (2) below as those duties apply in relation to persons who have or have had a mental disorder.

(2) Those enactments are—

    (a) sections 12(1) (provision of advice, guidance and assistance on an appropriate scale), 13A (provision of residential accommodation with nursing), 13B (provision of care and after-care) and 14 (provision of domiciliary and laundry services) of the Social Work (Scotland) Act 1968 (c.49); and

    (b) section 22(1) of the Children (Scotland) Act 1995 (c.36) (duty to provide services for children in need).

Co-operation and assistance

30 Co-operation with Health Boards and others

(1) In providing services for a person under any of sections 25 to 27 of this Act, a local authority shall co-operate with any—

    (a) Health Boards;

    (b) Special Health Boards;

    (c) National Health Service trusts; or

    (d) voluntary organisations,

that appear to the authority to have an interest, power or duty mentioned in subsection (2) below.

(2) Such an interest, power or duty is—

    (a) an interest in the provision of services by the local authority under any of sections 25 to 27 of this Act; or

    (b) a power or duty to provide or secure the provision of services, or an interest in the provision of services,

for the person.

31 Assistance from Health Boards and others

(1) Where it appears to a local authority that the assistance of a Health Board, a Special Health Board or a National Health Service trust—

18   *Mental Health (Care and Treatment) (Scotland) Act 2003 (asp 13)*
                  Part 4—Health Board and local authority functions
                                  Chapter 2—Local authority functions

(a) is necessary to enable the authority to perform any of their duties under section 25 or 26 of this Act; or

(b) would help the authority to perform any of those duties,

the authority may request the Health Board, Special Health Board or National Health Service trust to co-operate by providing the assistance specified in the request.

(2) A Health Board, a Special Health Board or a National Health Service trust receiving a request under subsection (1) above shall, if complying with the request—

(a) would be compatible with the discharge of its own functions (whether under any enactment or otherwise); and

(b) would not prejudice unduly the discharge by it of any of those functions,

comply with the request.

(3) This section is without prejudice to section 21 of the Children (Scotland) Act 1995 (c.36) (which enables a local authority to require assistance from a Health Board, a National Health Service trust or others in the exercise of the authority's functions under Part II of that Act).

Appointment of mental health officers

32   Appointment of mental health officers

(1) A local authority shall appoint a sufficient number of persons for the purpose of discharging, in relation to their area, the functions of mental health officers under—

(a) this Act;

(b) the 1995 Act; and

(c) the Adults with Incapacity (Scotland) Act 2000 (asp 4).

(2) A local authority shall appoint under subsection (1) above only persons—

(a) who are officers of a local authority; and

(b) who satisfy such requirements as the Scottish Ministers may direct as to—

(i)   registration;

(ii)   education and training;

(iii) experience;

(iv) competence as respects persons who have or have had a mental disorder; and

(v)   any other matters that may be specified in the direction.

(3) A person duly appointed by a local authority before the day on which this section comes into force to discharge the functions of a mental health officer shall, for the purposes of this Act, be deemed to have been appointed under subsection (1) above; and references in subsections (4) and (5) below to a person appointed under subsection (1) above shall include references to a person deemed by virtue of this subsection to have been so appointed.

Mental Health (Care and Treatment) (Scotland) Act 2003 (asp 13)   19
Part 4—Health Board and local authority functions
Chapter 2—Local authority functions

(4)   A local authority shall, in accordance with directions given by the Scottish Ministers, provide or secure the provision of training for persons appointed by them under subsection (1) above as respects requirements in directions under subsections (2) above and (5) below.

(5)   A local authority shall terminate the appointment of a person appointed under subsection (1) above if the person—

   (a)   ceases to be an officer of a local authority; or

   (b)   does not satisfy—

      (i)   any requirement in a direction under subsection (2) above; or

      (ii)   such other requirements as to any of the matters mentioned in paragraph (b) of that subsection as the Scottish Ministers may, from time to time, by direction specify.

(6)   The validity of any acts or omissions of a person appointed as a mental health officer in the discharge of the functions of such an officer prior to a termination of appointment by virtue of subsection (5) above is not affected by such termination.

(7)   Directions given by the Scottish Ministers under this section shall be given to local authorities collectively.

Duty to inquire into individual cases

33   Duty to inquire

(1)   Where it appears to a local authority that—

   (a)   a person in their area who is aged 16 years or over has a mental disorder; and

   (b)   any of the circumstances mentioned in subsection (2) below apply,

   the authority shall cause inquiries to be made into the person's case.

(2)   Those circumstances are—

   (a)   that the person may be, or may have been, subject, or exposed, at some place other than a hospital to—

      (i)   ill-treatment;

      (ii)   neglect; or

      (iii)   some other deficiency in care or treatment;

   (b)   that, because of the mental disorder, the person's property—

      (i)   may be suffering, or may have suffered, loss or damage; or

      (ii)   may be, or may have been, at risk of suffering loss or damage;

   (c)   that the person may be—

      (i)   living alone or without care; and

      (ii)   unable to look after himself or his property or financial affairs;

   (d)   that the person is not in hospital and, because of the mental disorder, the safety of some other person may be at risk.

20 *Mental Health (Care and Treatment) (Scotland) Act 2003 (asp 13)*
Part 4—Health Board and local authority functions
Chapter 2—Local authority functions

34   Inquiries under section 33: co-operation

(1)   This section applies where a local authority are required by section 33(1) of this Act to cause inquiries to be made into a person's case.

(2)   Where it appears to the local authority that the assistance of any of the persons mentioned in subsection (3) below—

    (a)   is necessary for the purposes of the inquiries; or

    (b)   would assist the inquiries,

the authority may request that person to provide the assistance specified in the request.

(3)   Those persons are—

    (a)   the Commission;

    (b)   the Public Guardian;

    (c)   the Scottish Commission for the Regulation of Care;

    (d)   a Health Board; and

    (e)   a National Health Service trust.

(4)   Where—

    (a)   a person receives a request under subsection (2) above; and

    (b)   complying with the request—

        (i)   would be compatible with the discharge of the person's functions (whether under any enactment or otherwise); and

        (ii)   would not prejudice unduly the discharge by the person of any of those functions,

the person shall comply with the request.

35   Inquiries under section 33: warrants

(1)   If a sheriff, or a justice of the peace, is satisfied by a relevant mental health officer's evidence on oath—

    (a)   that, for the purposes of inquiries under section 33 of this Act, it is necessary to enter premises; and

    (b)   that the mental health officer—

        (i)   is unable to obtain entry to those premises; or

        (ii)   reasonably apprehends that the mental health officer will be unable to obtain entry to those premises,

the sheriff or justice of the peace may grant a warrant under this subsection.

(2)   A warrant under subsection (1) above is a warrant—

    (a)   authorising—

        (i)   the mental health officer specified in the warrant;

        (ii)   any other persons so specified; and

Mental Health (Care and Treatment) (Scotland) Act 2003 (asp 13) 21
Part 4—Health Board and local authority functions
Chapter 2—Local authority functions

        (iii) any constable of the police force maintained for the area in which the premises are situated, .

before the expiry of the period of 8 days beginning with the day on which the warrant is granted, to enter, for the purposes of the inquiries, any premises so specified; and

  (b) authorising any such constable, before the expiry of that period, for the purpose of exercising the power mentioned in paragraph (a) above, to open lockfast places on premises so specified.

(3) An application for a warrant under subsection (1) above shall—

  (a) if made to the sheriff, be made to the sheriff of the sheriffdom; or

  (b) if made to a justice of the peace, be made to a justice for the commission area,

in which the premises to which the application relates are situated.

(4) If a sheriff, or a justice of the peace, is satisfied by a relevant mental health officer's evidence on oath—

  (a) that, for the purposes of inquiries under section 33 of this Act, it is necessary that a medical practitioner carry out a medical examination of the person who is the subject of the inquiries; and

  (b) that the mental health officer is unable to obtain the consent of that person to that matter,

the sheriff, or justice of the peace, may grant a warrant under this subsection.

(5) A warrant under subsection (4) above is a warrant authorising the detention of the person who is the subject of the inquiries for a period of 3 hours for the purposes of enabling a medical examination of the person to be carried out by the medical practitioner specified in the warrant.

(6) An application for a warrant under subsection (4) above shall—

  (a) if made to the sheriff, be made to the sheriff of the sheriffdom; or

  (b) if made to a justice of the peace, be made to a justice for the commission area,

in which the person who is the subject of the inquiries for the time being is.

(7) If a sheriff, or a justice of the peace, is satisfied by a relevant mental health officer's evidence on oath—

  (a) that, for the purposes of inquiries under section 33 of this Act, it is necessary that a medical practitioner have access to the person's medical records; and

  (b) that the mental health officer is unable to obtain the consent of that person to that matter,

the sheriff, or justice of the peace, may grant a warrant under this subsection.

(8) A warrant under subsection (7) above is a warrant requiring any person holding medical records of the person subject to the inquiries to produce them for inspection by the medical practitioner specified in the warrant on being required to do so by the practitioner.

(9) An application for a warrant under subsection (7) above shall—

  (a) if made to the sheriff, be made to the sheriff of the sheriffdom; or

(b)   if made to a justice, be made to a justice for the commission area,

in which the person who is the subject of the inquiries for the time being is.

(10)   A mental health officer shall as soon as practicable after the sheriff, or justice of the peace, decides to grant or refuse an application for a warrant under subsection (1), (4) or (7) above, give notice to the Commission as to whether a warrant was granted or refused.

(11)   No appeal shall be competent against a decision of a sheriff, or a justice of the peace, under this section granting, or refusing to grant, a warrant.

(12)   References to a relevant mental health officer—

     (a)   in subsection (1) above are to a mental health officer appointed by the local authority for the area in which the premises to which the application relates are situated;

     (b)   in subsections (4) and (7) above are to a mental health officer appointed by the local authority which is causing inquiries to be made.

PART 5

EMERGENCY DETENTION

Emergency detention certificate

36   Emergency detention in hospital

(1)   Where—

     (a)   a medical practitioner carries out a medical examination of a patient;

     (b)   the patient does not fall within subsection (2) below; and

     (c)   subsection (3) below applies,

the medical practitioner may, before the expiry of the appropriate period, grant an emergency detention certificate authorising, if the condition mentioned in subsection (7) below is satisfied, the measures mentioned in subsection (8) below.

(2)   The patient falls within this subsection if, immediately before the medical examination mentioned in subsection (1)(a) above is carried out, the patient is detained in hospital under authority of—

     (a)   an emergency detention certificate;

     (b)   a short-term detention certificate;

     (c)   an extension certificate;

     (d)   section 68 of this Act; or

     (e)   a certificate granted under section 114(2) or 115(2) of this Act.

(3)   Subject to subsection (6) below, this subsection applies where—

     (a)   there is no conflict of interest in relation to the medical examination;

     (b)   the medical practitioner considers that it is likely that the conditions mentioned in subsection (4) below are met in respect of the patient;

     (c)   the medical practitioner is satisfied that the conditions mentioned in subsection (5) below are met in respect of the patient; and

    (d) the medical practitioner has consulted a mental health officer and that mental health officer has consented to the grant of an emergency detention certificate.

(4)   The conditions referred to in subsection (3)(b) above are—

    (a) that the patient has a mental disorder; and

    (b) that, because of the mental disorder, the patient's ability to make decisions about the provision of medical treatment is significantly impaired.

(5)   The conditions referred to in subsection (3)(c) above are—

    (a) that it is necessary as a matter of urgency to detain the patient in hospital for the purpose of determining what medical treatment requires to be provided to the patient;

    (b) that if the patient were not detained in hospital there would be a significant risk—

        (i) to the health, safety or welfare of the patient; or

        (ii) to the safety of any other person; and

    (c) that making arrangements with a view to the grant of a short-term detention certificate would involve undesirable delay.

(6)   If it is impracticable for the medical practitioner to consult or seek consent under paragraph (d) of subsection (3) above, that paragraph need not be satisfied for the subsection to apply.

(7)   The condition referred to in subsection (1) above is that the measure mentioned in subsection (8)(b)(i) below is authorised by the certificate only if, before the patient is admitted under authority of the certificate to a hospital, the certificate is given to the managers of that hospital.

(8)   The measures referred to in subsection (1) above are—

    (a) the removal, before the expiry of the period of 72 hours beginning with the granting of the emergency detention certificate, of the patient to a hospital or to a different hospital; and

    (b) the detention of the patient in hospital for the period of 72 hours beginning with—

        (i) if, immediately before the certificate is granted, the patient is not in hospital, the first admission under authority of the certificate of the patient to hospital;

        (ii) if, immediately before the certificate is granted, the patient is in hospital, the granting of the certificate.

(9)   Regulations may specify—

    (a) the circumstances in which there is to be taken to be; and

    (b) the circumstances in which there is not to be taken to be,

a conflict of interest in relation to the medical examination.

(10)   The emergency detention certificate—

    (a) shall state the medical practitioner's reasons for believing the conditions mentioned in subsections (4) and (5) above to be met in respect of the patient; and

    (b) shall be signed by the medical practitioner.

(11) If a medical practitioner grants an emergency detention certificate in respect of a patient who, immediately before the certificate is granted, is in hospital, the medical practitioner shall, as soon as practicable after granting the certificate, give the certificate to the managers of that hospital.

(12) In subsection (1) above "appropriate period" means—

    (a) in a case where the medical examination of the patient is completed at least 4 hours before the end of the day (or, if it takes place on two days, the later of the days) on which it is carried out, the period beginning with completion of the examination and ending with the end of that day;

    (b) in any other case, the period of 4 hours beginning with the completion of the medical examination.

37   Notification by medical practitioner

(1) Subject to subsection (3) below, a medical practitioner who grants an emergency detention certificate shall, when the certificate is given to the managers of the hospital in which the patient is to be detained under authority of the certificate, give notice to them of the matters mentioned in subsection (2) below.

(2) Those matters are—

    (a) the reason for granting the certificate;

    (b) whether consent of a mental health officer was obtained to the granting of the certificate;

    (c) if the certificate was granted without consent to its granting having been obtained from a mental health officer, the reason why it was impracticable to consult a mental health officer;

    (d) the alternatives to granting the certificate that were considered by the medical practitioner; and

    (e) the reason for the medical practitioner determining that any such alternative was inappropriate.

(3) If it is impracticable for notice to be given when the certificate is given to the managers, the medical practitioner shall give notice as soon as practicable after that time.

Duties on hospital managers

38   Duties on hospital managers: examination, notification etc.

(1) This section applies where a patient is detained in hospital under authority of an emergency detention certificate.

(2) As soon as practicable after the period of detention authorised by the certificate begins as mentioned in section 36(8)(b) of this Act, the managers of the hospital shall make arrangements for an approved medical practitioner to carry out a medical examination of the patient.

(3) The managers of the hospital shall—

    (a) before the expiry of the period of 12 hours beginning with the giving of the certificate to them, inform the persons mentioned in subsection (4) below of the granting of the certificate; and

(b) before the expiry of the period of 7 days beginning with the day on which they receive notice under section 37 of this Act—

    (i) give notice to the persons mentioned in subsection (4) below of the matters notified to them under that section; and

    (ii) if the certificate was granted without consent to its granting having been obtained from a mental health officer, give notice of those matters to the persons mentioned in subsection (5) below.

(4) The persons referred to in subsection (3)(a) and (b)(i) above are—

    (a) the patient's nearest relative;

    (b) if that person does not reside with the patient, any person who resides with the patient;

    (c) if—

        (i) the managers know who the patient's named person is; and

        (ii) that named person is not any of the persons mentioned in paragraphs (a) and (b) above,

    the patient's named person; and

    (d) the Commission.

(5) The persons referred to in subsection (3)(b)(ii) above are—

    (a) if the managers know where the patient resides, the local authority for the area in which the patient resides; or

    (b) if the managers do not know where the patient resides, the local authority for the area in which the hospital is situated.

Revocation of certificate

39   Approved medical practitioner's duty to revoke emergency detention certificate

If the approved medical practitioner who carries out the medical examination required by section 38(2) of this Act is not satisfied—

    (a) that the conditions mentioned in section 36(4)(a) and (b) and (5)(b) of this Act continue to be met in respect of the patient; or

    (b) that it continues to be necessary for the detention in hospital of the patient to be authorised by the certificate,

the approved medical practitioner shall revoke the certificate.

40   Revocation of emergency detention certificate: notification

(1) Where an approved medical practitioner revokes a certificate under section 39 of this Act, the practitioner shall, as soon as practicable after doing so, inform—

    (a) the patient; and

    (b) the managers of the hospital in which the patient is detained,

of the revocation.

(2)   The managers of the hospital shall, as soon as practicable after being informed of the revocation, inform the persons mentioned in section 38(4) and (5) of this Act of the revocation.

Suspension of authority to detain

41   Suspension of authority to detain

(1)   Where—

     (a)   a patient is subject to an emergency detention certificate; and

     (b)   the patient's responsible medical officer grants a certificate specifying a period during which the emergency detention certificate shall not authorise the measure mentioned in section 36(8)(b) of this Act,

the emergency detention certificate does not authorise that measure during that period.

(2)   A period specified in a certificate granted under subsection (1) above may be expressed as—

     (a)   the duration of—

         (i)   an event; or

         (ii)   a series of events; or

     (b)   the duration of—

         (i)   an event; or

         (ii)   a series of events,

     and any associated travel.

(3)   If the responsible medical officer considers that it is necessary—

     (a)   in the interests of the patient; or

     (b)   for the protection of any other person,

a certificate granted under subsection (1) above may include conditions such as are mentioned in subsection (4) below; and any such conditions shall have effect.

(4)   Those conditions are—

     (a)   that, during the period specified in the certificate, the patient be kept in the charge of a person authorised in writing for the purpose by the responsible medical officer;

     (b)   such other conditions as may be specified by the responsible medical officer.

42   Certificate under section 41: revocation

(1)   Subsection (2) below applies where a certificate is granted under section 41(1) of this Act in respect of a patient.

(2)   If the patient's responsible medical officer is satisfied that it is necessary—

     (a)   in the interests of the patient; or

     (b)   for the protection of any other person,

that the certificate be revoked, the responsible medical officer may revoke the certificate.

(3)   Where a responsible medical officer revokes a certificate under subsection (2) above, the responsible medical officer shall, as soon as practicable after doing so, inform—

      (a)   the patient;

      (b)   if the certificate includes a condition such as is mentioned in section 41(4)(a) of this Act, any person authorised in accordance with that condition; and

      (c)   the managers of the hospital in which the patient is detained,

of the revocation.

(4)   The managers of the hospital shall, as soon as practicable after being informed of the revocation, inform the persons mentioned in section 38(4) and (5) of this Act of the revocation.

Effect of emergency detention certificate on compulsory treatment order

43   Effect of subsequent emergency detention certificate on compulsory treatment order

(1)   This section applies where—

      (a)   a patient is subject to a compulsory treatment order; and

      (b)   an emergency detention certificate is granted in respect of the patient.

(2)   The compulsory treatment order shall, subject to subsection (3) below, cease to authorise the measures specified in it for the period during which the patient is subject to the emergency detention certificate.

(3)   If the measure mentioned in section 66(1)(b) of this Act is specified in the compulsory treatment order, the compulsory treatment order shall continue to authorise that measure during the period mentioned in subsection (2) above.

PART 6

SHORT-TERM DETENTION

Short-term detention certificate

44   Short-term detention in hospital

(1)   Where—

      (a)   an approved medical practitioner carries out a medical examination of a patient;

      (b)   the patient does not fall within subsection (2) below; and

      (c)   subsection (3) below applies,

the approved medical practitioner may, before the expiry of the period of 3 days beginning with the completion of the medical examination, grant a short-term detention certificate authorising, if the condition mentioned in subsection (6) below is satisfied, the measures mentioned in subsection (5) below.

(2)   The patient falls within this subsection if, immediately before the medical examination mentioned in subsection (1)(a) above is carried out, the patient is detained in hospital under authority of—

      (a)   a short-term detention certificate;

      (b) an extension certificate;

      (c) section 68 of this Act; or

      (d) a certificate granted under section 114(2) or 115(2) of this Act.

(3)   This subsection applies where—

      (a) there is no conflict of interest in relation to the medical examination;

      (b) the approved medical practitioner considers that it is likely that the conditions mentioned in subsection (4) below are met in respect of the patient;

      (c) the approved medical practitioner consults a mental health officer; and

      (d) the mental health officer consents to the grant of a short-term detention certificate.

(4)   The conditions referred to subsection (3)(b) above are—

      (a) that the patient has a mental disorder;

      (b) that, because of the mental disorder, the patient's ability to make decisions about the provision of medical treatment is significantly impaired;

      (c) that it is necessary to detain the patient in hospital for the purpose of—

            (i)   determining what medical treatment should be given to the patient; or

            (ii)   giving medical treatment to the patient;

      (d) that if the patient were not detained in hospital there would be a significant risk—

            (i)   to the health, safety or welfare of the patient; or

            (ii)   to the safety of any other person; and

      (e) that the granting of a short-term detention certificate is necessary.

(5)   The measures referred to in subsection (1) above are—

      (a) the removal, before the expiry of the period of 3 days beginning with the granting of the short-term detention certificate, of the patient to a hospital or to a different hospital;

      (b) the detention of the patient in hospital for the period of 28 days beginning with—

            (i)   if, immediately before the certificate is granted, the patient is not in hospital, the beginning of the day on which admission under authority of the certificate of the patient to hospital first takes place;

            (ii)   if, immediately before the certificate is granted, the patient is in hospital, the beginning of the day on which the certificate is granted;

      (c) the giving to the patient, in accordance with Part 16 of this Act, of medical treatment.

(6)   The condition referred to in subsection (1) above is that the measure mentioned in subsection (5)(b)(i) above is authorised by the certificate only if, before the patient is admitted to hospital under authority of the certificate, the certificate is given to the managers of that hospital.

(7)   If an approved medical practitioner grants a short-term detention certificate in respect of a patient who, immediately before the certificate is granted, is in hospital, the approved medical practitioner shall, as soon as practicable after granting the certificate, give the certificate to the managers of that hospital.

(8)   Regulations may specify—

    (a)   the circumstances in which there is to be taken to be; and

    (b)   the circumstances in which there is not to be taken to be,

a conflict of interest in relation to the medical examination.

(9)   The short-term detention certificate—

    (a)   shall state the approved medical practitioner's reasons for believing the conditions mentioned in subsection (4) above to be met in respect of the patient; and

    (b)   shall be signed by the approved medical practitioner.

(10)   Before granting the short-term detention certificate, the approved medical practitioner shall, subject to subsection (11) below, consult the patient's named person about the proposed grant of the certificate; and the approved medical practitioner shall have regard to any views expressed by the named person.

(11)   The approved medical practitioner need not consult a named person as mentioned in subsection (10) above in any case where it is impracticable to do so.

45   Mental health officer's duty to interview patient etc.

(1)   Subject to subsection (2) below, before deciding whether to consent for the purposes of section 44(3)(d) of this Act, a mental health officer shall—

    (a)   interview the patient;

    (b)   ascertain the name and address of the patient's named person;

    (c)   inform the patient of the availability of independent advocacy services under section 259 of this Act; and

    (d)   take appropriate steps to ensure that the patient has the opportunity of making use of those services.

(2)   If it is impracticable for the mental health officer to—

    (a)   interview the patient; or

    (b)   ascertain the name and address of the patient's named person,

the mental health officer shall comply with the requirements in subsection (3) below.

(3)   Those requirements are—

    (a)   recording the steps taken by the mental health officer with a view to complying with the duty concerned; and

    (b)   before the expiry of the period of 7 days beginning with the day on which the mental health officer is consulted by an approved medical practitioner under section 44(3)(c) of this Act, giving a copy of the record to the approved medical practitioner.

Duties on hospital managers

46   Hospital managers' duties: notification

(1)   This section applies where a patient is detained in hospital under authority of a short-term detention certificate.

(2) The managers of the hospital shall as soon as practicable after the production to them of the short-term detention certificate, give notice of its granting to—

    (a) the patient;

    (b) the patient's named person;

    (c) any guardian of the patient; and

    (d) any welfare attorney of the patient.

(3) The managers of the hospital shall, before the expiry of the period of 7 days beginning with the day on which the certificate is granted, give notice of its granting, and send a copy of it, to—

    (a) the Tribunal; and

    (b) the Commission.

Extension certificate

47   Extension of detention pending application for compulsory treatment order

(1) Where—

    (a) a patient is detained in hospital under authority of a short-term detention certificate;

    (b) an approved medical practitioner carries out a medical examination of the patient; and

    (c) subsections (2) and (3) below apply,

the approved medical practitioner may, before the expiry of the period of 24 hours beginning with the completion of that medical examination, grant a certificate (any such certificate being referred to in this Act as an "extension certificate") authorising the measures mentioned in subsection (4) below.

(2) This subsection applies where—

    (a) there is no conflict of interest in relation to the medical examination; and

    (b) the approved medical practitioner considers—

        (i) that the conditions mentioned in paragraphs (a) to (d) of section 44(4) of this Act are met in respect of the patient; and

        (ii) that because of a change in the mental health of the patient, an application should be made under section 63 of this Act for a compulsory treatment order.

(3) This subsection applies where—

    (a) no application has been made under section 63 of this Act;

    (b) it would not be reasonably practicable to make an application under that section before the expiry of the period of detention authorised by the short-term detention certificate; and

    (c) subject to subsection (6) below—

        (i) the approved medical practitioner consults a mental health officer about the proposed grant of an extension certificate; and

        (ii) the mental health officer consents to the granting of the extension certificate.

(4) The measures referred to in subsection (1) above are—

    (a) the detention in hospital of the patient for the period of 3 days beginning with the expiry of the period for which the short-term detention certificate authorises the detention of the patient in hospital; and

    (b) the giving to the patient, in accordance with Part 16 of this Act, of medical treatment.

(5) Regulations may specify—

    (a) the circumstances in which there is to be taken to be; and

    (b) the circumstances in which there is not to be taken to be,

a conflict of interest in relation to the medical examination.

(6) An approved medical practitioner need not consult or seek consent under subsection (3)(c) above in any case where it is impracticable to do so.

(7) In reckoning the period of days mentioned in subsection (4)(a) above, there shall be left out of account any day which is not a working day.

(8) In this section "working day" means a day which is not—

    (a) Saturday;

    (b) Sunday; or

    (c) a day which is a bank holiday under the Banking and Financial Dealings Act 1971 (c.80) in Scotland.

48   Extension certificate: notification

(1) An approved medical practitioner who grants an extension certificate shall, before the expiry of the period of 24 hours beginning with the granting of the certificate, give the certificate to the managers of the hospital in which the patient is detained and give notice to the persons mentioned in subsection (2) below—

    (a) of the granting of the extension certificate;

    (b) of the approved medical practitioner's reasons for believing the conditions mentioned in paragraphs (a) to (d) of section 44(4) of this Act to be met in respect of the patient;

    (c) as to whether consent of a mental health officer was obtained to the granting of the certificate; and

    (d) if the certificate was granted without consent to its granting having been obtained from a mental health officer, the reason why it was impracticable to consult a mental health officer.

(2) Those persons are—

    (a) the patient;

    (b) the patient's named person;

    (c) the Tribunal;

    (d) the Commission;

(e) any guardian of the patient;

(f) any welfare attorney of the patient; and

(g) the mental health officer.

Revocation of certificates

49   Responsible medical officer's duty to review continuing need for detention

(1) Where a patient is detained in hospital under authority of a short-term detention certificate or an extension certificate, the patient's responsible medical officer shall, from time to time, consider—

   (a) whether the conditions mentioned in paragraphs (a), (b) and (d) of section 44(4) of this Act continue to be met in respect of the patient; and

   (b) whether it continues to be necessary for the detention in hospital of the patient to be authorised by the certificate.

(2) If, having complied with subsection (1) above, the responsible medical officer is not satisfied—

   (a) that the conditions referred to in paragraph (a) of that subsection continue to be met in respect of the patient; or

   (b) that it continues to be necessary for the detention in hospital of the patient to be authorised by the certificate,

the responsible medical officer shall revoke the certificate.

(3) The responsible medical officer shall, as soon as practicable after revoking a certificate under subsection (2) above, give notice of its revocation to—

   (a) the patient;

   (b) the patient's named person;

   (c) any guardian of the patient;

   (d) any welfare attorney of the patient; and

   (e) the mental health officer who was consulted under section 44(3)(c) of this Act.

(4) The responsible medical officer shall, before the expiry of the period of 7 days beginning with the day on which the certificate is revoked, give notice of its revocation to—

   (a) the Tribunal; and

   (b) the Commission.

50   Patient's right to apply for revocation of short-term detention certificate or extension certificate etc.

(1) Where a patient is in hospital under authority of a short-term detention certificate or an extension certificate—

   (a) the patient; or

   (b) the patient's named person,

may apply to the Tribunal for revocation of the certificate.

(2) Before determining an application under subsection (1) above, the Tribunal shall afford the persons mentioned in subsection (3) below the opportunity—

    (a) of making representations (whether orally or in writing); and

    (b) of leading, or producing, evidence.

(3) Those persons are—

    (a) the patient;

    (b) the patient's named person;

    (c) any guardian of the patient;

    (d) any welfare attorney of the patient;

    (e) the approved medical practitioner who granted the short-term detention certificate;

    (f) the mental health officer who was consulted under section 44(3)(c) of this Act;

    (g) if the patient has a responsible medical officer, that responsible medical officer;

    (h) any curator *ad litem* appointed in respect of the patient by the Tribunal; and

    (i) any other person appearing to the Tribunal to have an interest in the application.

(4) On an application under subsection (1) above, the Tribunal shall, if not satisfied—

    (a) that the conditions mentioned in paragraphs (a), (b) and (d) of section 44(4) of this Act continue to be met in respect of the patient; or

    (b) that it continues to be necessary for the detention in hospital of the patient to be authorised by the certificate,

revoke the certificate.

(5) Where, before a short-term detention certificate is revoked under subsection (4) above an extension certificate has been granted in respect of the patient, the revocation of the short-term detention certificate shall have the effect of revoking the extension certificate, notwithstanding that there has been no application under subsection (1) above in relation to the extension certificate.

51 Commission's power to revoke short-term detention certificate or extension certificate

Where—

    (a) the detention of a patient in hospital is authorised by a short-term detention certificate or an extension certificate; and

    (b) the Commission is satisfied—

        (i) that not all of the conditions mentioned in paragraphs (a), (b) and (d) of section 44(4) of this Act continue to be met in respect of the patient; or

        (ii) that it does not continue to be necessary for the detention in hospital of the patient to be authorised by the certificate,

the Commission may revoke the certificate.

52   Revocation of short-term detention certificate or extension certificate: notification

Where the Commission revokes a certificate under section 51 of this Act, it shall, as soon as practicable after doing so, give notice of the revocation to—

   (a) the patient;

   (b) the patient's named person;

   (c) any guardian of the patient;

   (d) any welfare attorney of the patient;

   (e) the managers of the hospital in which the patient is detained;

   (f) the mental health officer who was consulted under section 44(3)(c) of this Act; and

   (g) the Tribunal.

Suspension of detention

53   Suspension of measure authorising detention

(1)   Where—

   (a) a patient is subject to a short-term detention certificate; and

   (b) the patient's responsible medical officer grants a certificate specifying a period during which the short-term detention certificate shall not authorise the measures mentioned in section 44(5)(b) of this Act,

the short-term detention certificate does not authorise that measure during that period.

(2)   A period specified in a certificate granted under subsection (1) above may be expressed as—

   (a) the duration of—

      (i) an event; or

      (ii) a series of events; or

   (b) the duration of—

      (i) an event; or

      (ii) a series of events,

   and any associated travel.

(3)   If the responsible medical officer considers that it is necessary—

   (a) in the interests of the patient; or

   (b) for the protection of any other person,

a certificate granted under subsection (1) above may include conditions such as are mentioned in subsection (4) below; and any such conditions shall have effect.

(4)   Those conditions are—

   (a) that, during the period specified in the certificate, the patient be kept in the charge of a person authorised in writing for the purpose by the responsible medical officer;

   (b) such other conditions as may be specified by the responsible medical officer.

54   **Certificate under section 53: revocation**

(1)   Subsection (2) below applies where a certificate is granted under section 53(1) of this Act in respect of a patient.

(2)   If the patient's responsible medical officer is satisfied that it is necessary—

     (a)   in the interests of the patient; or

     (b)   for the protection of any other person,

that the certificate be revoked, the responsible medical officer may revoke the certificate.

(3)   Where a responsible medical officer revokes a certificate under subsection (2) above, the responsible medical officer shall, as soon as practicable after doing so, give notice of the revocation to—

     (a)   the patient;

     (b)   the patient's named person;

     (c)   the mental health officer;

     (d)   if the certificate includes a condition such as is mentioned in section 53(4)(a) of this Act, any person authorised in accordance with that condition; and

     (e)   the Commission.

Effect of short-term detention certificate on emergency detention certificate

55   **Effect of subsequent short-term detention certificate on emergency detention certificate**

If a short-term detention certificate is granted in respect of a patient who is in hospital under authority of an emergency detention certificate, the emergency detention certificate shall, on the granting of the short-term detention certificate, be revoked.

Effect of short-term detention certificate on compulsory treatment order

56   **Effect of subsequent short-term detention certificate on compulsory treatment order**

(1)   Subsection (2) below applies where—

     (a)   a patient is subject to a compulsory treatment order; and

     (b)   a short-term detention certificate is granted in respect of the patient.

(2)   The compulsory treatment order shall cease to authorise the measures specified in it for the period during which the patient is subject to the short-term detention certificate.

36   *Mental Health (Care and Treatment) (Scotland) Act 2003 (asp 13)*
Part 7—Compulsory treatment orders
Chapter 1—Application for, and making of, orders

PART 7

COMPULSORY TREATMENT ORDERS

CHAPTER 1

APPLICATION FOR, AND MAKING OF, ORDERS

Pre-application procedures

57   **Mental health officer's duty to apply for compulsory treatment order**

(1)   Where subsections (2) to (5) below apply in relation to a patient, a mental health officer shall apply to the Tribunal under section 63 of this Act for a compulsory treatment order in respect of that patient.

(2)   This subsection applies where two medical practitioners carry out medical examinations of the patient in accordance with the requirements of section 58 of this Act.

(3)   This subsection applies where each of the medical practitioners who carries out a medical examination mentioned in subsection (2) above is satisfied—

     (a)   that the patient has a mental disorder;

     (b)   that medical treatment which would be likely to—

         (i)   prevent the mental disorder worsening; or

         (ii)   alleviate any of the symptoms, or effects, of the disorder,

       is available for the patient;

     (c)   that if the patient were not provided with such medical treatment there would be a significant risk—

         (i)   to the health, safety or welfare of the patient; or

         (ii)   to the safety of any other person;

     (d)   that because of the mental disorder the patient's ability to make decisions about the provision of such medical treatment is significantly impaired; and

     (e)   that the making of a compulsory treatment order is necessary.

(4)   This subsection applies where each of the medical practitioners who carries out a medical examination mentioned in subsection (2) above submits to the mental health officer a report (any such report being referred to in this Act as a "mental health report")—

     (a)   stating that the medical practitioner submitting the report is satisfied that the conditions mentioned in paragraphs (a) to (e) of subsection (3) above are met in respect of the patient;

     (b)   stating, in relation to each of the conditions mentioned in paragraphs (b) to (e) of subsection (3) above, the medical practitioner's reasons for believing the condition to be met in respect of the patient;

     (c)   specifying (by reference to the appropriate paragraph (or paragraphs) of the definition of "mental disorder" in section 328(1) of this Act) the type (or types) of mental disorder that the patient has;

     (d)   setting out a description of—

Mental Health (Care and Treatment) (Scotland) Act 2003 (asp 13)   37
Part 7—Compulsory treatment orders
Chapter 1—Application for, and making of, orders

(i) the symptoms that the patient has of the mental disorder; and

(ii) the ways in which the patient is affected by the mental disorder;

(e) specifying the measures that should, in the medical practitioner's opinion, be authorised by the compulsory treatment order;

(f) specifying the date or dates on which the medical practitioner carried out the medical examination mentioned in subsection (2) above; and

(g) setting out any other information that the medical practitioner considers to be relevant.

(5) This subsection applies where—

(a) for the purposes of subsection (4)(c) above each of the mental health reports specifies at least one type of mental disorder that is also specified in the other report;

(b) for the purposes of subsection (4)(e) above each of the mental health reports specifies the same measures; and

(c) one of the mental health reports (being a report by an approved medical practitioner) states the views of that medical practitioner as to—

(i) subject to subsection (6) below, whether notice should be given to the patient under section 60(1)(a) of this Act; and

(ii) whether the patient is capable of arranging for a person to represent the patient in connection with the application under section 63 of this Act.

(6) A medical practitioner may state the view that notice should not be given under section 60(1)(a) of this Act only if, in the opinion of that medical practitioner, the giving of notice would be likely to cause significant harm to the patient or any other person.

(7) Where a mental health officer is required by subsection (1) above to make an application for a compulsory treatment order, the mental health officer shall make the application before the expiry of the period of 14 days beginning with—

(a) in the case where each of the mental health reports specifies the same date (or dates) for the purposes of subsection (4)(f) above, that date (or the later, or latest, of those dates); or

(b) in the case where each of those reports specifies for those purposes a different date (or different dates), the later (or latest) of those dates.

58   Medical examination: requirements

(1) The requirements referred to in section 57(2) of this Act are set out in subsections (2) to (6) below.

(2) Subject to subsection (4) below and to regulations under subsection (5) below—

(a) each medical examination of the patient shall be carried out by an approved medical practitioner; and

(b) subject to subsection (6) below, each such examination shall be carried out separately.

(3) Where the medical examinations are carried out separately, the second shall be completed no more than five days after the first.

38   *Mental Health (Care and Treatment) (Scotland) Act 2003 (asp 13)*
Part 7—Compulsory treatment orders
Chapter 1—Application for, and making of, orders

(4)   The patient's general medical practitioner may carry out one of the medical examinations of the patient although not an approved medical practitioner.

(5)   Except in circumstances specified in regulations, there must not be a conflict of interest in relation to the medical examination; and regulations shall specify the circumstances in which there is to be taken to be such a conflict of interest.

(6)   The medical examinations need not be carried out separately if—

     (a)   where the patient is capable of consenting to the examinations, the patient consents to the examinations being carried out at the same time; or

     (b)   where the patient is incapable of consenting to the examinations—

         (i)   the patient's named person;

         (ii)   any guardian of the patient; or

         (iii)   any welfare attorney of the patient,

     consents to the examinations being carried out at the same time.

59   Mental health officer's duty to identify named person

Where a mental health officer is required by 57(1) of this Act to make an application under section 63 of this Act in respect of a patient, the mental health officer shall, as soon as practicable after the duty to make the application arises, take such steps as are reasonably practicable to ascertain the name and address of the patient's named person.

60   Application for compulsory treatment order: notification

(1)   Where a mental health officer is required by section 57(1) of this Act to make an application under section 63 of this Act in respect of a patient, the mental health officer shall, as soon as practicable after the duty to make the application arises (and, in any event, before making the application) give notice that the application is to be made—

     (a)   subject to subsection (2) below, to the patient in respect of whom the application is to be made;

     (b)   to the patient's named person; and

     (c)   to the Commission.

(2)   If the view set out in one of the mental health reports by virtue of section 57(5)(c) of this Act is that notice should not be given under paragraph (a) of subsection (1) above, the mental health officer—

     (a)   need not give such notice; but

     (b)   may, if the mental health officer considers it appropriate to do so, give such notice.

61   Mental health officer's duty to prepare report

(1)   This section applies where a mental health officer is required by section 57(1) of this Act to make an application under section 63 of this Act in respect of a patient.

(2)   The mental health officer shall, before the date on which, by virtue of section 57(7) of this Act, the application is to be made—

Mental Health (Care and Treatment) (Scotland) Act 2003 (asp 13)   39
Part 7—Compulsory treatment orders
Chapter 1—Application for, and making of, orders

    (a) subject to subsection (3) below, interview the patient;

    (b) if the patient has not been given notice under section 60(1)(a) of this Act, inform the patient that the application is to be made;

    (c) inform the patient of—

        (i) the patient's rights in relation to the application; and

        (ii) the availability of independent advocacy services under section 259 of this Act;

    (d) take appropriate steps to ensure that the patient has the opportunity of making use of those services; and

    (e) prepare in relation to the patient a report in accordance with subsection (4) below.

(3)   If it is impracticable for the mental health officer to comply with the requirement in subsection (2)(a) above, the mental health officer need not do so.

(4)   The report shall state—

    (a) the name and address of the patient;

    (b) if known by the mental health officer, the name and address of—

        (i) the patient's named person; and

        (ii) the patient's primary carer;

    (c) the steps that the mental health officer has taken in pursuance of the requirements imposed by subsection (2) above;

    (d) if it was impracticable for the mental health officer to comply with the requirement in subsection (2)(a) above, the reason for that being the case;

    (e) in so far as relevant for the purposes of the application, details of the personal circumstances of the patient;

    (f) the mental health officer's views on the mental health reports relating to the patient;

    (g) if known by the mental health officer, details of any advance statement that the patient has made (and not withdrawn); and

    (h) any other information that the mental health officer considers relevant to the determination by the Tribunal of the application.

62   Mental health officer's duty to prepare proposed care plan

(1)   This section applies where a mental health officer is required by section 57(1) of this Act to make an application under section 63 of this Act in respect of a patient.

(2)   The mental health officer shall, before the date on which, by virtue of section 57(7) of this Act, the application is to be made, prepare a plan (a "proposed care plan") relating to the patient.

(3)   Before preparing the proposed care plan, the mental health officer shall consult—

    (a) the medical practitioners who provided the mental health reports relating to the patient;

40   *Mental Health (Care and Treatment) (Scotland) Act 2003 (asp 13)*
Part 7—Compulsory treatment orders
Chapter 1—Application for, and making of, orders

         (b)   subject to subsection (7) below, the persons mentioned in subsection (4) below; and

         (c)   such other persons as the mental health officer considers appropriate.

(4)   The persons referred to in subsection (3)(b) above are persons who appear to the mental health officer to provide—

         (a)   medical treatment of the kind that it is proposed to specify, by virtue of paragraph (d) of subsection (5) below, in the proposed care plan;

         (b)   community care services, or relevant services, of the kind that it is proposed to specify, by virtue of paragraph (e) of that subsection, in that plan; or

         (c)   other treatment, care or services of the kind that it is proposed to specify, by virtue of paragraph (f) of that subsection, in that plan.

(5)   The proposed care plan shall specify—

         (a)   (by reference to the appropriate paragraph (or paragraphs) of the definition of "mental disorder" in section 328(1) of this Act), the type (or types) of mental disorder which the patient has;

         (b)   the needs of the patient for medical treatment that have been assessed by the medical practitioners who submitted the mental health reports relating to the patient;

         (c)   in so far as relevant for the purposes of the application—

             (i)   where the patient is a child, the needs of the patient that have been assessed under section 23(3) of the Children (Scotland) Act 1995 (c.36);

             (ii)   where the patient is not a child, the needs of the patient that have been assessed under section 12A(1)(a) of the Social Work (Scotland) Act 1968 (c.49);

         (d)   the medical treatment which it is proposed to give to the patient in relation to each of the needs specified by virtue of paragraph (b) above (including the names of the persons who would give the treatment and the addresses at which the treatment would be given);

         (e)   any community care services or relevant services which it is proposed to provide to the patient in relation to each of the needs specified by virtue of paragraph (c) above (including the names of the persons who would provide such services and the addresses at which such services would be provided);

         (f)   in so far as relevant for the purposes of the application—

             (i)   any treatment or care (other than treatment or care specified, by virtue of paragraph (d) above, in the proposed care plan); or

             (ii)   any service (other than a service specified, by virtue of paragraph (e) above, in the proposed care plan),

         which it is proposed to provide to the patient (including the names of the persons who would provide such treatment, care or service and the addresses at which such treatment, care or service would be provided);

         (g)   which of the measures mentioned in section 66(1) of this Act it is proposed that the compulsory treatment order should authorise;

Mental Health (Care and Treatment) (Scotland) Act 2003 (asp 13) 41
Part 7—Compulsory treatment orders
Chapter 1—Application for, and making of, orders

(h) where it is proposed that the compulsory treatment order should authorise the detention of the patient in hospital, the name and address of the hospital;

(i) where it is proposed that the compulsory treatment order should authorise any of the measures mentioned in section 66(1)(c) to (h) of this Act, details of the measure (or measures);

(j) where it is proposed that the compulsory treatment order should specify—

    (i) any medical treatment specified, by virtue of paragraph (d) above, in the proposed care plan;

    (ii) any community care services, or relevant services, specified, by virtue of paragraph (e) above, in the proposed care plan; or

    (iii) any treatment, care or service specified, by virtue of paragraph (f) above, in the proposed care plan,

that medical treatment, those services or that treatment, care, or service, as the case may be;

(k) where it is proposed that the compulsory treatment order should authorise measures other than the detention of the patient in hospital, the name of the hospital the managers of which should have responsibility for appointing the patient's responsible medical officer; and

(l) the objectives of—

    (i) the medical treatment which it is proposed, by virtue of paragraph (d) above, to give to the patient;

    (ii) any community care services or relevant services which it is proposed, by virtue of paragraph (e) above, to provide to the patient;

    (iii) any treatment, care or service which, by virtue of paragraph (f) above, it is proposed to provide to the patient; and

    (iv) the measures (other than detention of the patient in hospital) that it is proposed that the compulsory treatment order should authorise.

(6) The proposed care plan shall be signed by the mental health officer.

(7) The mental health officer need not consult any person such as is mentioned in subsection (4) above in any case where it is impracticable to do so.

(8) In this section "child" has the same meaning as in section 23(3) of the Children (Scotland) Act 1995 (c.36).

Application for order

63   **Application for compulsory treatment order**

(1) An application to the Tribunal for a compulsory treatment order may be made by, and only by, a mental health officer.

(2) An application—

    (a) shall specify—

        (i) the measures that are sought in relation to the patient in respect of whom the application is made;

42

Mental Health (Care and Treatment) (Scotland) Act 2003 (asp 13)
Part 7—Compulsory treatment orders
Chapter 1—Application for, and making of, orders

     (ii) any medical treatment, community care services, relevant services or other treatment, care or service specified in the proposed care plan by virtue of section 62(5)(j) of this Act; and

     (iii) where it is proposed that the order should authorise measures other than the detention of the patient in hospital, the name of the hospital the managers of which should have responsibility for appointing the patient's responsible medical officer; and

  (b) shall be accompanied by the documents that are mentioned in subsection (3) below.

(3) Those documents are—

  (a) the mental health reports;

  (b) the report prepared under section 61 of this Act; and

  (c) the proposed care plan,

relating to the patient.

Making of order etc.

64   **Powers of Tribunal on application under section 63: compulsory treatment order**

(1) This section applies where an application is made under section 63 of this Act.

(2) Before determining the application, the Tribunal shall afford the persons mentioned in subsection (3) below the opportunity—

  (a) of making representations (whether orally or in writing); and

  (b) of leading, or producing, evidence.

(3) Those persons are—

  (a) the patient;

  (b) the patient's named person;

  (c) any guardian of the patient;

  (d) any welfare attorney of the patient;

  (e) the mental health officer;

  (f) the medical practitioners who submitted the mental health reports which accompany the application;

  (g) if the patient has a responsible medical officer, that officer;

  (h) the patient's primary carer;

  (i) any curator *ad litem* appointed in respect of the patient by the Tribunal; and

  (j) any other person appearing to the Tribunal to have an interest in the application.

(4) The Tribunal may—

  (a) if satisfied that all of the conditions mentioned in subsection (5) below are met, make an order—

Mental Health (Care and Treatment) (Scotland) Act 2003 (asp 13)   43
Part 7—Compulsory treatment orders
Chapter 1—Application for, and making of, orders

(i)   authorising, for the period of 6 months beginning with the day on which the order is made, such of the measures mentioned in section 66(1) of this Act as may be specified in the order;

(ii)   specifying such medical treatment, community care services, relevant services, other treatment, care or service as the Tribunal considers appropriate (any such medical treatment, community care services, relevant services, other treatment, care or service so specified being referred to in this Act as a "recorded matter");

(iii)   recording (by reference to the appropriate paragraph (or paragraphs) of the definition of "mental disorder" in section 328(1) of this Act) the type (or types) of mental disorder that the patient has; and

(iv)   if the order does not authorise the detention of the patient in hospital, specifying the name of the hospital the managers of which are to have responsibility for appointing the patient's responsible medical officer; or

(b)   refuse the application.

(5)   The conditions referred to in subsection (4)(a) above are—

     (a)   that the patient has a mental disorder;

     (b)   that medical treatment which would be likely to—

        (i)   prevent the mental disorder worsening; or

        (ii)   alleviate any of the symptoms, or effects, of the disorder,

      is available for the patient;

     (c)   that if the patient were not provided with such medical treatment there would be a significant risk—

        (i)   to the health, safety or welfare of the patient; or

        (ii)   to the safety of any other person;

     (d)   that because of the mental disorder the patient's ability to make decisions about the provision of such medical treatment is significantly impaired;

     (e)   that the making of a compulsory treatment order in respect of the patient is necessary; and

     (f)   where the Tribunal does not consider it necessary for the patient to be detained in hospital, such other conditions as may be specified in regulations.

(6)   Subject to subsection (7) below, an order under subsection (4)(a) above may, in addition to, or instead of, specifying some or all of the measures sought in the application to which the order relates, specify measures other than those set out in that application.

(7)   The Tribunal may specify in the order under subsection (4)(a) above measures other than those set out in the application only if, before making the order—

     (a)   subject to subsection (8) below, the Tribunal gives notice to the persons mentioned in subsection (3) above—

        (i)   stating what it is proposing to do; and

        (ii)   setting out what those measures are;

     (b)   the Tribunal affords those persons the opportunity—

44   *Mental Health (Care and Treatment) (Scotland) Act 2003 (asp 13)*
Part 7—Compulsory treatment orders
Chapter 1—Application for, and making of, orders

           (i)   of making representations (whether orally or in writing) in relation to the proposal; and

           (ii)   of leading, or producing, evidence.

(8)   Where the duty under subsection (7)(a) above arises during a hearing of the application, notice need not be given under that subsection to any person mentioned in subsection (3) above who is present at the hearing.

(9)   Before making regulations under subsection (5)(f) above, the Scottish Ministers shall consult such persons as they consider appropriate.

65   Powers of Tribunal on application under section 63: interim compulsory treatment order

(1)   This section applies where an application is made under section 63 of this Act.

(2)   Subject to subsections (3) and (4) below and to section 69 of this Act, on the application of any person having an interest in the proceedings, or *ex proprio motu*, the Tribunal may, if satisfied as to the matters mentioned in subsection (6) below, make an order (an "interim compulsory treatment order")—

     (a)   authorising for such period not exceeding 28 days as may be specified in the order such of the measures mentioned in section 66(1) of this Act as may be so specified; and

     (b)   if the order does not authorise the detention of the patient in hospital, specifying the name of the hospital the managers of which are to have responsibility for appointing the patient's responsible medical officer.

(3)   The Tribunal may not make an interim compulsory treatment order if its effect, when taken with any other interim compulsory treatment order made in respect of the patient, would be to authorise measures in respect of the patient for a continuous period of more than 56 days.

(4)   Before making an interim compulsory treatment order, the Tribunal shall afford the persons mentioned in subsection (5) below the opportunity—

     (a)   of making representations (whether orally or in writing); and

     (b)   of leading, or producing, evidence.

(5)   Those persons are—

     (a)   the persons referred to in section 64(3)(a) to (e) and (g) to (i) of this Act;

     (b)   the medical practitioners who submitted the mental health reports which accompany the application under section 63 of this Act; and

     (c)   any other person appearing to the Tribunal to have an interest in that application.

(6)   The matters referred to in subsection (2) above are—

     (a)   that the conditions mentioned in paragraphs (a) to (d) of section 64(5) of this Act are met in respect of the patient; and

     (b)   that it is necessary to make an interim compulsory treatment order.

Mental Health (Care and Treatment) (Scotland) Act 2003 (asp 13)   45
Part 7—Compulsory treatment orders
Chapter 1—Application for, and making of, orders

66   **Measures that may be authorised**

(1)   Subject to subsection (2) below, the measures referred to in sections 64(4)(a)(i) and 65(2)(a) of this Act are—

    (a)   the detention of the patient in the specified hospital;

    (b)   the giving to the patient, in accordance with Part 16 of this Act, of medical treatment;

    (c)   the imposition of a requirement on the patient to attend—

       (i)   on specified or directed dates; or

       (ii)   at specified or directed intervals,

    specified or directed places with a view to receiving medical treatment;

    (d)   the imposition of a requirement on the patient to attend—

       (i)   on specified or directed dates; or

       (ii)   at specified or directed intervals,

    specified or directed places with a view to receiving community care services, relevant services or any treatment, care or service;

    (e)   the imposition of a requirement on the patient to reside at a specified place;

    (f)   the imposition of a requirement on the patient to allow—

       (i)   the mental health officer;

       (ii)   the patient's responsible medical officer; or

       (iii)   any person responsible for providing medical treatment, community care services, relevant services or any treatment, care or service to the patient who is authorised for the purposes of this paragraph by the patient's responsible medical officer,

    to visit the patient in the place where the patient resides;

    (g)   the imposition of a requirement on the patient to obtain the approval of the mental health officer to any proposed change of address; and

    (h)   the imposition of a requirement on the patient to inform the mental health officer of any change of address before the change takes effect.

(2)   Regulations may make provision for measures prescribed by the regulations to be treated as included among the measures mentioned in subsection (1) above.

(3)   In this section—

    "directed" means in accordance with directions given by the patient's responsible medical officer; and

    "specified" means specified in the compulsory treatment order or, as the case may be, the interim compulsory treatment order.

67   **Order authorising detention: ancillary authorisation**

(1)   Where a compulsory treatment order or an interim compulsory treatment order—

    (a)   authorises the detention of a patient in a hospital specified in the order; or

46   *Mental Health (Care and Treatment) (Scotland) Act 2003 (asp 13)*
Part 7—Compulsory treatment orders
Chapter 1—Application for, and making of, orders

(b) imposes a requirement on a patient to reside at a place specified in the order,

this section authorises the removal, before the expiry of the period of 7 days beginning with the appropriate day, of the patient in respect of whom the order is made to that hospital or, as the case may be, place.

(2) In subsection (1) above, "appropriate day" means the day on which—

    (a) a compulsory treatment order or, as the case may be, an interim compulsory treatment order authorising detention of a patient in hospital is made; or

    (b) a compulsory treatment order is varied so as to authorise the detention of a patient in the hospital specified in the order.

Extension of short-term detention: special case

68   Extension of short-term detention pending determination of application

(1) Where—

    (a) the detention of a patient in hospital is authorised by—

        (i) a short-term detention certificate; or

        (ii) an extension certificate; and

    (b) before the expiry of the period of detention so authorised, an application is made under section 63 of this Act,

the measures mentioned in subsection (2) below are authorised.

(2) Those measures are—

    (a) the detention in hospital of the patient for the period of 5 days beginning with the expiry of the period for which the certificate authorises the detention of the patient in hospital; and

    (b) the giving to the patient, in accordance with Part 16 of this Act, of medical treatment.

(3) In reckoning the period of days mentioned in subsection (2)(a) above, there shall be left out of account any day which is not a working day.

(4) In this section "working day" has the meaning given by section 47(8) of this Act.

Time limit for Tribunal's determination: special case

69   Time limit for determining application etc. where section 68 applies

Where section 68 of this Act applies, the Tribunal shall, before the expiry of the period of 5 days referred to in section 68(2)(a) of this Act—

    (a) determine whether an interim compulsory treatment order should be made; and

    (b) if it determines that an interim compulsory treatment order should not be made, determine the application.

Mental Health (Care and Treatment) (Scotland) Act 2003 (asp 13) 47
Part 7—Compulsory treatment orders
Chapter 2—Interim compulsory treatment orders: review and revocation

Effect of making of orders on short-term detention

70   Effect of subsequent order on short-term detention certificate

If a compulsory treatment order, or an interim compulsory treatment order, is made in respect of a patient who is in hospital under authority of a short-term detention certificate, the certificate shall, on the making of the order, be revoked.

Application of Chapter where patient subject to hospital direction or transfer for treatment direction

71   Application of Chapter where patient subject to hospital direction or transfer for treatment direction

Where a patient is subject to—

(a)   a hospital direction; or

(b)   a transfer for treatment direction,

this Chapter shall have effect in accordance with schedule 3 to this Act.

CHAPTER 2

INTERIM COMPULSORY TREATMENT ORDERS: REVIEW AND REVOCATION

72   Interim compulsory treatment order: responsible medical officer's duty to keep under review

(1)   Where a patient is subject to an interim compulsory treatment order, the patient's responsible medical officer shall from time to time consider—

(a)   whether the conditions mentioned in paragraphs (a) to (d) of section 64(5) of this Act continue to apply in respect of the patient; and

(b)   whether it continues to be necessary for the patient to be subject to an interim compulsory treatment order.

(2)   If, having considered the matters mentioned in paragraphs (a) and (b) of subsection (1) above, the responsible medical officer is not satisfied—

(a)   that the conditions mentioned in paragraphs (a) to (d) of section 64(5) of this Act continue to apply in respect of the patient; or

(b)   that it continues to be necessary for the patient to be subject to an interim compulsory treatment order,

the responsible medical officer shall make a determination revoking the interim compulsory treatment order.

(3)   A determination under this section shall be made as soon as practicable after the duty to make it arises.

73   Commission's power to revoke interim compulsory treatment order

(1)   This section applies where a patient is subject to an interim compulsory treatment order.

(2)   If the Commission is satisfied—

48   *Mental Health (Care and Treatment) (Scotland) Act 2003 (asp 13)*
Part 7—Compulsory treatment orders
Chapter 3—Compulsory treatment orders: care plan

(a) that not all of the conditions mentioned in paragraphs (a) to (d) of section 64(5) of this Act continue to apply in respect of the patient; or

(b) that it does not continue to be necessary for the patient to be subject to an interim compulsory treatment order,

the Commission may revoke the interim compulsory treatment order.

74   Revocation under section 72 or 73: notification

(1) Where a patient's responsible medical officer makes a determination under section 72 of this Act, the responsible medical officer shall, as soon as practicable after doing so—

    (a) give notice of the determination; and

    (b) send a statement of the reasons for it,

to the Commission and to the persons mentioned in subsection (3) below.

(2) Where the Commission makes a determination under section 73 of this Act, it shall, as soon as practicable after doing so—

    (a) give notice of the determination; and

    (b) send a statement of the reasons for it,

to the patient's responsible medical officer and to the persons mentioned in subsection (3) below.

(3) The persons referred to in subsections (1) and (2) above are—

    (a) the patient;

    (b) the patient's named person;

    (c) any guardian of the patient;

    (d) any welfare attorney of the patient;

    (e) the mental health officer; and

    (f) the Tribunal.

75   Effect of subsequent compulsory treatment order on interim compulsory treatment order

If a compulsory treatment order is made in respect of a patient who is subject to an interim compulsory treatment order, the interim compulsory treatment order shall, on the making of the compulsory treatment order, be revoked.

CHAPTER 3

COMPULSORY TREATMENT ORDERS: CARE PLAN

76   Care plan: preparation, placing in medical records etc.

(1) As soon as practicable after a patient's responsible medical officer is appointed under section 230 of this Act, the responsible medical officer shall—

    (a) prepare a plan (any such plan being referred to in this Act as a "care plan") relating to the patient; and

Mental Health (Care and Treatment) (Scotland) Act 2003 (asp 13)
Part 7—Compulsory treatment orders
Chapter 4—Review of orders

49

    (b) ensure that the patient's care plan is included in the patient's medical records.

(2) The care plan shall set out—

    (a) the medical treatment—

        (i) which it is proposed to give; and

        (ii) which is being given,

    to the patient while the patient is subject to the compulsory treatment order; and

    (b) such other information relating to the care of the patient as may be prescribed by regulations.

(3) Subject to subsection (4)(b) below, a patient's responsible medical officer may from time to time amend the patient's care plan.

(4) Regulations may prescribe—

    (a) circumstances in which a patient's responsible medical officer is required to amend the patient's care plan;

    (b) information in a care plan which may not be amended.

(5) Where a patient's responsible medical officer amends the patient's care plan—

    (a) the responsible medical officer shall ensure that, as soon as practicable after it is amended, the amended care plan is included in the patient's medical records; and

    (b) subsections (2) to (4) above and this subsection shall apply as if references to the care plan were references to the amended care plan.

CHAPTER 4

REVIEW OF ORDERS

Mandatory reviews by responsible medical officer

77   First mandatory review

(1) This section applies where a compulsory treatment order is made in respect of a patient.

(2) The patient's responsible medical officer shall, during the appropriate period, carry out a review in respect of the order (such review being referred to in this Part of this Act as the "first review") by complying with the requirements in subsection (3) below.

(3) Those requirements are—

    (a) to—

        (i) carry out a medical examination of the patient; or

        (ii) make arrangements for an approved medical practitioner to carry out such a medical examination;

    (b) to consider—

        (i) whether the conditions mentioned in paragraphs (a) to (d) of section 64(5) of this Act continue to apply in respect of the patient; and

        (ii) whether it continues to be necessary for the patient to be subject to a compulsory treatment order; and

50   *Mental Health (Care and Treatment) (Scotland) Act 2003 (asp 13)*
Part 7—Compulsory treatment orders
Chapter 4—Review of orders

     (c) to consult—

        (i)   the mental health officer;

        (ii) such persons as are mentioned in subsection (4) below as the responsible medical officer considers appropriate; and

        (iii) such other persons as the responsible medical officer considers appropriate.

(4)   The persons referred to in subsection (3)(c)(ii) above are—

     (a) persons who appear to the responsible medical officer to provide medical treatment of the kind that is set out in the patient's care plan;

     (b) if any community care services or relevant services are set out in that plan, persons who appear to the responsible medical officer to provide services of that kind;

     (c) if any other treatment, care or service is set out in that plan, persons who appear to the responsible medical officer to provide treatment, care or a service of that kind.

(5)   In subsection (2) above, "appropriate period" means the period of 2 months ending with the day on which the compulsory treatment order ceases to authorise the measures specified in it.

78   Further mandatory reviews

(1)   This section applies where a compulsory treatment order is extended—

     (a) by a determination under section 86 of this Act; or

     (b) by virtue of an order under section 103 of this Act.

(2)   The patient's responsible medical officer shall, during the period mentioned in subsection (3) below, carry out a review in respect of the compulsory treatment order (such review being referred to in this Part of this Act as a "further review") by complying with the requirements set out in section 77(3) of this Act.

(3)   The period referred to in subsection (2) above is the period of 2 months ending with the day on which the compulsory treatment order as extended by the determination, or by virtue of the order under section 103 of this Act, ceases to authorise the measures specified in it.

Revocation of order by responsible medical officer or Commission

79   Responsible medical officer's duty to revoke order: mandatory reviews

(1)   This section applies where a patient's responsible medical officer is carrying out—

     (a) the first review of the compulsory treatment order to which the patient is subject; or

     (b) a further review of that order.

(2)   If, having regard to any views expressed by persons consulted under section 77(3)(c) of this Act for the purpose of the review being carried out, the responsible medical officer is not satisfied—

     (a) that the conditions mentioned in paragraphs (a) to (d) of section 64(5) of this Act continue to apply in respect of the patient; or

Mental Health (Care and Treatment) (Scotland) Act 2003 (asp 13) 51
Part 7—Compulsory treatment orders
Chapter 4—Review of orders

(b) that it continues to be necessary for the patient to be subject to a compulsory treatment order,

the responsible medical officer shall make a determination revoking the compulsory treatment order.

(3) A determination under this section shall be made as soon as practicable after the duty to make it arises.

80   Revocation of order: responsible medical officer's duty to keep under review

(1) This section applies where a patient is subject to a compulsory treatment order.

(2) Without prejudice to the duties imposed on the patient's responsible medical officer by sections 77(2), 78(2), 79(2) and 93(2) of this Act, the responsible medical officer shall from time to time consider—

    (a) whether the conditions mentioned in paragraphs (a) to (d) of section 64(5) of this Act continue to apply in respect of the patient; and

    (b) whether it continues to be necessary for the patient to be subject to a compulsory treatment order.

(3) If, having considered the matters mentioned in paragraphs (a) and (b) of subsection (2) above, the responsible medical officer is not satisfied—

    (a) that the conditions mentioned in paragraphs (a) to (d) of section 64(5) of this Act continue to apply in respect of the patient; or

    (b) that it continues to be necessary for the patient to be subject to a compulsory treatment order,

the responsible medical officer shall make a determination revoking the compulsory treatment order.

(4) A determination under this section shall be made as soon as practicable after the duty to make it arises.

81   Commission's power to revoke order

(1) This section applies where a patient is subject to a compulsory treatment order.

(2) If the Commission is satisfied—

    (a) that not all of the conditions mentioned in paragraphs (a) to (d) of section 64(5) of this Act continue to apply in respect of the patient; or

    (b) that it does not continue to be necessary for the patient to be subject to a compulsory treatment order,

it may make a determination revoking the compulsory treatment order.

82   Revocation of order: notification

(1) Where a patient's responsible medical officer makes a determination under section 79 or 80 of this Act, that officer shall—

    (a) give notice of the determination; and

    (b) send a statement of the reasons for it,

52   *Mental Health (Care and Treatment) (Scotland) Act 2003 (asp 13)*
Part 7—Compulsory treatment orders
Chapter 4—Review of orders

to the Commission and to the persons mentioned in subsection (3) below.

(2)   Where the Commission makes a determination under section 81 of this Act, it shall—

      (a)   give notice of the determination; and

      (b)   send a statement of the reasons for it,

to the patient's responsible medical officer and to the persons mentioned in subsection (3) below.

(3)   The persons referred to in subsections (1) and (2) above are—

      (a)   the patient;

      (b)   the patient's named person;

      (c)   any guardian of the patient;

      (d)   any welfare attorney of the patient;

      (e)   the mental health officer; and

      (f)   the Tribunal.

(4)   Notice under subsection (1) or (2) above—

      (a)   to the persons mentioned in paragraphs (a) to (d) of subsection (3) above shall be given as soon as practicable after the determination is made and, in any event, before the expiry of the period of 7 days beginning with the day on which the determination is made; and

      (b)   to—

           (i)   the Commission;

           (ii)   the patient's responsible medical officer; and

           (iii)   the persons mentioned in paragraphs (e) and (f) of that subsection,

shall be given before the expiry of the period of 7 days beginning with the day on which the determination is made.

Further steps to be taken where order not revoked

83   **Mandatory reviews: further steps to be taken where order not revoked**

(1)   This section applies where a patient's responsible medical officer is carrying out—

      (a)   the first review of the compulsory treatment order to which the patient is subject; or

      (b)   a further review of that order.

(2)   If, having regard to any views expressed by persons consulted under section 77(3)(c) of this Act for the purpose of the review being carried out, the patient's responsible medical officer is satisfied—

      (a)   that the conditions mentioned in paragraphs (a) to (d) of section 64(5) of this Act continue to apply in respect of the patient; and

      (b)   that it continues to be necessary for the patient to be subject to a compulsory treatment order,

Mental Health (Care and Treatment) (Scotland) Act 2003 (asp 13)   53
Part 7—Compulsory treatment orders
Chapter 4—Review of orders

the responsible medical officer shall comply with the requirements in subsection (3) below.

(3)   Those requirements are—

   (a)   to consider whether it will continue to be necessary for the patient to be subject to a compulsory treatment order after the day on which the order to which the patient is subject will cease (unless extended) to authorise the measures specified in it;

   (b)   to assess the needs of the patient for medical treatment;

   (c)   to consider—

      (i)   whether the compulsory treatment order should be varied by modifying the measures, or any recorded matter, specified in it; and

      (ii)   if the order should be varied, what modification is appropriate;

   (d)   to consider any views expressed on the matters mentioned in paragraphs (a) to (c) above by persons consulted under section 77(3)(c) of this Act.

Extension of order by responsible medical officer

84   Responsible medical officer's duty where extension of order appears appropriate

(1)   This section applies where a patient's responsible medical officer is carrying out—

   (a)   the first review of the compulsory treatment order to which the patient is subject; or

   (b)   a further review of that order.

(2)   If, having regard to any views expressed by persons consulted under section 77(3)(c) of this Act for the purpose of the review being carried out, it appears to the responsible medical officer—

   (a)   that it will continue to be necessary for the patient to be subject to a compulsory treatment order after the day on which the order will cease (unless extended) to authorise the measures specified in it; and

   (b)   that the order should not be varied by modifying the measures, or any recorded matter, specified in it,

the responsible medical officer shall give notice to the mental health officer that the responsible medical officer is proposing to make a determination under section 86 of this Act extending the order.

85   Mental health officer's duties: extension of order

(1)   The mental health officer shall, as soon as practicable after receiving notice under section 84(2) of this Act, comply with the requirements in subsection (2) below.

(2)   Those requirements are—

   (a)   subject to subsection (3) below, to interview the patient;

   (b)   to inform the patient—

54   *Mental Health (Care and Treatment) (Scotland) Act 2003 (asp 13)*
Part 7—Compulsory treatment orders
Chapter 4—Review of orders

(i)   that the patient's responsible medical officer is proposing to make a determination under section 86 of this Act extending the compulsory treatment order to which the patient is subject for the period mentioned in section 86(2) of this Act;

(ii) of the patient's rights in relation to such a determination; and

(iii) of the availability of independent advocacy services under section 259 of this Act;

(c) to take appropriate steps to ensure that the patient has the opportunity of making use of those services; and

(d) to inform the patient's responsible medical officer—

(i)   of whether the mental health officer agrees, or disagrees, that the determination that is proposed should be made;

(ii) if the mental health officer disagrees, of the reason why that is the case; and

(iii) of any other matters that the mental health officer considers relevant.

(3)   If it is impracticable for the mental health officer to comply with the requirement in subsection (2)(a) above, the mental health officer need not do so.

86   Responsible medical officer's duty to extend order

(1)   If, having regard to—

(a) any views expressed by persons consulted under section 77(3)(c) of this Act for the purpose of the review being carried out; and

(b) any views expressed by the mental health officer under section 85(2)(d) of this Act for the purpose of that review,

the responsible medical officer is satisfied as to the matters mentioned in section 84(2)(a) and (b) of this Act, the responsible medical officer shall make a determination extending the compulsory treatment order for the period mentioned in subsection (2) below.

(2)   The period referred to in subsection (1) above is—

(a) where a determination is made in respect of the first review, the period of 6 months beginning with the day on which the compulsory treatment order will cease (unless extended) to authorise the measures specified in it;

(b) where a determination is made in respect of the first further review, the period of 12 months beginning with the expiry of the period mentioned in paragraph (a) above;

(c) where a determination is made in respect of a subsequent further review, the period of 12 months beginning with the expiry of the period of 12 months for which the order is extended as a result of the immediately preceding further review.

Mental Health (Care and Treatment) (Scotland) Act 2003 (asp 13) 55
Part 7—Compulsory treatment orders
Chapter 4—Review of orders

87   Determination extending order: notification etc.

(1)   Where a patient's responsible medical officer makes a determination under section 86 of this Act, that officer shall, as soon as practicable after the determination is made and, in any event, before the day on which the compulsory treatment order will cease, if it is not extended by the determination, to authorise the measures specified in it, comply with the requirements in subsection (2) below.

(2)   Those requirements are—

(a)   to prepare a record stating—

(i)   the determination;

(ii)   the reasons for it;

(iii)   whether the mental health officer agrees, or disagrees, with the determination or has failed to comply with the duty imposed by section 85(2)(d)(i) of this Act;

(iv)   if the mental health officer disagrees with the determination, the reasons for the disagreement;

(v)   (by reference to the appropriate paragraph (or paragraphs) of the definition of "mental disorder" in section 328(1) of this Act) the type (or types) of mental disorder that the patient has; and if there is a difference between that type (or types) and the type (or types) of mental disorder recorded in the compulsory treatment order in respect of which the determination is made, what that difference is; and

(vi)   such other matters as may be prescribed by regulations;

(b)   to submit the record to the Tribunal; and

(c)   at the same time as the responsible medical officer submits the record to the Tribunal, to give notice of the determination and send a copy of the record—

(i)   subject to subsection (3) below, to the patient;

(ii)   to the patient's named person;

(iii)   to the mental health officer; and

(iv)   to the Commission.

(3)   If the responsible medical officer considers that there would be a risk of significant harm to the patient, or to others, if a copy of the record were sent to the patient, that officer need not send a copy to the patient.

(4)   At the same time as the responsible medical officer submits the record to the Tribunal, that officer shall send to the Tribunal, and to the persons mentioned in subsection (2)(c)(ii) to (iv) above, a statement of the matters mentioned in subsection (5) below.

(5)   Those matters are—

(a)   whether the responsible medical officer is sending a copy of the record to the patient; and

(b)   if the responsible medical officer is not sending a copy of the record to the patient, the reason for not doing so.

56   *Mental Health (Care and Treatment) (Scotland) Act 2003 (asp 13)*
Part 7—Compulsory treatment orders
Chapter 4—Review of orders

Extension and variation of order: application by responsible medical officer

88   Responsible medical officer's duty where extension and variation of order appear appropriate

(1)   This section applies where a patient's responsible medical officer is carrying out—

    (a)   the first review of the compulsory treatment order to which the patient is subject; or

    (b)   a further review of that order.

(2)   If, having regard to any views expressed by persons consulted under section 77(3)(c) of this Act for the purpose of the review being carried out, it appears to the responsible medical officer—

    (a)   that it will continue to be necessary for the patient to be subject to a compulsory treatment order after the day on which the order will cease (unless extended) to authorise the measures specified in it; but

    (b)   that the order should be varied by modifying the measures, or any recorded matter, specified in it,

the responsible medical officer shall comply with the requirement in subsection (3) below.

(3)   That requirement is to give notice to the mental health officer—

    (a)   that the responsible medical officer is proposing to make an application to the Tribunal under section 92 of this Act for an order under section 103 of this Act—

        (i)   extending the compulsory treatment order for the period mentioned in subsection (4) below; and

        (ii)   varying that order by modifying the measures, or a recorded matter, specified in it; and

    (b)   of the modification of the measures, or any recorded matter, specified in that order that the responsible medical officer is proposing.

(4)   The period referred to in subsection (3) above is—

    (a)   where the application is made in respect of the first review, the period of 6 months beginning with the day on which the compulsory treatment order will (unless extended) cease to authorise the measures specified in it;

    (b)   where the application is made in respect of the first further review, the period of 12 months beginning with the expiry of the period mentioned in paragraph (a) above;

    (c)   where the application is made in respect of a subsequent further review, the period of 12 months beginning with the expiry of the period of 12 months for which the order is extended as a result of the immediately preceding further review.

89   Mental health officer's duties: extension and variation of order

(1)   The mental health officer shall, as soon as practicable after receiving notice under section 88(3) of this Act, comply with the requirements in subsection (2) below.

(2)   Those requirements are—

Mental Health (Care and Treatment) (Scotland) Act 2003 (asp 13) 57
Part 7—Compulsory treatment orders
Chapter 4—Review of orders

(a) subject to subsection (3) below, to interview the patient;

(b) to inform the patient of the matters mentioned in subsection (4) below;

(c) to inform the patient of the availability of independent advocacy services under section 259 of this Act;

(d) to take appropriate steps to ensure that the patient has the opportunity of making use of those services; and

(e) to inform the patient's responsible medical officer—

    (i) of whether the mental health officer agrees, or disagrees, that the application that is proposed should be made;

    (ii) if the mental health officer disagrees, of the reason why that is the case; and

    (iii) of any other matters that the mental health officer considers relevant.

(3) If it is impracticable for the mental health officer to comply with the requirement in subsection (2)(a) above, the mental health officer need not do so.

(4) The matters referred to in subsection (2)(b) above are—

(a) that the patient's responsible medical officer is proposing to make an application to the Tribunal under section 92 of this Act for an order—

    (i) extending the compulsory treatment order to which the patient is subject for the period mentioned in section 88(4) of this Act; and

    (ii) varying the compulsory treatment order by modifying the measures or a recorded matter specified in it;

(b) the modification of the measures or any recorded matter specified in that order that the responsible medical officer is proposing; and

(c) the patient's rights in relation to such an application.

90 Responsible medical officer's duty to apply for extension and variation of order

(1) If, having regard to—

(a) any views expressed by persons consulted under section 77(3)(c) of this Act for the purpose of the review being carried out; and

(b) any views expressed by the mental health officer under section 89(2)(e) of this Act for the purpose of that review,

the responsible medical officer is satisfied as to the matters mentioned in section 88(2)(a) and (b) of this Act, the responsible medical officer shall comply with the requirement in subsection (2) below.

(2) That requirement is to make an application to the Tribunal under section 92 of this Act for an order—

(a) extending the compulsory treatment order for the period mentioned in section 88(4) of this Act; and

(b) varying that order by modifying the measures, or a recorded matter, specified in it.

(3) An application made under section 92 of this Act, by virtue of subsection (1) above, for an order mentioned in subsection (2) above shall be made as soon as practicable after the duty to make it arises.

58   *Mental Health (Care and Treatment) (Scotland) Act 2003 (asp 13)*
Part 7—Compulsory treatment orders
Chapter 4—Review of orders

91   **Application for extension and variation of order: notification**

Where, by virtue of section 90(1) of this Act, an application is to be made under section 92 of this Act, the patient's responsible medical officer shall, as soon as practicable after the duty to make the application arises (and, in any event, before making the application), give notice that the application is to be made to—

    (a) the patient;

    (b) the patient's named person;

    (c) any guardian of the patient;

    (d) any welfare attorney of the patient;

    (e) the mental health officer; and

    (f) the Commission.

92   **Application to Tribunal**

An application under this section to the Tribunal by a patient's responsible medical officer for an order extending and varying a compulsory treatment order—

    (a) shall state—

        (i)   the name and address of the patient;

        (ii)   the name and address of the patient's named person;

        (iii) the modification of the measures, or any recorded matter, specified in the compulsory treatment order that is proposed by the responsible medical officer;

        (iv) the reasons for seeking that modification;

        (v)   whether the mental health officer agrees, or disagrees, that the application should be made, or has failed to comply with the duty imposed by section 89(2)(e)(i) of this Act; and

        (vi) if the mental health officer disagrees, the reason for that disagreement; and

    (b) shall be accompanied by such documents as may be prescribed by regulations.

Variation of order: application by responsible medical officer

93   **Responsible medical officer's duties: variation of order**

  (1)   This section applies where a patient is subject to a compulsory treatment order.

  (2)   Without prejudice to the duties imposed on the patient's responsible medical officer by sections 77(2), 78(2) and 83(2) of this Act, the responsible medical officer shall from time to time consider whether the compulsory treatment order should be varied by modifying the measures, or any recorded matter, specified in it.

  (3)   If it appears to the responsible medical officer that the compulsory treatment order should be varied as mentioned in subsection (2) above, the responsible medical officer shall, as soon as practicable, comply with the requirements in subsection (4) below.

  (4)   Those requirements are—

Mental Health (Care and Treatment) (Scotland) Act 2003 (asp 13)
Part 7—Compulsory treatment orders
Chapter 4—Review of orders

59

    (a) to assess the needs of the patient for medical treatment;

    (b) to consider what modification, if any, of the measures, or any recorded matter, specified in the compulsory treatment order is appropriate;

    (c) to consult—

        (i) the mental health officer; and

        (ii) such persons as the responsible medical officer considers appropriate.

(5) If, having regard to any views expressed by persons consulted under subsection (4)(c) above, the responsible medical officer is satisfied that the compulsory treatment order should be varied as mentioned in subsection (2) above, the responsible medical officer shall make an application to the Tribunal under section 95 of this Act for an order under section 103 of this Act varying the compulsory treatment order in that way.

(6) An application made under section 95 of this Act, by virtue of subsection (5) above, for an order mentioned in that subsection shall be made as soon as practicable after the duty to make it arises.

94   Application by responsible medical officer for variation of order: notification

Where, by virtue of section 93(5) of this Act, an application is to be made under section 95 of this Act, the patient's responsible medical officer shall, as soon as practicable after the duty to make the application arises (and, in any event, before making the application), give notice that the application is to be made to the persons mentioned in section 91(a) to (f) of this Act.

95   Application to Tribunal by responsible medical officer

An application under this section to the Tribunal by a patient's responsible medical officer for an order varying a compulsory treatment order—

    (a) shall state the matters mentioned in section 92(a)(i) to (vi) of this Act; and

    (b) shall be accompanied by such documents as may be prescribed by regulations.

Recorded matters: reference to Tribunal by responsible medical officer

96   Recorded matters: reference to Tribunal by responsible medical officer

(1) This section applies where a patient is subject to a compulsory treatment order which specifies one or more recorded matters.

(2) Without prejudice to the duties imposed on the patient's responsible medical officer by sections 77(2), 78(2) and 83(2) of this Act and subject to subsection (6) below, if it appears to the responsible medical officer that any recorded matter specified in the compulsory treatment order is not being provided, the responsible medical officer shall, as soon as practicable, consult—

    (a) the mental health officer; and

    (b) such other persons as the responsible medical officer considers appropriate.

60   *Mental Health (Care and Treatment) (Scotland) Act 2003 (asp 13)*
Part 7—Compulsory treatment orders
Chapter 4—Review of orders

(3)   If, having regard to any views expressed by persons consulted under subsection (2) above, the responsible medical officer is satisfied that a recorded matter specified in the compulsory treatment order is not being provided, the responsible medical officer shall make a reference to the Tribunal.

(4)   A reference under subsection (3) above—

    (a)   shall state—

        (i)   the name and address of the patient;

        (ii) the name and address of the patient's named person; and

        (iii) the reason for making the reference; and

    (b)   shall be accompanied by such documents as may be prescribed by regulations.

(5)   A reference under subsection (3) above shall be made as soon as practicable after the duty to make it arises.

(6)   Subsections (2) to (5) above do not apply where—

    (a)   the responsible medical officer is required, by virtue of section 79 or 80 of this Act, to revoke the compulsory treatment order; or

    (b)   the responsible medical officer is making an application under section 92 or 95 of this Act in respect of the compulsory treatment order.

97   Reference to Tribunal under section 96(3): notification

Where a patient's responsible medical officer is required by section 96(3) of this Act to make a reference to the Tribunal, the responsible medical officer shall, as soon as practicable after the duty to make the reference arises, give notice that the reference is to be made to the persons mentioned in section 91(a) to (f) of this Act.

Reference to Tribunal by Commission

98   Reference to Tribunal by Commission

(1)   This section applies where a patient is subject to a compulsory treatment order.

(2)   If it appears to the Commission that it is appropriate to do so, it may make a reference to the Tribunal in respect of the compulsory treatment order to which the patient is subject.

(3)   Where a reference is to be made under subsection (2) above, the Commission shall, as soon as practicable, give notice that a reference is to be made to—

    (a)   the patient's responsible medical officer; and

    (b)   the persons mentioned in section 91(a) to (e) of this Act.

(4)   A reference under subsection (2) above shall state—

    (a)   the name and address of the patient;

    (b)   the name and address of the patient's named person; and

    (c)   the reason for making the reference.

Mental Health (Care and Treatment) (Scotland) Act 2003 (asp 13)   61
Part 7—Compulsory treatment orders
Chapter 4—Review of orders

Applications by patient etc.

99   **Application by patient etc. for revocation of determination extending order**

(1)   Where a patient's responsible medical officer makes a determination under section 86 of this Act, subject to subsection (3) below, either of the persons mentioned in subsection (2) below may make an application under this section to the Tribunal for an order under section 103 of this Act revoking the determination.

(2)   Those persons are—

    (a)   the patient;

    (b)   the patient's named person.

(3)   Subsection (1) above does not apply where the Tribunal is required, by virtue of section 101 of this Act, to review the determination.

100   **Application by patient etc. for revocation or variation of order**

(1)   This section applies where a patient is subject to a compulsory treatment order.

(2)   Either of the persons mentioned in subsection (3) below may, subject to subsections (4) and (6) below, make an application under this section to the Tribunal for an order under section 103 of this Act—

    (a)   revoking the compulsory treatment order; or

    (b)   varying that order by modifying—

       (i)   the measures; or

       (ii)   any recorded matter,

    specified in it.

(3)   Those persons are—

    (a)   the patient;

    (b)   the patient's named person.

(4)   An application under this section may not be made during the period of 3 months beginning with the making of any of the orders mentioned in subsection (5) below.

(5)   Those orders are—

    (a)   the compulsory treatment order;

    (b)   an order in respect of the compulsory treatment order made under section 102 of this Act;

    (c)   an order in respect of the compulsory treatment order made, by virtue of section 92 of this Act, under section 103 of this Act.

(6)   If—

    (a)   an application under this section for revocation of a compulsory treatment order is refused; or

    (b)   an application is made under this section for variation of a compulsory treatment order,

62   *Mental Health (Care and Treatment) (Scotland) Act 2003 (asp 13)*
Part 7—Compulsory treatment orders
Chapter 4—Review of orders

the person who made the application shall not be entitled to make more than one further application under this section in respect of the compulsory treatment order during the period mentioned in subsection (8) below.

(7)   If an application under section 99 of this Act for revocation of a determination under section 86 of this Act is refused, the person who made the application shall not be entitled to make more than one application under this section in respect of the compulsory treatment order which is the subject of the determination during the period mentioned in subsection (8) below.

(8)   The period referred to in subsections (6) and (7) above is—

    (a)   where the application mentioned in subsection (6)(a) or (b) or (7) above is made before the expiry of the period of 6 months beginning with the day on which the compulsory treatment order was made, that period of 6 months; or

    (b)   where that application is made before the expiry of—

        (i)   the period of 6 months beginning with the expiry of the period mentioned in paragraph (a) above, that period of 6 months; or

        (ii)   any subsequent period of 12 months that begins with, or with an anniversary of, the expiry of the period of 6 months mentioned in sub-paragraph (i) above, that subsequent period of 12 months.

Review by Tribunal of determination extending order

101   Tribunal's duty to review determination under section 86

(1)   This section applies where a patient's responsible medical officer makes a determination under section 86 of this Act.

(2)   If—

    (a)   the record submitted to the Tribunal under section 87(2)(b) of this Act states—

        (i)   that there is a difference between the type (or types) of mental disorder that the patient has and the type (or types) of mental disorder recorded in the compulsory treatment order in respect of which the determination is made; or

        (ii)   that the mental health officer disagrees with the determination or has failed to comply with the duty imposed by section 85(2)(d)(i) of this Act; or

    (b)   no decision has been made by the Tribunal under this section or section 103 of this Act in respect of the compulsory treatment order to which the determination relates during the period of 2 years ending with the day on which the order, had it not been extended by the determination, would have ceased to authorise the measures specified in it,

the Tribunal shall review the determination.

Powers of Tribunal

102   Powers of Tribunal on review under section 101

(1)   On the review of a determination under section 101 of this Act, the Tribunal may make an order under this section—

Mental Health (Care and Treatment) (Scotland) Act 2003 (asp 13)   63
Part 7—Compulsory treatment orders
Chapter 4—Review of orders

      (a) revoking the determination;

      (b) revoking both the determination and the compulsory treatment order;

      (c) confirming the determination; or

      (d) confirming the determination and varying the compulsory treatment order by modifying—

          (i) the measures; or

          (ii) any recorded matter,

      specified in it.

(2)   Before making a decision under subsection (1) above, the Tribunal shall allow the persons mentioned in subsection (3) below the opportunity—

      (a) of making representations (whether orally or in writing); and

      (b) of leading, or producing, evidence.

(3)   Those persons are—

      (a) the patient;

      (b) the patient's named person;

      (c) any guardian of the patient;

      (d) any welfare attorney of the patient;

      (e) the mental health officer;

      (f) the patient's responsible medical officer;

      (g) the patient's primary carer;

      (h) any curator *ad litem* appointed in respect of the patient by the Tribunal; and

      (i) any other person appearing to the Tribunal to have an interest in the determination.

103   **Powers of Tribunal on application under section 92, 95, 99 or 100**

(1)   Where an application is made under section 92 of this Act, the Tribunal may make an order—

      (a) extending the compulsory treatment order to which the application relates for the period mentioned in section 88(4) of this Act and varying the compulsory treatment order by modifying—

          (i) the measures; or

          (ii) any recorded matter,

      specified in it;

      (b) extending the compulsory treatment order for that period;

      (c) refusing the application; or

      (d) refusing the application and revoking the compulsory treatment order.

(2)   Where an application is made under section 99 of this Act, the Tribunal may make an order—

64   *Mental Health (Care and Treatment) (Scotland) Act 2003 (asp 13)*
Part 7—Compulsory treatment orders
Chapter 4—Review of orders

    (a) revoking the determination to which the application relates;

    (b) revoking—

        (i) the determination; and

        (ii) the compulsory treatment order to which the determination relates;

    (c) confirming the determination; or

    (d) confirming the determination and varying the compulsory treatment order by modifying—

        (i) the measures; or

        (ii) any recorded matter,

    specified in it.

(3)   Where an application is made under section 100(2)(a) of this Act, the Tribunal may make an order—

    (a) revoking the compulsory treatment order to which the application relates;

    (b) varying the compulsory treatment order by modifying—

        (i) the measures; or

        (ii) any recorded matter,

    specified in it; or

    (c) refusing the application.

(4)   Where an application is made under section 95 or 100(2)(b) of this Act, the Tribunal may make an order—

    (a) varying the compulsory treatment order to which the application relates by modifying—

        (i) the measures; or

        (ii) any recorded matter,

    specified in it;

    (b) refusing the application; or

    (c) refusing the application and revoking that order.

(5)   Before making a decision under any of subsections (1) to (4) above, the Tribunal shall afford the persons mentioned in subsection (6) below the opportunity—

    (a) of making representations (whether orally or in writing); and

    (b) of leading, or producing, evidence.

(6)   Those persons are—

    (a) the persons mentioned in section 102(3)(a) to (h) of this Act; and

    (b) any other person appearing to the Tribunal to have an interest in the application.

Mental Health (Care and Treatment) (Scotland) Act 2003 (asp 13) 65
Part 7—Compulsory treatment orders
Chapter 4—Review of orders

104   Powers of Tribunal on reference under section 96 or 98

(1)   Where a reference is made under section 96 or 98 of this Act, the Tribunal may make an order—

    (a)   varying the compulsory treatment order in respect of which the reference is made by modifying—

        (i)   the measures; or

        (ii)   any recorded matter,

    specified in it; or

    (b)   revoking the compulsory treatment order.

(2)   Before making an order under subsection (1) above, the Tribunal shall allow the persons mentioned in subsection (3) below the opportunity—

    (a)   of making representations (whether orally or in writing); and

    (b)   of leading, or producing, evidence.

(3)   Those persons are—

    (a)   the persons mentioned in section 102(3)(a) to (h) of this Act; and

    (b)   any other person appearing to the Tribunal to have an interest in the reference.

105   Interim extension etc. of order: application under section 92

(1)   This section applies where an application is made under section 92 of this Act.

(2)   Subject to section 107 of this Act, on the application of any person having an interest in the proceedings, or *ex proprio motu*, the Tribunal may, if it considers—

    (a)   that it will be unable to determine the application before the compulsory treatment order to which the application relates ceases to authorise the measures specified in it; and

    (b)   that it is appropriate, pending its determining the application, to—

        (i)   extend the order; or

        (ii)   extend and vary the order by modifying the measures, or any recorded matter, specified in it,

make an interim order extending, or extending and varying, the compulsory treatment order for such period not exceeding 28 days as may be specified in the order of the Tribunal.

106   Interim variation of order: application, reference or review under Chapter

(1)   This section applies where—

    (a)   an application is made under section 92, 95, 99 or 100 of this Act;

    (b)   a reference is made under section 96 or 98 of this Act; or

    (c)   the Tribunal is reviewing a determination under section 101 of this Act.

66   *Mental Health (Care and Treatment) (Scotland) Act 2003 (asp 13)*
Part 7—Compulsory treatment orders
Chapter 4—Review of orders

(2)   Subject to section 107 of this Act, on the application of any person having an interest in the proceedings, or *ex proprio motu*, the Tribunal may, if it considers that it is appropriate to do so pending its—

     (a)   determining the application or reference; or

     (b)   making its decision on the review;

make an interim order varying the compulsory treatment order by modifying the measures, or any recorded matter, specified in it, for such period not exceeding 28 days as may be specified in the order of the Tribunal.

107   Limit on Tribunal's power to make interim orders

The Tribunal may not make an interim order under section 105 or 106 of this Act if the effect of making the order would be that interim orders under either, or both, of those sections would be in force for a continuous period of more than 56 days.

108   Tribunal's order varying compulsory treatment order

Where the Tribunal makes—

     (a)   an order under section 102, 103, 104 or 106 of this Act varying a compulsory treatment order; or

     (b)   an order under section 103 or 105 of this Act extending and varying such an order,

the Tribunal shall specify in its order the modifications made by its order to the measures, and any recorded matter, specified in the compulsory treatment order.

109   Ancillary powers of Tribunal

(1)   This section applies where—

     (a)   an application is made to the Tribunal under section 92, 95, 99 or 100 of this Act;

     (b)   the Tribunal is, under section 101 of this Act, reviewing a determination; or

     (c)   a reference is made to the Tribunal under section 96 or 98 of this Act.

(2)   Regulations may prescribe circumstances in which the Tribunal may require—

     (a)   the patient's responsible medical officer; or

     (b)   the mental health officer,

to prepare and submit to the Tribunal reports on such matters as may be prescribed.

Effect of interim orders on calculation of time periods in Chapter

110   Effect of interim orders on calculation of time periods in Chapter

(1)   Subject to subsection (2) below, in calculating, for the purpose of this Chapter, the day on which a compulsory treatment order—

     (a)   ceases;

     (b)   will cease; or

     (c)   would have ceased,

Mental Health (Care and Treatment) (Scotland) Act 2003 (asp 13)
Part 7—Compulsory treatment orders
Chapter 5—Breach of orders

67

to authorise the measures specified in it, there shall be left out of account any period for which the order is extended (or extended and varied) by an interim order under section 105 of this Act.

(2) Subsection (1) above does not apply as respects calculating that day for the purpose of that section.

Meaning of "modify"

111   Meaning of "modify"

In this Chapter, any reference to modifying measures, or recorded matters, specified in a compulsory treatment order includes a reference to—

(a) amending those measures or recorded matters;

(b) removing from the order any measure or recorded matter;

(c) adding to the order any measure or recorded matter;

(d) specifying a recorded matter in an order which does not specify a recorded matter.

CHAPTER 5

BREACH OF ORDERS

Failure to attend for medical treatment

112   Failure to attend for medical treatment

(1) Subject to subsection (2) below, where—

(a) a patient is subject to—

(i) a compulsory treatment order; or

(ii) an interim compulsory treatment order,

that imposes on the patient a requirement mentioned in section 66(1)(c) of this Act ("the attendance requirement"); and

(b) the patient fails to comply with the attendance requirement,

the patient's responsible medical officer may exercise the power conferred by subsection (3) below.

(2) The responsible medical officer may exercise the power conferred by subsection (3) below only if—

(a) the responsible medical officer has consulted a mental health officer; and

(b) the mental health officer consents to the power being exercised.

(3) The responsible medical officer may take, or may cause a person authorised for the purpose by the responsible medical officer to take, the patient into custody and convey the patient—

(a) to the place the patient is required to attend by the attendance requirement; or

(b) to any hospital.

(4) Subject to subsection (5) below, where by virtue of subsection (3) above the patient is conveyed to the place the patient is required to attend or a hospital—

68   *Mental Health (Care and Treatment) (Scotland) Act 2003 (asp 13)*
Part 7—Compulsory treatment orders
Chapter 5—Breach of orders

(a) if the order to which the patient is subject authorises the measure mentioned in section 66(1)(b) of this Act, the patient may be detained there for so long as is necessary for the purpose of giving to the patient any medical treatment that could have been given to the patient had the patient complied with the attendance requirement;

(b) if the order to which the patient is subject does not authorise that measure, the patient may be detained there for so long as is necessary to determine whether the patient is capable of consenting to medical treatment and, if so, whether the patient consents to receive any medical treatment.

(5) The patient may not be detained by virtue of subsection (4) above for more than a period of 6 hours beginning with the arrival of the patient in the place or hospital.

Non-compliance generally with order

113   Non-compliance generally with order

(1) Where—

     (a) a patient is subject to—

         (i) a compulsory treatment order; or

         (ii) an interim compulsory treatment order,

     that does not authorise the detention of the patient in hospital;

     (b) the patient fails to comply with any measure authorised by the order; and

     (c) subsection (2) or (3) below applies,

the power conferred by subsection (4) below may be exercised.

(2) This subsection applies if the patient's responsible medical officer considers that—

     (a) reasonable steps have been taken to contact the patient following the patient's failure to comply with the measure;

     (b) if contact has been made with the patient, the patient has been afforded a reasonable opportunity to comply with the measure; and

     (c) if the patient were to continue to fail to comply with the measure, it is reasonably likely that there would be a significant deterioration in the patient's mental health.

(3) This subsection applies if the patient's responsible medical officer considers that—

     (a) if the patient were to continue to fail to comply with the measure, it is reasonably likely that there would be a significant deterioration in the patient's mental health; and

     (b) it is necessary as a matter of urgency that the power conferred by subsection (4) below be exercised.

(4) The patient's responsible medical officer may take, or may cause a person authorised for the purpose by the responsible medical officer to take, the patient into custody and convey the patient to a hospital.

(5) Where the power conferred by subsection (4) above is exercised in relation to a patient, the patient may be detained in hospital for the period of 72 hours beginning with the arrival by virtue of that subsection of the patient in hospital.

Mental Health (Care and Treatment) (Scotland) Act 2003 (asp 13)
Part 7—Compulsory treatment orders
Chapter 5—Breach of orders

69

(6) As soon as reasonably practicable after the patient has been conveyed to a hospital, the responsible medical officer shall—

    (a) carry out a medical examination of the patient; or

    (b) make arrangements for an approved medical practitioner to carry out such an examination.

114 Compulsory treatment order: detention pending review or application for variation

(1) Subsection (2) below applies where—

    (a) a patient who is subject to an order such as is mentioned in subsection (1)(a)(i) of section 113 of this Act is detained in hospital by virtue of subsection (5) of that section;

    (b) the patient has been examined under subsection (6) of that section;

    (c) the patient's responsible medical officer—

        (i) is considering under subsection (2) of section 93 of this Act whether that order should be varied by modifying the measures specified in it; or

        (ii) by virtue of subsection (5) of that section, is required to make an application to the Tribunal; and

    (d) the patient's responsible medical officer considers that if the patient does not continue to be detained in hospital it is reasonably likely that there will be a significant deterioration in the patient's mental health.

(2) Subject to subsections (3) and (4) below, the responsible medical officer may grant a certificate authorising the continued detention in hospital of the patient for the period of 28 days beginning with the granting of the certificate.

(3) The power in subsection (2) above may be exercised only if—

    (a) the responsible medical officer has consulted the mental health officer; and

    (b) the mental health officer consents to the power being exercised.

(4) Before granting a certificate under subsection (2) above the responsible medical officer shall, if it is practicable to do so, consult the patient's named person.

(5) A certificate under subsection (2) above—

    (a) shall state the responsible medical officer's reasons for believing that paragraph (d) of subsection (1) applies in the patient's case; and

    (b) shall be signed by the responsible medical officer.

115 Interim compulsory treatment order: detention pending further procedure

(1) Subsection (2) below applies where—

    (a) a patient who is subject to an order such as is mentioned in subsection (1)(a)(ii) of section 113 of this Act is detained in hospital by virtue of subsection (5) of that section;

    (b) the patient has been examined under subsection (6) of that section;

70   *Mental Health (Care and Treatment) (Scotland) Act 2003 (asp 13)*
Part 7—Compulsory treatment orders
Chapter 5—Breach of orders

(c)   the patient's responsible medical officer considers that if the patient does not continue to be detained in hospital it is reasonably likely that there will be a significant deterioration in the patient's mental health; and

(d)   on the expiry of the period of detention authorised by subsection (5) of that section the period for which the order authorises the measures specified in it will not have expired.

(2)   Subject to subsections (3) and (4) below, the responsible medical officer may grant a certificate authorising the continued detention in hospital of the patient for the period beginning with the granting of the certificate and ending with the expiry of the period for which the order authorises the measures specified in it.

(3)   The power in subsection (2) above may be exercised only if—

(a)   the patient's responsible medical officer has consulted a mental health officer; and

(b)   the mental health officer consents to the power being exercised.

(4)   Before granting a certificate the responsible medical officer shall, if it is practicable to do so, consult the patient's named person.

(5)   A certificate under subsection (2) above—

(a)   shall state the responsible medical officer's reasons for believing that subsection (1)(c) above applies in the patient's case; and

(b)   shall be signed by the responsible medical officer.

116   Certificate under section 114(2) or 115(2): notification

(1)   This section applies where a certificate is granted under section 114(2) or 115(2) of this Act in respect of a patient.

(2)   The managers of the hospital in which the patient is detained shall, as soon as practicable after the granting of the certificate, give notice of its granting to—

(a)   the patient;

(b)   the patient's named person;

(c)   any guardian of the patient; and

(d)   any welfare attorney of the patient.

(3)   The managers of the hospital in which the patient is detained shall, before the expiry of the period of 7 days beginning with the granting of the certificate, give notice of its granting, and send a copy of it, to—

(a)   the Tribunal; and

(b)   the Commission.

Revocation of certificates

117   Certificate under section 114(2): responsible medical officer's duty to revoke

(1)   Where—

(a)   a patient's responsible medical officer grants, by virtue of subsection (1)(c)(i) of section 114 of this Act, a certificate under subsection (2) of that section; and

Mental Health (Care and Treatment) (Scotland) Act 2003 (asp 13)   71
Part 7—Compulsory treatment orders
Chapter 5—Breach of orders

    (b) the responsible medical officer determines that the order should not be varied as mentioned in section 93(2) of this Act,

the responsible medical officer shall revoke the certificate.

(2) Where—

    (a) a patient's responsible medical officer grants, by virtue of subsection (1)(c)(ii) of section 114 of this Act, a certificate under subsection (2) of that section; and

    (b) the responsible medical officer is not satisfied that if the patient does not continue to be detained in hospital it is reasonably likely that there will be a significant deterioration in the patient's mental health,

the responsible medical officer shall revoke the certificate.

118   Certificate under section 115(2): responsible medical officer's duty to revoke

Where—

    (a) a patient's responsible medical officer grants a certificate under section 115(2) of this Act; and

    (b) the responsible medical officer is not satisfied that if the patient does not continue to be detained in hospital it is reasonably likely that there will be a significant deterioration in the patient's mental health,

the responsible medical officer shall revoke the certificate.

119   Revocation of certificate granted under section 114(2) or 115(2): notification

Where a patient's responsible medical officer revokes, under section 117 or 118 of this Act, a certificate, the responsible medical officer shall—

    (a) as soon as practicable after the revocation, give notice of the revocation to the persons mentioned in subsection (2) of section 116 of this Act; and

    (b) before the expiry of the period of 7 days beginning with the revocation, give notice of the revocation to the persons mentioned in subsection (3) of that section.

120   Certificates under sections 114(2) and 115(2): patient's right to apply to Tribunal

(1) This section applies where a certificate is granted under section 114(2) or 115(2) of this Act in respect of a patient.

(2) On the application of the patient or the patient's named person, the Tribunal shall, if not satisfied that if the patient does not continue to be detained in hospital it is reasonably likely that there will be a significant deterioration in the patient's mental health, revoke the certificate.

Effect of section 113(5) on order

121   Effect of section 113(5) on order

(1) Subject to subsection (2) below, where a patient is detained in hospital under section 113(5) of this Act, the compulsory treatment order or, as the case may be, interim compulsory treatment order to which the patient is subject shall cease, during the period mentioned in that section, to authorise the measures specified in it.

72   *Mental Health (Care and Treatment) (Scotland) Act 2003 (asp 13)*
Part 7—Compulsory treatment orders
Chapter 6—Transfers

(2)   If the measure mentioned in section 66(1)(b) of this Act is specified in the order, the order shall continue to authorise that measure during the period referred to in subsection (1) above.

Effect of certificate under section 114(2) on order

122   Effect of certificate under section 114(2) on order

(1)   Subject to subsection (2) below, where a certificate is granted under section 114(2) of this Act in respect of a patient, the compulsory treatment order to which the patient is subject shall cease, during the period mentioned in that section, to authorise the measures specified in it.

(2)   If the measure mentioned in section 66(1)(b) of this Act is specified in the order, the order shall continue to authorise that measure during the period referred to in subsection (1) above.

Effect of certificate under section 115(2) on order

123   Effect of certificate under section 115(2) on order

(1)   Subject to subsection (2) below, where a certificate is granted under section 115(2) of this Act in respect of a patient, the interim compulsory treatment order to which the patient is subject shall cease, during the period mentioned in that section, to authorise the measures specified in it.

(2)   If the measure mentioned in section 66(1)(b) of this Act is specified in the order, the order shall continue to authorise that measure during the period referred to in subsection (1) above.

CHAPTER 6

TRANSFERS

124   Transfer to other hospital

(1)   This section applies where the detention of a patient in hospital is authorised by a compulsory treatment order.

(2)   The managers of the hospital in which the patient is detained may, where the condition mentioned in subsection (3) below is satisfied, transfer the patient to another hospital.

(3)   The condition is that the managers of the hospital to which it is proposed to transfer the patient consent to the transfer.

(4)   Where the managers of a hospital propose to transfer the patient under subsection (2) above, they shall, subject to subsections (5) and (7) below, give the persons mentioned in subsection (8) below at least 7 days' notice of the transfer.

(5)   The managers of a hospital need not give notice under subsection (4) above where it is necessary that the patient be transferred urgently.

(6)   Where, by virtue of subsection (5) above, notice is not given under subsection (4) above, the managers of the hospital shall, subject to subsection (7) below, give the persons mentioned in subsection (8) below notice—

        (a)   where the proposed transfer has not taken place, of the proposed transfer; or

Mental Health (Care and Treatment) (Scotland) Act 2003 (asp 13)
Part 7—Compulsory treatment orders
Chapter 6—Transfers

73

(b)   where the transfer has taken place, of the transfer,

as soon as practicable before, on or, as the case may be, after the transfer.

(7)   The managers of the hospital need not give notice to the patient under subsection (4) or, as the case may be, (6) above where the patient consents to the transfer.

(8)   The persons referred to in subsections (4) and (6) above are—

(a)   the patient;

(b)   the patient's named person; and

(c)   the patient's primary carer.

(9)   Where—

(a)   notice is given under subsection (4) or (6)(a) above of a proposed transfer under subsection (2) above; and

(b)   the proposed transfer does not take place before the end of the period of 3 months beginning with the day on which notice is given,

the managers of the hospital may transfer the patient as proposed only if subsection (10) below applies.

(10)   This subsection applies where—

(a)   the condition mentioned in subsection (3) above continues to be satisfied; and

(b)   the persons mentioned in subsection (8) above are given at least 7 days' notice of the proposed transfer.

(11)   Subsections (5) to (7) above shall apply to the giving of notice under subsection (10)(b) above as they apply to the giving of notice under subsection (4) above.

(12)   Where the patient is transferred under subsection (2) above, the managers of the hospital from which the patient is transferred shall, before the expiry of the period of 7 days beginning with the transfer, give notice to the Commission of the matters mentioned in subsection (13) below.

(13)   Those matters are—

(a)   the date on which the patient was transferred;

(b)   the hospital to which the patient was transferred;

(c)   that—

(i)   notice was given under subsection (4) above; or

(ii)   if no such notice was given, the reasons why it was necessary that the patient be transferred urgently; and

(d)   whether notice was given under subsection (6) or (10)(b) above.

(14)   Where the patient is transferred under subsection (2) above, the compulsory treatment order shall, for the purposes of this Act (other than sections 125 and 126), be taken to specify the hospital to which the patient is transferred.

125   Transfer to hospital other than state hospital: appeal to Tribunal

(1)   This section applies where a patient—

74   *Mental Health (Care and Treatment) (Scotland) Act 2003 (asp 13)*
Part 7—Compulsory treatment orders
Chapter 6—Transfers

        (a)   receives notice under subsection (4), (6)(a) or (10)(b) of section 124 of this Act that it is proposed to transfer the patient; or

        (b)   is transferred under subsection (2) of that section,

to any hospital other than a state hospital.

(2)   The patient, or the patient's named person, may, during the period mentioned in subsection (3) below, appeal to the Tribunal against the proposed transfer or, as the case may be, the transfer.

(3)   That period is—

        (a)   in the case of the patient—

           (i)   where notice is given to the patient before the proposed transfer, the period beginning with the day on which notice is given and ending 28 days after the transfer;

           (ii) where notice is given to the patient on or after the transfer, the period beginning with the day on which the patient is transferred and ending 28 days after the day on which notice is given; or

           (iii) where notice is not given to the patient, the period of 28 days beginning with the day on which the patient is transferred;

        (b)   in the case of the patient's named person—

           (i)   where notice is given to the patient's named person before the proposed transfer, the period beginning with the day on which notice is given and ending 28 days after the transfer; or

           (ii) where notice is given to the patient's named person on or after the transfer, the period of 28 days beginning with the day on which notice is given.

(4)   If, when an appeal under subsection (2) above against a proposed transfer is made to the Tribunal, the proposed transfer has not taken place—

        (a)   the managers of the hospital shall not transfer the patient as proposed; but

        (b)   the Tribunal may, if satisfied that, pending the determination of the appeal, the patient should be transferred as proposed, make an order that the patient be so transferred.

(5)   On an appeal under subsection (2) above, the Tribunal may make an order that the proposed transfer not take place or, as the case may be, that the patient be returned to the hospital from which the patient was transferred.

126   **Transfer to state hospital: appeal to Tribunal**

(1)   This section applies where a patient—

        (a)   receives notice under subsection (4), (6)(a) or (10)(b) of section 124 of this Act that it is proposed to transfer the patient; or

        (b)   is transferred under subsection (2) of that section,

to a state hospital.

Mental Health (Care and Treatment) (Scotland) Act 2003 (asp 13)   75
Part 7—Compulsory treatment orders
Chapter 7—Suspension

(2)   The patient, or the patient's named person, may, during the period mentioned in subsection (3) below, appeal to the Tribunal against the proposed transfer or, as the case may be, the transfer.

(3)   That period is—

    (a)   in the case of the patient—

        (i)   where notice is given to the patient before the proposed transfer, the period beginning with the day on which notice is given and ending 12 weeks after the transfer;

        (ii)   where notice is given to the patient on or after the transfer, the period beginning with the day on which the patient is transferred and ending 12 weeks after the day on which notice is given; or

        (iii)   where notice is not given to the patient, the period of 12 weeks beginning with the day on which the patient is transferred;

    (b)   in the case of the patient's named person—

        (i)   where notice is given to the patient's named person before the proposed transfer, the period beginning with the day on which notice is given and ending 12 weeks after the transfer; or

        (ii)   where notice is given to the patient's named person on or after the transfer, the period of 12 weeks beginning with the day on which notice is given.

(4)   If, when an appeal under subsection (2) above against a proposed transfer is made to the Tribunal, the proposed transfer has not taken place—

    (a)   the managers of the hospital shall not transfer the patient as proposed; but

    (b)   the Tribunal may, if satisfied that, pending determination of the appeal, the patient should be transferred as proposed, make an order that the patient be so transferred.

(5)   On an appeal under subsection (2) above, the Tribunal may, if not satisfied as to the matter mentioned in subsection (6) below, make an order that the proposed transfer not take place or, as the case may be, that the patient be returned to the hospital from which the patient was transferred.

(6)   That matter is—

    (a)   that the patient requires to be detained in hospital under conditions of special security; and

    (b)   that those conditions of special security can be provided only in a state hospital.

CHAPTER 7

SUSPENSION

127   Suspension of measure authorising detention

(1)   Where—

    (a)   a patient is subject to a compulsory treatment order that authorises the measure mentioned in section 66(1)(a) of this Act; and

76   *Mental Health (Care and Treatment) (Scotland) Act 2003 (asp 13)*
Part 7—Compulsory treatment orders
Chapter 7—Suspension

    (b) subject to subsection (2) below, the patient's responsible medical officer grants a certificate specifying a period not exceeding 6 months during which the order shall not authorise that measure,

the order does not authorise that measure during that period.

(2)   If the sum of—

    (a) the period that the responsible medical officer proposes to specify in a certificate under subsection (1) above; and

    (b) the period specified in any other certificate granted under that subsection in respect of the same patient,

would exceed 9 months in the period of 12 months ending with the expiry of the period mentioned in paragraph (a) above, the responsible medical officer may not grant a certificate under that subsection.

(3)   Where—

    (a) a patient is subject to an interim compulsory treatment order that authorises the measure mentioned in section 66(1)(a) of this Act; and

    (b) the patient's responsible medical officer grants a certificate specifying a period during which the order shall not authorise that measure,

the order does not authorise that measure during that period.

(4)   A period specified in a certificate under subsection (1) or (3) above may be expressed as—

    (a) the duration of—

        (i) an event; or

        (ii) a series of events; or

    (b) the duration of—

        (i) an event; or

        (ii) a series of events,

    and any associated travel.

(5)   If the responsible medical officer considers that it is necessary—

    (a) in the interests of the patient; or

    (b) for the protection of any other person,

a certificate under subsection (1) or (3) above may include conditions such as are mentioned in subsection (6) below; and any such conditions shall have effect.

(6)   Those conditions are—

    (a) that, during the period specified in the certificate, the patient be kept in the charge of a person authorised in writing for the purpose by the patient's responsible medical officer; and

    (b) such other conditions as may be specified by the patient's responsible medical officer.

(7)   Where a patient's responsible medical officer proposes to grant a certificate under subsection (1) above specifying—

Mental Health (Care and Treatment) (Scotland) Act 2003 (asp 13)
Part 7—Compulsory treatment orders
Chapter 7—Suspension

77

    (a) a period of more than 28 days; or

    (b) a period which, when taken together with the period specified in any other certificate granted under that subsection, would exceed 28 days,

the responsible medical officer shall, before granting such a certificate, give notice of the proposal to the persons mentioned in subsection (8) below.

(8)   Those persons are—

    (a) the patient;

    (b) the patient's named person;

    (c) the patient's general medical practitioner; and

    (d) the mental health officer.

(9)   Where a certificate is granted under subsection (1) above specifying a period of more than 28 days, the patient's responsible medical officer shall, before the expiry of the period of 14 days beginning with the day on which the certificate is granted, give notice of it to the Commission.

128   Suspension of other measures

(1)   Where—

    (a) a patient is subject to a compulsory treatment order that authorises any of the measures mentioned in section 66(1)(b) to (h) of this Act; and

    (b) subject to subsection (2) below, the patient's responsible medical officer grants a certificate specifying a period not exceeding 3 months during which the order shall not authorise such of those measures as are specified in the certificate,

the order does not authorise the measures specified in the certificate during that period.

(2)   If the sum of—

    (a) the period that the responsible medical officer proposes to specify in a certificate under subsection (1) above; and

    (b) the period specified in any other certificate granted under that subsection in respect of the same patient,

would exceed 3 months, the responsible medical officer may not grant a certificate under that subsection.

(3)   Where a patient's responsible medical officer proposes to grant a certificate under subsection (1) above, the responsible medical officer shall, before granting such a certificate, give notice to the persons mentioned in subsection (4) below of—

    (a) the measures and the period that the responsible medical officer proposes to specify in the certificate; and

    (b) the responsible medical officer's reasons for proposing to specify those measures.

(4)   Those persons are—

    (a) the patient;

    (b) the patient's named person; and

    (c) the mental health officer.

78   *Mental Health (Care and Treatment) (Scotland) Act 2003 (asp 13)*
Part 7—Compulsory treatment orders
Chapter 7—Suspension

(5)   Where a certificate is granted under subsection (1) above, the patient's responsible medical officer shall, before the expiry of the period of 14 days beginning with the day on which the certificate is granted, give notice to the Commission of—

         (a)   the granting of the certificate;

         (b)   the measures and the period specified in the certificate; and

         (c)   the responsible medical officer's reasons for specifying those measures.

129   Certificates under sections 127 and 128: revocation

(1)   Subsection (2) below applies where a certificate is granted under section 127(1) or (3) or 128(1) of this Act.

(2)   If the patient's responsible medical officer is satisfied that it is necessary—

         (a)   in the interests of the patient; or

         (b)   for the protection of any other person,

that the certificate be revoked, the responsible medical officer may revoke the certificate.

(3)   Where the responsible medical officer revokes under subsection (2) above a certificate granted under subsection (1) or (3) of section 127 of this Act, the responsible medical officer shall, as soon as practicable after the revocation, give notice of it to—

         (a)   the patient;

         (b)   the patient's named person;

         (c)   the mental health officer;

         (d)   where a person is authorised for the purposes of subsection (6)(a) of that section, that person; and

         (e)   the patient's general medical practitioner.

(4)   Where the responsible medical officer revokes under subsection (2) above a certificate granted under section 128(1) of this Act, the responsible medical officer shall, as soon as practicable after the revocation, give notice to the persons mentioned in paragraphs (a) to (c) of subsection (3) above of—

         (a)   the revocation; and

         (b)   the responsible medical officer's reasons for revoking the certificate.

(5)   Where the responsible medical officer revokes under subsection (2) above a certificate granted under section 127(1) or (3) or 128(1) of this Act, the responsible medical officer shall, before the expiry of the period of 14 days beginning with the day on which the certificate is revoked, give notice of the revocation to the Commission.

Mental Health (Care and Treatment) (Scotland) Act 2003 (asp 13)   79
Part 8—Mentally disordered persons: criminal proceedings
Chapter 1—Pre-sentence orders

PART 8

MENTALLY DISORDERED PERSONS: CRIMINAL PROCEEDINGS

CHAPTER 1

PRE-SENTENCE ORDERS

Assessment orders and treatment orders

130   **Mentally disordered persons subject to criminal proceedings: assessment and treatment**

After section 52 of the 1995 Act there shall be inserted—

"Remit of mentally disordered persons from district court

52A   **Remit of certain mentally disordered persons from district court to sheriff court**

Where—

(a) a person has been charged in a district court with an offence punishable by imprisonment; and

(b) it appears to the court that the person has a mental disorder,

the district court shall remit the person to the sheriff in the manner provided by section 7(9) and (10) of this Act.

Assessment orders

52B   **Prosecutor's power to apply for assessment order**

(1) Where—

(a) a person has been charged with an offence;

(b) a relevant disposal has not been made in the proceedings in respect of the offence; and

(c) it appears to the prosecutor that the person has a mental disorder,

the prosecutor may apply to the court for an order under section 52D(2) of this Act (in this Act referred to as an "assessment order") in respect of that person.

(2) Where the prosecutor applies for an assessment order under subsection (1) above, the prosecutor shall, as soon as reasonably practicable after making the application, inform the persons mentioned in subsection (3) below of the making of the application.

(3) Those persons are—

(a) the person in respect of whom the application is made;

(b) any solicitor acting for the person; and

(c) in a case where the person is in custody, the Scottish Ministers.

(4) In this section—

"court" means any court, other than a district court, competent to deal with the case; and

80   *Mental Health (Care and Treatment) (Scotland) Act 2003 (asp 13)*
Part 8—Mentally disordered persons: criminal proceedings
Chapter 1—Pre-sentence orders

"relevant disposal" means—

    (a)   the liberation in due course of law of the person charged;

    (b)   the desertion of summary proceedings *pro loco et tempore* or *simpliciter*;

    (c)   the desertion of solemn proceedings *simpliciter*;

    (d)   the acquittal of the person charged; or

    (e)   the conviction of the person charged.

52C   Scottish Ministers' power to apply for assessment order

(1)   Where—

    (a) a person has been charged with an offence;

    (b) the person has not been sentenced;

    (c) the person is in custody; and

    (d) it appears to the Scottish Ministers that the person has a mental disorder,

the Scottish Ministers may apply to the court for an assessment order in respect of that person.

(2)   Where the Scottish Ministers apply for an order under subsection (1) above, they shall, as soon as reasonably practicable after making the application, inform the persons mentioned in subsection (3) below of the making of the application.

(3)   Those persons are—

    (a) the person in respect of whom the application is made;

    (b) any solicitor acting for the person; and

    (c) in a case where a relevant disposal has not been made in the proceedings in respect of the offence with which the person is charged, the prosecutor.

(4)   In this section, "court" and "relevant disposal" have the same meanings as in section 52B of this Act.

52D   Assessment order

(1)   This section applies where an application for an assessment order is made under section 52B(1) or 52C(1) of this Act.

(2)   If the court is satisfied—

    (a) on the written or oral evidence of a medical practitioner, as to the matters mentioned in subsection (3) below; and

    (b) that, having regard to the matters mentioned in subsection (4) below, it is appropriate,

it may, subject to subsection (5) below, make an assessment order authorising the measures mentioned in subsection (6) below and specifying any matters to be included in the report under section 52G(1) of this Act.

Mental Health (Care and Treatment) (Scotland) Act 2003 (asp 13)
Part 8—Mentally disordered persons: criminal proceedings
Chapter 1—Pre-sentence orders

81

(3) The matters referred to in subsection (2)(a) above are—

   (a) that there are reasonable grounds for believing—

      (i) that the person in respect of whom the application is made has a mental disorder;

      (ii) that it is necessary to detain the person in hospital to assess whether the conditions mentioned in subsection (7) below are met in respect of the person; and

      (iii) that if the assessment order were not made there would be a significant risk to the health, safety or welfare of the person or a significant risk to the safety of any other person;

   (b) that the hospital proposed by the medical practitioner is suitable for the purpose of assessing whether the conditions mentioned in subsection (7) below are met in respect of the person;

   (c) that, if an assessment order were made, the person could be admitted to such hospital before the expiry of the period of 7 days beginning with the day on which the order is made; and

   (d) that it would not be reasonably practicable to carry out the assessment mentioned in paragraph (b) above unless an order were made.

(4) The matters referred to in subsection (2)(b) above are—

   (a) all the circumstances (including the nature of the offence with which the person in respect of whom the application is made is charged or, as the case may be, of which the person was convicted); and

   (b) any alternative means of dealing with the person.

(5) The court may make an assessment order only if the person in respect of whom the application is made has not been sentenced.

(6) The measures are—

   (a) in the case of a person who, when the assessment order is made, has not been admitted to the specified hospital, the removal, before the expiry of the period of 7 days beginning with the day on which the order is made, of the person to the specified hospital by—

      (i) a constable;

      (ii) a person employed in, or contracted to provide services in or to, the specified hospital who is authorised by the managers of that hospital to remove persons to hospital for the purposes of this section; or

      (iii) a specified person;

   (b) the detention, for the period of 28 days beginning with the day on which the order is made, of the person in the specified hospital; and

   (c) during the period of 28 days beginning with the day on which the order is made, the giving to the person, in accordance with Part 16 of the Mental Health (Care and Treatment) (Scotland) Act 2003 (asp 13), of medical treatment.

82   *Mental Health (Care and Treatment) (Scotland) Act 2003 (asp 13)*
Part 8—Mentally disordered persons: criminal proceedings
Chapter 1—Pre-sentence orders

(7)   The conditions referred to in paragraphs (a)(ii) and (b) of subsection (3) above are—

    (a)   that the person in respect of whom the application is made has a mental disorder;

    (b)   that medical treatment which would be likely to—

        (i)   prevent the mental disorder worsening; or

        (ii)   alleviate any of the symptoms, or effects, of the disorder,

      is available for the person; and

    (c)   that if the person were not provided with such medical treatment there would be a significant risk—

        (i)   to the health, safety or welfare of the person; or

        (ii)   to the safety of any other person.

(8)   The court may make an assessment order in the absence of the person in respect of whom the application is made only if—

    (a)   the person is represented by counsel or a solicitor;

    (b)   that counsel or solicitor is given an opportunity of being heard; and

    (c)   the court is satisfied that it is—

        (i)   impracticable; or

        (ii)   inappropriate,

      for the person to be brought before it.

(9)   An assessment order may include such directions as the court thinks fit for the removal of the person subject to the order to, and detention of the person in, a place of safety pending the person's admission to the specified hospital.

(10)   The court shall, as soon as reasonably practicable after making an assessment order, give notice of the making of the order to—

    (a)   the person subject to the order;

    (b)   any solicitor acting for the person;

    (c)   in a case where—

        (i)   the person has been charged with an offence; and

        (ii)   a relevant disposal has not been made in the proceedings in respect of the offence,

      the prosecutor;

    (d)   in a case where the person, immediately before the order was made, was in custody, the Scottish Ministers; and

    (e)   the Mental Welfare Commission.

(11)   In this section—

      "court" has the same meaning as in section 52B of this Act;

Mental Health (Care and Treatment) (Scotland) Act 2003 (asp 13)   83
Part 8—Mentally disordered persons: criminal proceedings
Chapter 1—Pre-sentence orders

"medical treatment" has the meaning given by section 329(1) of the Mental Health (Care and Treatment) (Scotland) Act 2003 (asp 13);

"relevant disposal" has the same meaning as in section 52B of this Act; and

"specified" means specified in the assessment order.

52E   **Assessment order made *ex proprio motu*: application of section 52D**

(1)   Where—

      (a)   a person has been charged with an offence;

      (b)   the person has not been sentenced; and

      (c)   it appears to the court that the person has a mental disorder,

      the court may, subject to subsections (2) and (3) below, make an assessment order in respect of that person.

(2)   The court may make an assessment order under subsection (1) above only if it would make one under subsections (2) to (11) of section 52D of this Act; and those subsections shall apply for the purposes of subsection (1) above as they apply for the purposes of subsection (1) of that section, references in those subsections to the person in respect of whom the application is made being construed as references to the person in respect of whom it is proposed to make an assessment order.

(3)   An assessment order made under subsection (1) above shall, for the purposes of this Act and the Mental Health (Care and Treatment) (Scotland) Act 2003 (asp 13), be treated as if made under section 52D(2) of this Act.

(4)   In this section, "court" has the same meaning as in section 52B of this Act.

52F   **Assessment order: supplementary**

(1)   If, before the expiry of the period of 7 days beginning with the day on which an assessment order is made—

      (a)   in the case of a person who, immediately before the order was made, was in custody, it appears to the Scottish Ministers; or

      (b)   in any other case, it appears to the court,

      that, by reason of emergency or other special circumstances, it is not reasonably practicable for the person to be admitted to the hospital specified in the order, the Scottish Ministers, or, as the case may be, the court, may direct that the person be admitted to the hospital specified in the direction.

(2)   Where the court makes a direction under subsection (1) above, it shall, as soon as reasonably practicable after making the direction, inform the person having custody of the person subject to the assessment order of the making of the direction.

(3)   Where the Scottish Ministers make a direction under subsection (1) above, they shall, as soon as reasonably practicable after making the direction, inform—

      (a)   the court;

84   *Mental Health (Care and Treatment) (Scotland) Act 2003 (asp 13)*
Part 8—Mentally disordered persons: criminal proceedings
Chapter 1—Pre-sentence orders

    (b) the person having custody of the person subject to the assessment order; and

    (c) in a case where—

        (i)   the person has been charged with an offence; and

        (ii) a relevant disposal has not been made in the proceedings in respect of the offence,

    the prosecutor,

of the making of the direction.

(4)   Where a direction is made under subsection (1) above, the assessment order shall have effect as if the hospital specified in the direction were the hospital specified in the order.

(5)   In this section—

    "court" means the court which made the assessment order; and

    "relevant disposal" has the same meaning as in section 52B of this Act.

52G   Review of assessment order

(1)   The responsible medical officer shall, before the expiry of the period of 28 days beginning with the day on which the assessment order is made, submit a report in writing to the court—

    (a) as to whether the conditions mentioned in section 52D(7) of this Act are met in respect of the person subject to the order; and

    (b) as to any matters specified by the court under section 52D(2) of this Act.

(2)   The responsible medical officer shall, at the same time as such officer submits the report to the court, send a copy of such report—

    (a) to the person in respect of whom the report is made;

    (b) to any solicitor acting for the person;

    (c) in a case where—

        (i)   the person has been charged with an offence; and

        (ii) a relevant disposal has not been made in the proceedings in respect of the offence,

    to the prosecutor; and

    (d) to the Scottish Ministers.

(3)   Subject to subsection (4) below, the court shall, on receiving a report submitted under subsection (1) above, revoke the assessment order and—

    (a) subject to subsections (7) and (8) below, make a treatment order; or

    (b) commit the person to prison or such other institution to which the person might have been committed had the assessment order not been made or otherwise deal with the person as the court considers appropriate.

Mental Health (Care and Treatment) (Scotland) Act 2003 (asp 13)
Part 8—Mentally disordered persons: criminal proceedings
Chapter 1—Pre-sentence orders

85

(4)   If, on receiving a report submitted under subsection (1) above, the court is satisfied that further time· is necessary to assess whether the conditions mentioned in section 52D(7) of this Act are met in respect of the person subject to the assessment order, it may, on one occasion only, make an order extending the assessment order for a period not exceeding 7 days beginning with the day on which the order otherwise would cease to authorise the detention of the person in hospital.

(5)   The court may, under subsection (4) above, extend an assessment order in the absence of the person subject to the order only if—

(a)   the person is represented by counsel or a solicitor;

(b)   that counsel or solicitor is given an opportunity of being heard; and

(c)   the court is satisfied that it is—

(i)   impracticable; or

(ii)   inappropriate,

for the person to be brought before it.

(6)   Where the court makes an order under subsection (4) above, it shall, as soon as reasonably practicable after making the order, give notice of the making of the order to—

(a)   the persons mentioned in paragraphs (a) and (b) of subsection (2) above;

(b)   in a case where—

(i)   the person has been charged with an offence; and

(ii)   a relevant disposal has not been made in the proceedings in respect of the offence,

the prosecutor;

(c)   the Scottish Ministers; and

(d)   the person's responsible medical officer.

(7)   The court shall make a treatment order under subsection (3)(a) above only if it would make one under subsections (2) to (10) of section 52M of this Act; and those subsections shall apply for the purposes of subsection (3)(a) above as they apply for the purposes of that section, references in those subsections to the person in respect of whom the application is made being construed as references to the person in respect of whom it is proposed to make a treatment order.

(8)   A treatment order made under subsection (3)(a) above shall, for the purposes of this Act and the Mental Health (Care and Treatment) (Scotland) Act 2003 (asp 13), be treated as if made under section 52M(2) of this Act.

(9)   The responsible medical officer shall, where that officer is satisfied that there has been a change of circumstances since the assessment order was made which justifies the variation of the order, submit a report to the court in writing.

(10)   Where a report is submitted under subsection (9) above, the court shall—

86   *Mental Health (Care and Treatment) (Scotland) Act 2003 (asp 13)*
Part 8—Mentally disordered persons: criminal proceedings
Chapter 1—Pre-sentence orders

    (a) if satisfied that the person need not be subject to an assessment order, revoke the order and take any action mentioned in subsection (3)(b) above; or

    (b) if not so satisfied—

        (i) confirm the order;

        (ii) vary the order; or

        (iii) revoke the order and take any action mentioned in subsection (3)(b) above.

(11) Sections 52D, 52F, 52H and 52J of this Act and subsections (1) to (3) above apply to the variation of an order under subsection (10)(b)(ii) above as they apply to an assessment order.

(12) In this section—

    "court" means the court which made the assessment order;

    "relevant disposal" has the same meaning as in section 52B of this Act; and

    "responsible medical officer" means the person's responsible medical officer appointed under section 230 of the Mental Health (Care and Treatment) (Scotland) Act 2003 (asp 13).

52H   Early termination of assessment order

(1) This section applies where—

    (a) in the case of a person who, when the assessment order is made, has not been removed to the hospital specified in the order, the period of 7 days beginning with the day on which the order is made has not expired;

    (b) in the case of a person—

        (i) who, when the assessment order is made, has been admitted to the hospital specified in the order; or

        (ii) who has been removed under paragraph (a) of subsection (6) of section 52D of this Act to the hospital so specified,

    the period of 28 days beginning with the day on which the order is made has not expired; or

    (c) in the case of a person in respect of whom the court has made an order under section 52G(4) of this Act extending the assessment order for a period, the period for which the order was extended has not expired.

(2) An assessment order shall cease to have effect on the occurrence of any of the following events—

    (a) the making of a treatment order in respect of the person subject to the assessment order;

    (b) in a case where—

        (i) the person subject to the assessment order has been charged with an offence; and

Mental Health (Care and Treatment) (Scotland) Act 2003 (asp 13)
Part 8—Mentally disordered persons: criminal proceedings
Chapter 1—Pre-sentence orders

87

(ii) a relevant disposal had not been made in the proceedings in respect of that offence when the order was made,

the making of a relevant disposal in such proceedings;

(c) in a case where the person subject to the assessment order has been convicted of an offence but has not been sentenced—

(i) the deferral of sentence by the court under section 202(1) of this Act;

(ii) the making of one of the orders mentioned in subsection (3) below or

(iii) the imposition of any sentence.

(3) The orders are—

(a) an interim compulsion order;

(b) a compulsion order;

(c) a guardianship order;

(d) a hospital direction;

(e) any order under section 57 of this Act; or

(f) a probation order which includes a requirement imposed by virtue of section 230(1) of this Act.

(4) In this section, "relevant disposal" has the same meaning as in section 52B of this Act.

52J   Power of court on assessment order ceasing to have effect

(1) Where, otherwise than by virtue of section 52G(3) or (10) or 52H(2) of this Act, an assessment order ceases to have effect the court shall commit the person who was subject to the order to prison or such other institution to which the person might have been committed had the order not been made or otherwise deal with the person as the court considers appropriate.

(2) In this section, "court" has the same meaning as in section 52B of this Act.

Treatment orders

52K   Prosecutor's power to apply for treatment order

(1) Where—

(a) a person has been charged with an offence;

(b) a relevant disposal has not been made in the proceedings in respect of the offence; and

(c) it appears to the prosecutor that the person has a mental disorder,

the prosecutor may apply to the court for an order under section 52M of this Act (in this Act referred to as a "treatment order") in respect of that person.

88   *Mental Health (Care and Treatment) (Scotland) Act 2003 (asp 13)*
Part 8—Mentally disordered persons: criminal proceedings
Chapter 1—Pre-sentence orders

(2) Where the prosecutor applies for a treatment order under subsection (1) above, the prosecutor shall, as soon as reasonably practicable after making the application, inform the persons mentioned in subsection (3) below of the making of the application.

(3) Those persons are—

(a) the person in respect of whom the application is made;

(b) any solicitor acting for the person; and

(c) in a case where the person is in custody, the Scottish Ministers.

(4) In this section, "court" and "relevant disposal" have the same meanings as in section 52B of this Act.

52L   Scottish Ministers' power to apply for treatment order

(1) Where—

(a) a person has been charged with an offence;

(b) the person has not been sentenced;

(c) the person is in custody; and

(d) it appears to the Scottish Ministers that the person has a mental disorder,

the Scottish Ministers may apply to the court for a treatment order in respect of that person.

(2) Where the Scottish Ministers apply for an order under subsection (1) above, they shall, as soon as reasonably practicable after making the application, inform the persons mentioned in subsection (3) below of the making of the application.

(3) Those persons are—

(a) the person in respect of whom the application is made;

(b) any solicitor acting for the person; and

(c) in a case where a relevant disposal has not been made in the proceedings in respect of the offence with which the person is charged, the prosecutor.

(4) In this section, "court" and "relevant disposal" have the same meanings as in section 52B of this Act.

52M   Treatment order

(1) This section applies where an application for a treatment order is made under section 52K(1) or 52L(1) of this Act.

(2) If the court is satisfied—

(a) on the written or oral evidence of two medical practitioners, as to the matters mentioned in subsection (3) below; and

(b) that, having regard to the matters mentioned in subsection (4) below, it is appropriate,

Mental Health (Care and Treatment) (Scotland) Act 2003 (asp 13)
Part 8—Mentally disordered persons: criminal proceedings
Chapter 1—Pre-sentence orders

89

it may, subject to subsection (5) below, make a treatment order authorising the measures mentioned in subsection (6) below.

(3) The matters referred to in subsection (2)(a) above are—

    (a) that the conditions mentioned in subsection (7) of section 52D of this Act are met in relation to the person in respect of whom the application is made;

    (b) that the hospital proposed by the approved medical practitioner and the medical practitioner is suitable for the purpose of giving medical treatment to the person; and

    (c) that, if a treatment order were made, such person could be admitted to such hospital before the expiry of the period of 7 days beginning with the day on which the order is made.

(4) The matters referred to in subsection (2)(b) above are—

    (a) all the circumstances (including the nature of the offence with which the person in respect of whom the application is made is charged or, as the case may be, of which the person was convicted); and

    (b) any alternative means of dealing with the person.

(5) The court may make a treatment order only if the person in respect of whom the application is made has not been sentenced.

(6) The measures are—

    (a) in the case of a person who, when the treatment order is made, has not been admitted to the specified hospital, the removal, before the expiry of the period of 7 days beginning with the day on which the order is made, of the person to the specified hospital by—

        (i) a constable;

        (ii) a person employed in, or contracted to provide services in or to, the specified hospital who is authorised by the managers of that hospital to remove persons to hospital for the purposes of this section; or

        (iii) a specified person;

    (b) the detention of the person in the specified hospital; and

    (c) the giving to the person, in accordance with Part 16 of the Mental Health (Care and Treatment) (Scotland) Act 2003 (asp 13), of medical treatment.

(7) The court may make a treatment order in the absence of the person in respect of whom the application is made only if—

    (a) the person is represented by counsel or solicitor;

    (b) that counsel or solicitor is given an opportunity of being heard; and

    (c) the court is satisfied that it is—

        (i) impracticable; or

        (ii) inappropriate,

90

Mental Health (Care and Treatment) (Scotland) Act 2003 (asp 13)
Part 8—Mentally disordered persons: criminal proceedings
Chapter 1—Pre-sentence orders

for the person to be brought before it.

(8) A treatment order may include such directions as the court thinks fit for the removal of the person subject to the order to, and detention of the person in, a place of safety pending the person's admission to the specified hospital.

(9) The court shall, as soon as reasonably practicable after making a treatment order, give notice of the making of the order to—

    (a) the person subject to the order;

    (b) any solicitor acting for the person;

    (c) in a case where—

        (i) the person has been charged with an offence; and

        (ii) a relevant disposal has not been made in the proceedings in respect of the offence,

    the prosecutor;

    (d) in a case where the person, immediately before the order was made—

        (i) was in custody; or

        (ii) was subject to an assessment order and, immediately before that order was made, was in custody,

    the Scottish Ministers; and

    (e) the Mental Welfare Commission.

(10) In this section—

    "court" has the same meaning as in section 52B of this Act;

    "medical treatment" has the same meaning as in section 52D of this Act; and

    "specified" means specified in the treatment order.

52N   **Treatment order made *ex proprio motu*: application of section 52M**

(1) Where—

    (a) a person has been charged with an offence;

    (b) the person has not been sentenced; and

    (c) it appears to the court that the person has a mental disorder,

the court may, subject to subsections (2) and (3) below, make a treatment order in respect of that person.

(2) The court may make a treatment order under subsection (1) above only if it would make one under subsections (2) to (10) of section 52M of this Act; and those subsections shall apply for the purposes of subsection (1) above as they apply for the purposes of subsection (1) of that section, references in those subsections to the person in respect of whom the application is made being construed as references to the person in respect of whom it is proposed to make a treatment order.

Mental Health (Care and Treatment) (Scotland) Act 2003 (asp 13)   91
Part 8—Mentally disordered persons: criminal proceedings
Chapter 1—Pre-sentence orders

(3)   A treatment order made under subsection (1) above shall, for the purposes of this Act and the Mental Health (Care and Treatment) (Scotland) Act 2003 (asp 13), be treated as if made under section 52M(2) of this Act.

(4)   In this section, "court" has the same meaning as in section 52B of this Act.

52P   **Treatment order: supplementary**

(1)   If, before the expiry of the period of 7 days beginning with the day on which the treatment order is made—

     (a)   in the case of a person to whom subsection (2) below applies, it appears to the Scottish Ministers; or

     (b)   in any other case, it appears to the court,

that, by reason of emergency or other special circumstances, it is not reasonably practicable for the person to be admitted to the hospital specified in the order, the Scottish Ministers, or, as the case may be, the court, may direct that the person be admitted to the hospital specified in the direction.

(2)   This subsection applies to—

     (a)   a person who is in custody immediately before the treatment order is made; or

     (b)   a person—

         (i)   who was subject to an assessment order immediately before the treatment order is made; and

         (ii)   who was in custody immediately before that assessment order was made.

(3)   Where the court makes a direction under subsection (1) above, it shall, as soon as reasonably practicable after making the direction, inform the person having custody of the person subject to the treatment order of the making of the direction.

(4)   Where the Scottish Ministers make a direction under subsection (1) above, they shall, as soon as reasonably practicable after making the direction, inform—

     (a)   the court;

     (b)   the person having custody of the person subject to the treatment order; and

     (c)   in a case where—

         (i)   the person has been charged with an offence; and

         (ii)   a relevant disposal has not been made in the proceedings in respect of the offence,

     the prosecutor,

of the making of the direction.

(5)   Where a direction is made under subsection (1) above, the treatment order shall have effect as if the hospital specified in the direction were the hospital specified in the order.

92   *Mental Health (Care and Treatment) (Scotland) Act 2003 (asp 13)*
Part 8—Mentally disordered persons: criminal proceedings
Chapter 1—Pre-sentence orders

(6)   In this section—

"court" means the court which made the treatment order; and

"relevant disposal" has the same meaning as in section 52B of this Act.

52Q   Review of treatment order

(1)   The responsible medical officer shall, where that officer is satisfied—

(a)   that any of the conditions mentioned in section 52D(7) of this Act are no longer met in respect of the person subject to the treatment order; or

(b)   that there has otherwise been a change of circumstances since the order was made which makes the continued detention of the person in hospital by virtue of the order no longer appropriate,

submit a report in writing to the court.

(2)   Where a report is submitted under subsection (1) above, the court shall—

(a)   if satisfied that the person need not be subject to the treatment order—

(i)   revoke the order; and

(ii)   commit the person to prison or such other institution to which the person might have been committed had the order not been made or otherwise deal with the person as the court considers appropriate; or

(b)   if not so satisfied—

(i)   confirm the order;

(ii)   vary the order; or

(iii)   revoke the order and take any action mentioned in paragraph (a)(ii) above.

(3)   Sections 52M, 52P, this section and sections 52R and 52S of this Act apply to the variation of a treatment order under subsection (2)(b)(ii) above as they apply to a treatment order.

(4)   In this section—

"court" means the court which made the treatment order; and

"responsible medical officer" means the person's responsible medical officer appointed under section 230 of the Mental Health (Care and Treatment) (Scotland) Act 2003 (asp 13).

52R   Termination of treatment order

(1)   This section applies—

(a)   where, in the case of a person who, when the treatment order is made, has not been removed to the hospital specified in the order, the period of 7 days beginning with the day on which the order is made has not expired; or

(b)   in the case of a person—

Mental Health (Care and Treatment) (Scotland) Act 2003 (asp 13)   93
Part 8—Mentally disordered persons: criminal proceedings
Chapter 1—Pre-sentence orders

(i)   who, when the treatment order is made, has been admitted to the hospital specified in the order; or

(ii)   who has been removed under paragraph (a) of subsection (6) of section 52M of this Act to the hospital so specified.

(2)   A treatment order shall cease to have effect on the occurrence of any of the following events—

    (a)   in a case where—

       (i)   the person subject to the treatment order has been charged with an offence; and

       (ii)   a relevant disposal had not been made in the proceedings in respect of such offence when the order was made,

     the making of a relevant disposal in such proceedings;

    (b)   in a case where the person subject to the treatment order has been convicted of an offence but has not been sentenced—

       (i)   the deferral of sentence by the court under section 202(1) of this Act;

       (ii)   the making of one of the orders mentioned in subsection (3) below; or

       (iii) the imposition of any sentence.

(3)   The orders are—

    (a)   an interim compulsion order;

    (b)   a compulsion order;

    (c)   a guardianship order;

    (d)   a hospital direction;

    (e)   any order under section 57 of this Act; or

    (f)   a probation order which includes a requirement imposed by virtue of section 230(1) of this Act.

(4)   In this section, "relevant disposal" has the same meaning as in section 52B of this Act.

52S   Power of court on treatment order ceasing to have effect

(1)   Where, otherwise than by virtue of section 52Q(2) or 52R(2) of this Act, a treatment order ceases to have effect the court shall commit the person who was subject to the order to prison or such other institution to which the person might have been committed had the order not been made or otherwise deal with the person as the court considers appropriate.

(2)   In this section, "court" has the same meaning as in section 52B of this Act.

94   *Mental Health (Care and Treatment) (Scotland) Act 2003 (asp 13)*
                    Part 8—Mentally disordered persons: criminal proceedings
                                        Chapter 1—Pre-sentence orders

Prevention of delay in trials

52T   Prevention of delay in trials: assessment orders and treatment orders

(1)   Subsections (4) to (9) of section 65 of this Act shall apply in the case of a person charged on indictment who is detained in hospital by virtue of an assessment order or a treatment order as those subsections apply in the case of an accused who is—

    (a)   committed for an offence until liberated in due course of law; and

    (b)   detained by virtue of that committal.

(2)   Section 147 of this Act shall apply in the case of a person charged with an offence in summary proceedings who is detained in hospital by virtue of an assessment order or a treatment order as it applies in the case of an accused who is detained in respect of that offence.

(3)   Any period during which, under—

    (a)   section 221 (as read with sections 222 and 223) of the Mental Health (Care and Treatment) (Scotland) Act 2003 (asp 13); or

    (b)   section 224 (as read with sections 225 and 226) of that Act,

a patient's detention is not authorised shall be taken into account for the purposes of the calculation of any of the periods mentioned in subsection (4) below.

(4)   Those periods are—

    (a)   the total periods of 80 days and 110 days referred to respectively in paragraphs (a) and (b) of subsection (4) of section 65 of this Act as applied by subsection (1) above;

    (b)   those total periods as extended under subsection (5) or (7) respectively or, on appeal, under subsection (8) of that section as so applied;

    (c)   the total of 40 days referred to in section 147 of this Act (prevention of delay in trials in summary proceedings) as applied by subsection (2) above; and

    (d)   that period as extended under subsection (2) of that section or, on appeal, under subsection (3) of that section as so applied.

Effect of assessment and treatment orders on pre-existing mental health orders

52U   Effect of assessment order and treatment order on pre-existing mental health order

(1)   This section applies where—

    (a)   a patient is subject to a relevant order; and

    (b)   an assessment order or a treatment order is made in respect of the patient.

(2)   The relevant order shall, subject to subsection (3) below, cease to authorise the measures specified in it for the period during which the patient is subject to the assessment order or, as the case may be, treatment order.

Mental Health (Care and Treatment) (Scotland) Act 2003 (asp 13)   95
· Part 8—Mentally disordered persons: criminal proceedings
Chapter 1—Pre-sentence orders

(3) For the purposes of sections 112 to 120, and Part 20, of the Mental Health (Care and Treatment) (Scotland) Act 2003 (asp 13) (the "2003 Act"), the patient shall be deemed not to be subject to the relevant order during the period mentioned in subsection (2) above.

(4) In this section, a "relevant order" means—

     (a) an interim compulsory treatment order made under section 65(2) of the 2003 Act; and

     (b) a compulsory treatment order made under section 64(4)(a) of that Act.".

Interim compulsion orders

131   **Mentally disordered offenders: interim compulsion orders**

For section 53 of the 1995 Act (interim hospital orders), there shall be substituted—

"Interim compulsion orders

53   **Interim compulsion order**

(1) This section applies where a person (referred to in this section and in sections 53A to 53D of this Act as an "offender")—

     (a) is convicted in the High Court or the sheriff court of an offence punishable by imprisonment (other than an offence the sentence for which is fixed by law); or

     (b) is remitted to the High Court by the sheriff under any enactment for sentence for such an offence.

(2) If the court is satisfied—

     (a) on the written or oral evidence of two medical practitioners—

         (i) that the offender has a mental disorder; and

         (ii) as to the matters mentioned in subsection (3) below; and

     (b) that, having regard to the matters mentioned in subsection (4) below, it is appropriate,

it may, subject to subsection (7) below, make an order (in this Act referred to as an "interim compulsion order") authorising the measures mentioned in subsection (8) below and specifying any matters to be included in the report under section 53B(1) of this Act.

(3) The matters referred to in subsection (2)(a)(ii) above are—

     (a) that there are reasonable grounds for believing—

         (i) that the conditions mentioned in subsection (5) below are likely to be met in respect of the offender; and

         (ii) that the offender's mental disorder is such that it would be appropriate to make one of the disposals mentioned in subsection (6) below in relation to the offender;

     (b) that the hospital to be specified in the order is suitable for the purpose of assessing whether the conditions mentioned in subsection (5) below are met in respect of the offender;

96   *Mental Health (Care and Treatment) (Scotland) Act 2003 (asp 13)*
Part 8—Mentally disordered persons: criminal proceedings
Chapter 1—Pre-sentence orders

    (c) that, were an interim compulsion order made, the offender could be admitted to such hospital before the expiry of the period of 7 days beginning with the day on which the order is made; and

    (d) that it would not be reasonably practicable for the assessment mentioned in paragraph (b) above to be made unless an order were made.

(4)   The matters referred to in subsection (2)(b) above are—

    (a) all the circumstances (including the nature of the offence of which the offender is convicted); and

    (b) any alternative means of dealing with the offender.

(5)   The conditions referred to in paragraphs (a)(i) and (b) of subsection (3) above are—

    (a) that medical treatment which would be likely to—

        (i) prevent the mental disorder worsening; or

        (ii) alleviate any of the symptoms, or effects, of the disorder,

    is available for the offender;

    (b) that if the offender were not provided with such medical treatment there would be a significant risk—

        (i) to the health, safety or welfare of the offender; or

        (ii) to the safety of any other person; and

    (c) that the making of an interim compulsion order in respect of the offender is necessary.

(6)   The disposals are—

    (a) both a compulsion order that authorises detention in hospital by virtue of section 57A(8)(a) of this Act and a restriction order; or

    (b) a hospital direction.

(7)   An interim compulsion order may authorise detention in a state hospital only if, on the written or oral evidence of the two medical practitioners mentioned in subsection (2)(a) above, it appears to the court—

    (a) that the offender requires to be detained in hospital under conditions of special security; and

    (b) that such conditions of special security can be provided only in a state hospital.

(8)   The measures are—

    (a) in the case of an offender who, when the interim compulsion order is made, has not been admitted to the specified hospital, the removal, before the expiry of the period of 7 days beginning with the day on which the order is made, of the offender to the specified hospital by—

        (i) a constable;

        (ii) a person employed in, or contracted to provide services in or to, the specified hospital who is authorised by the managers of that

Mental Health (Care and Treatment) (Scotland) Act 2003 (asp 13) 97
Part 8—Mentally disordered persons: criminal proceedings
Chapter 1—Pre-sentence orders

hospital to remove persons to hospital for the purposes of this section; or

    (iii) a specified person;

(b) the detention, for a period not exceeding 12 weeks beginning with the day on which the order is made, of the offender in the specified hospital; and

(c) during the period of 12 weeks beginning with the day on which the order is made, the giving to the offender, in accordance with Part 16 of the Mental Health (Care and Treatment) (Scotland) Act 2003 (asp 13), of medical treatment.

(9) An interim compulsion order may include such directions as the court thinks fit for the removal of the offender to, and the detention of the offender in, a place of safety pending the offender's admission to the specified hospital.

(10) The court may make an interim compulsion order in the absence of the offender only if—

(a) the offender is represented by counsel or solicitor;

(b) that counsel or solicitor is given an opportunity of being heard; and

(c) the court is satisfied that it is—

    (i) impracticable; or

    (ii) inappropriate,

for the offender to be brought before it.

(11) The court shall, as soon as reasonably practicable after making an interim compulsion order, give notice of the making of the order to—

(a) the person subject to the order;

(b) any solicitor acting for that person;

(c) the Scottish Ministers; and

(d) the Mental Welfare Commission.

(12) Where a court makes an interim compulsion order in relation to an offender, the court—

(a) shall not, at the same time—

    (i) make an order under section 200 of this Act;

    (ii) impose a fine;

    (iii) pass sentence of imprisonment;

    (iv) make a compulsion order;

    (v) make a guardianship order;

    (vi) make a probation order; or

    (vii) make a community service order,

in relation of the offender;

98   *Mental Health (Care and Treatment) (Scotland) Act 2003 (asp 13)*
Part 8—Mentally disordered persons: criminal proceedings
Chapter 1—Pre-sentence orders

(b) may make any other order which it has power to make apart from this section.

(13) In this section—

"medical treatment" has the same meaning as in section 52D of this Act;

"sentence of imprisonment" includes any sentence or order for detention; and

"specified" means specified in the interim compulsion order.

53A   Interim compulsion order: supplementary

(1) If, before the expiry of the period of 7 days beginning with the day on which the interim compulsion order is made, it appears to the court, or, as the case may be, the Scottish Ministers, that, by reason of emergency or other special circumstances, it is not reasonably practicable for the offender to be admitted to the hospital specified in the order, the court, or, as the case may be, the Scottish Ministers, may direct that the offender be admitted to the hospital specified in the direction.

(2) Where—

(a) the court makes a direction under subsection (1) above, it shall, as soon as reasonably practicable after making the direction, inform the person having custody of the offender; and

(b) the Scottish Ministers make such a direction, they shall, as soon as reasonably practicable after making the direction, inform—

(i) the court; and

(ii) the person having custody of the offender.

(3) Where a direction is made under subsection (1) above, the interim compulsion order shall have effect as if the hospital specified in the direction were the hospital specified in the order.

(4) In this section, "court" means the court which made the interim compulsion order.

53B   Review and extension of interim compulsion order

(1) The responsible medical officer shall, before the expiry of the period specified by the court under section 53(8)(b) of this Act, submit a report in writing to the court—

(a) as to the matters mentioned in subsection (2) below; and

(b) as to any matters specified by the court under section 53(2) of this Act.

(2) The matters are—

(a) whether the conditions mentioned in section 53(5) of this Act are met in respect of the offender;

(b) the type (or types) of mental disorder that the offender has; and

Mental Health (Care and Treatment) (Scotland) Act 2003 (asp 13)
Part 8—Mentally disordered persons: criminal proceedings
Chapter 1—Pre-sentence orders

99

(c) whether it is necessary to extend the interim compulsion order to allow further time for the assessment mentioned in section 53(3)(b) of this Act.

(3) The responsible medical officer shall, at the same time as such officer submits the report to the court, send a copy of such report to—

(a) the offender; and

(b) any solicitor acting for the offender.

(4) The court may, on receiving the report submitted under subsection (1) above, if satisfied that the extension of the order is necessary, extend the order for such period (not exceeding 12 weeks beginning with the day on which the order would cease to have effect were such an extension not made) as the court may specify.

(5) The court may extend an interim compulsion order under subsection (4) above for a period only if, by doing so, the total period for which the offender will be subject to the order does not exceed 12 months beginning with the day on which the order was first made.

(6) The court may, under subsection (4) above, extend an interim compulsion order in the absence of the offender only if—

(a) the offender is represented by counsel or a solicitor;

(b) that counsel or solicitor is given an opportunity of being heard; and

(c) the court is satisfied that it is—

(i) impracticable; or

(ii) inappropriate,

for the offender to be brought before it.

(7) Subsections (1) to (9) of this section shall apply for the purposes of an interim compulsion order extended under subsection (4) above as they apply for the purposes of an interim compulsion order, references in those subsections to the period specified by the court under section 53(8)(b) of this Act being construed as references to the period specified by the court under subsection (4) above.

(8) Where a report is submitted under subsection (1) above, the court may, before the expiry of the period specified by the court under section 53(8)(b) of this Act—

(a) revoke the interim compulsion order and make one of the disposals mentioned in section 53(6) of this Act; or

(b) revoke the interim compulsion order and deal with the offender in any way (other than by making an interim compulsion order) in which the court could have dealt with the offender if no such order had been made.

(9) In this section—

"court" means the court which made the interim compulsion order; and

"responsible medical officer" means the responsible medical officer appointed in respect of the offender under section 230 of the Mental Health (Care and Treatment) (Scotland) Act 2003 (asp 13).

100   *Mental Health (Care and Treatment) (Scotland) Act 2003 (asp 13)*
Part 8—Mentally disordered persons: criminal proceedings
Chapter 2—Disposals on conviction and acquittal

53C   **Early termination of interim compulsion order**

(1)   An interim compulsion order shall cease to have effect if the court—

(a)   makes a compulsion order in relation to the offender;

(b)   makes a hospital direction in relation to the offender; or

(c)   deals with the offender in some other way, including the imposing of a sentence of imprisonment on the offender.

(2)   In this section, "court" means the court which made the interim compulsion order.

53D   **Power of court on interim compulsion order ceasing to have effect**

(1)   Where, otherwise than by virtue of section 53B(8) or 53C of this Act, an interim compulsion order ceases to have effect the court may deal with the offender who was subject to the order in any way (other than the making of a new interim compulsion order) in which it could have dealt with the offender if no such order had been made.

(2)   In this section, "court" means the court which made the interim compulsion order.".

Remand for inquiry into mental condition

132   **Remand for inquiry into mental condition: time-limit for appeals**

In section 200 of the 1995 Act (remand for inquiry into physical or mental condition), in subsection (9)—

(a)   after the word "may", where it first occurs, there shall be inserted ", before the expiry of the period of 24 hours beginning with his remand,";

(b)   after the word "may", where it second occurs, there shall be inserted ", at any time during the period when the order for his committal, or, as the case may be, renewal of such order, is in force,"; and

(c)   the words "within 24 hours of his remand or, as the case may be, committal," shall cease to have effect.

CHAPTER 2

DISPOSALS ON CONVICTION AND ACQUITTAL

Compulsion orders

133   **Mentally disordered offenders: compulsion orders**

After section 57 of the 1995 Act there shall be inserted—

"Compulsion orders

57A   **Compulsion order**

(1)   This section applies where a person (in this section and in sections 57C and 57D of this Act, referred to as the "offender")—

Mental Health (Care and Treatment) (Scotland) Act 2003 (asp 13) 101
Part 8—Mentally disordered persons: criminal proceedings
Chapter 2—Disposals on conviction and acquittal

(a) is convicted in the High Court or the sheriff court of an offence punishable by imprisonment (other than an offence the sentence for which is fixed by law); or

(b) is remitted to the High Court by the sheriff under any enactment for sentence for such an offence.

(2) If the court is satisfied—

(a) on the written or oral evidence of two medical practitioners, that the conditions mentioned in subsection (3) below are met in respect of the offender; and

(b) that, having regard to the matters mentioned in subsection (4) below, it is appropriate,

it may, subject to subsection (5) below, make an order (in this Act referred to as a "compulsion order") authorising, subject to subsection (7) below, for the period of 6 months beginning with the day on which the order is made such of the measures mentioned in subsection (8) below as may be specified in the order.

(3) The conditions referred to in subsection (2)(a) above are—

(a) that the offender has a mental disorder;

(b) that medical treatment which would be likely to—

(i) prevent the mental disorder worsening; or

(ii) alleviate any of the symptoms, or effects, of the disorder,

is available for the offender;

(c) that if the offender were not provided with such medical treatment there would be a significant risk—

(i) to the health, safety or welfare of the offender; or

(ii) to the safety of any other person; and

(d) that the making of a compulsion order in respect of the offender is necessary.

(4) The matters referred to in subsection (2)(b) above are—

(a) the mental health officer's report, prepared in accordance with section 57C of this Act, in respect of the offender;

(b) all the circumstances, including—

(i) the nature of the offence of which the offender was convicted; and

(ii) the antecedents of the offender; and

(c) any alternative means of dealing with the offender.

(5) The court may, subject to subsection (6) below, make a compulsion order authorising the detention of the offender in a hospital by virtue of subsection (8)(a) below only if satisfied, on the written or oral evidence of the two medical practitioners mentioned in subsection (2)(a) above, that—

(a) the medical treatment mentioned in subsection (3)(b) above can be provided only if the offender is detained in hospital;

102   *Mental Health (Care and Treatment) (Scotland) Act 2003 (asp 13)*
                           Part 8—Mentally disordered persons: criminal proceedings
                                  Chapter 2—Disposals on conviction and acquittal

   (b) the offender could be admitted to the hospital to be specified in the order before the expiry of the period of 7 days beginning with the day on which the order is made; and

   (c) the hospital to be so specified is suitable for the purpose of giving the medical treatment to the offender.

(6) A compulsion order may authorise detention in a state hospital only if, on the written or oral evidence of the two medical practitioners mentioned in subsection (2)(a) above, it appears to the court—

   (a) that the offender requires to be detained in hospital under conditions of special security; and

   (b) that such conditions of special security can be provided only in a state hospital.

(7) Where the court—

   (a) makes a compulsion order in respect of an offender; and

   (b) also makes a restriction order in respect of the offender,

the compulsion order shall authorise the measures specified in it without limitation of time.

(8) The measures mentioned in subsection (2) above are—

   (a) the detention of the offender in the specified hospital;

   (b) the giving to the offender, in accordance with Part 16 of the Mental Health (Care and Treatment) (Scotland) Act 2003 (asp 13), of medical treatment;

   (c) the imposition of a requirement on the offender to attend—

      (i) on specified or directed dates; or

      (ii) at specified or directed intervals,

      specified or directed places with a view to receiving medical treatment;

   (d) the imposition of a requirement on the offender to attend—

      (i) on specified or directed dates; or

      (ii) at specified or directed intervals,

      specified or directed places with a view to receiving community care services, relevant services or any treatment, care or service;

   (e) subject to subsection (9) below, the imposition of a requirement on the offender to reside at a specified place;

   (f) the imposition of a requirement on the offender to allow—

      (i) the mental health officer;

      (ii) the offender's responsible medical officer; or

      (iii) any person responsible for providing medical treatment, community care services, relevant services or any treatment, care or service to the offender who is authorised for the purposes of this paragraph by the offender's responsible medical officer,

Mental Health (Care and Treatment) (Scotland) Act 2003 (asp 13)
Part 8—Mentally disordered persons: criminal proceedings
Chapter 2—Disposals on conviction and acquittal

103

to visit the offender in the place where the offender resides;

    (g) the imposition of a requirement on the offender to obtain the approval of the mental health officer to any change of address; and

    (h) the imposition of a requirement on the offender to inform the mental health officer of any change of address before the change takes effect.

(9) The court may make a compulsion order imposing, by virtue of subsection (8)(e) above, a requirement on an offender to reside at a specified place which is a place used for the purpose of providing a care home service only if the court is satisfied that the person providing the care home service is willing to receive the offender.

(10) The Scottish Ministers may, by regulations made by statutory instrument, make provision for measures prescribed by the regulations to be treated as included among the measures mentioned in subsection (8) above.

(11) The power conferred by subsection (10) above may be exercised so as to make different provision for different cases or descriptions of case or for different purposes.

(12) No regulations shall be made under subsection (10) above unless a draft of the statutory instrument containing them has been laid before, and approved by a resolution of, the Scottish Parliament.

(13) The court shall be satisfied as to the condition mentioned in subsection (3)(a) above only if the description of the offender's mental disorder by each of the medical practitioners mentioned in subsection (2)(a) above specifies, by reference to the appropriate paragraph (or paragraphs) of the definition of "mental disorder" in section 328(1) of the Mental Health (Care and Treatment) (Scotland) Act 2003 (asp 13), at least one type of mental disorder that the offender has that is also specified by the other.

(14) A compulsion order—

    (a) shall specify—

        (i) by reference to the appropriate paragraph (or paragraphs) of the definition of "mental disorder" in section 328(1) of the Mental Health (Care and Treatment) (Scotland) Act 2003 (asp 13), the type (or types) of mental disorder that each of the medical practitioners mentioned in subsection (2)(a) above specifies that the offender has that is also specified by the other; and

        (ii) if the order does not, by virtue of subsection (8)(a) above, authorise the detention of the offender in hospital, the name of the hospital the managers of which are to have responsibility for appointing the offender's responsible medical officer; and

    (b) may include—

        (i) in a case where a compulsion order authorises the detention of the offender in a specified hospital by virtue of subsection (8)(a) above; or

        (ii) in a case where a compulsion order imposes a requirement on the offender to reside at a specified place by virtue of subsection (8)(e) above,

104   *Mental Health (Care and Treatment) (Scotland) Act 2003 (asp 13)*
Part 8—Mentally disordered persons: criminal proceedings
Chapter 2—Disposals on conviction and acquittal

such directions as the court thinks fit for the removal of the offender to, and the detention of the offender in, a place of safety pending the offender's admission to the specified hospital or, as the case may be, place.

(15)   Where the court makes a compulsion order in relation to an offender, the court—

    (a)   shall not—

        (i)   make an order under section 200 of this Act;

        (ii)   make an interim compulsion order;

        (iii) make a guardianship order;

        (iv)   pass a sentence of imprisonment;

        (v)   impose a fine;

        (vi)   make a probation order; or

        (vii) make a community service order,

        in relation to the offender;

    (b)   may make any other order that the court has power to make apart from this section.

(16)   In this section—

"care home service" has the meaning given by section 2(3) of the Regulation of Care (Scotland) Act 2001 (asp 8);

"community care services" has the meaning given by section 5A(4) of the Social Work (Scotland) Act 1968 (c.49);

"medical treatment" has the same meaning as in section 52D of this Act;

"relevant services" has the meaning given by section 19(2) of the Children (Scotland) Act 1995 (c.36);

"responsible medical officer", in relation to an offender, means the responsible medical officer appointed in respect of the offender under section 230 of the Mental Health (Care and Treatment) (Scotland) Act 2003 (asp 13);

"restriction order" means an order under section 59 of this Act;

"sentence of imprisonment" includes any sentence or order for detention; and

"specified" means specified in the compulsion order.

57B   Compulsion order authorising detention in hospital or requiring residence at place: ancillary provision

(1)   Where a compulsion order—

    (a)   authorises the detention of an offender in a specified hospital; or

    (b)   imposes a requirement on an offender to reside at a specified place,

Mental Health (Care and Treatment) (Scotland) Act 2003 (asp 13)   105
Part 8—Mentally disordered persons: criminal proceedings
Chapter 2—Disposals on conviction and acquittal

this section authorises the removal, before the expiry of the period of 7 days beginning with the day on which the order is made, of the offender to the specified hospital or place, by any of the persons mentioned in subsection (2) below.

(2)   Those persons are—

     (a)   a constable;

     (b)   a person employed in, or contracted to provide services in or to, the specified hospital who is authorised by the managers of that hospital to remove persons to hospital for the purposes of this section; and

     (c)   a specified person.

(3)   In this section, "specified" means specified in the compulsion order.

57C   Mental health officer's report

(1)   This section applies where the court is considering making a compulsion order in relation to an offender under section 57A of this Act.

(2)   If directed to do so by the court, the mental health officer shall—

     (a)   subject to subsection (3) below, interview the offender; and

     (b)   prepare a report in relation to the offender in accordance with subsection (4) below.

(3)   If it is impracticable for the mental health officer to comply with the requirement in subsection (2)(a) above, the mental health officer need not do so.

(4)   The report shall state—

     (a)   the name and address of the offender;

     (b)   if known by the mental health officer, the name and address of the offender's primary carer;

     (c)   in so far as relevant for the purposes of section 57A of this Act, details of the personal circumstances of the offender; and

     (d)   any other information that the mental health officer considers relevant for the purposes of that section.

(5)   In this section—

"carer", and "primary", in relation to a carer, have the meanings given by section 329(1) of the Mental Health (Care and Treatment) (Scotland) Act 2003 (asp 13);

"mental health officer" means a person appointed (or deemed to be appointed) under section 32(1) of that Act; and

"named person" has the meaning given by section 329(1) of that Act.

57D   Compulsion order: supplementary

(1)   If, before the expiry of the period of 7 days beginning with the day on which a compulsion order authorising detention of the offender in a hospital is made, it

106   *Mental Health (Care and Treatment) (Scotland) Act 2003 (asp 13)*
Part 8—Mentally disordered persons: criminal proceedings
Chapter 2—Disposals on conviction and acquittal

appears to the court, or, as the case may be, the Scottish Ministers, that, by reason of emergency or other special circumstances, it is not reasonably practicable for the offender to be admitted to the hospital specified in the order, the court, or, as the case may be, the Scottish Ministers, may direct that the offender be admitted to the hospital specified in the direction.

(2)   Where—

    (a)   the court makes a direction under subsection (1) above, it shall inform the person having custody of the offender; and

    (b)   the Scottish Ministers make such a direction, they shall inform—

        (i)   the court; and

        (ii)   the person having custody of the offender.

(3)   Where a direction is made under subsection (1) above, the compulsion order shall have effect as if the hospital specified in the direction were the hospital specified in the order.

(4)   In this section, "court" means the court which made the compulsion order.".

Urgent detention of acquitted persons

134   Power of court to detain acquitted persons

After section 60B of the 1995 Act, there shall be inserted—

"60C   Acquitted persons: detention for medical examination

(1)   Subject to subsection (7) below, this section applies where a person charged with an offence is acquitted.

(2)   If the court by or before which the person is acquitted is satisfied—

    (a)   on the written or oral evidence of two medical practitioners that the conditions mentioned in subsection (3) below are met in respect of the person; and

    (b)   that it is not practicable to secure the immediate examination of the person by a medical practitioner,

the court may, immediately after the person is acquitted, make an order authorising the measures mentioned in subsection (4) below for the purpose of enabling arrangements to be made for a medical practitioner to carry out a medical examination of the person.

(3)   The conditions referred to in subsection (2)(a) above are—

    (a)   that the person has a mental disorder;

    (b)   that medical treatment which would be likely to—

        (i)   prevent the mental disorder worsening; or

        (ii)   alleviate any of the symptoms, or effects, of the disorder,

    is available for the person; and

    (c)   that if the person were not provided with such medical treatment there would be a significant risk—

Mental Health (Care and Treatment) (Scotland) Act 2003 (asp 13) 107
Part 8—Mentally disordered persons: criminal proceedings
Chapter 2—Disposals on conviction and acquittal

> (i) to the health, safety or welfare of the person; or
>
> (ii) to the safety of any other person.

(4) The measures referred to in subsection (2) above are—

  (a) the removal of the person to a place of safety by—

   (i) a constable; or

   (ii) a person specified by the court; and

  (b) the detention, subject to subsection (6) below, of the person in that place of safety for a period of 6 hours beginning with the time at which the order under subsection (2) above is made.

(5) If the person absconds—

  (a) while being removed to a place of safety under subsection (4) above; or

  (b) from the place of safety,

  a constable or the person specified by the court under paragraph (a) of that subsection may, at any time during the period mentioned in paragraph (b) of that subsection, take the person into custody and remove the person to a place of safety.

(6) An order under this section ceases to authorise detention of a person if, following the medical examination of the person, a medical practitioner grants—

  (a) an emergency detention certificate under section 36 of the Mental Health (Care and Treatment) (Scotland) Act 2003 (asp 13); or

  (b) a short-term detention certificate under section 44 of that Act.

(7) This section does not apply—

  (a) in a case where a declaration is made by virtue of section 54(6) of this Act that the person is acquitted on account of the person's insanity at the time of doing the act or making the omission constituting the offence with which the person was charged; or

  (b) in a case where the court states under section 55(4) of this Act that the person is so acquitted on the ground of such insanity.

(8) In this section, "medical treatment" has the same meaning as in section 52D of this Act.

60D Notification of detention under section 60C

(1) This section applies where a person has been removed to a place of safety under section 60C of this Act.

(2) The court shall, before the expiry of the period of 14 days beginning with the day on which the order under section 60C(2) of this Act is made, ensure that the Mental Welfare Commission is given notice of the matters mentioned in subsection (3) below.

(3) Those matters are—

  (a) the name and address of the person removed to the place of safety;

108   *Mental Health (Care and Treatment) (Scotland) Act 2003 (asp 13)*
Part 8—Mentally disordered persons: criminal proceedings
Chapter 3—Mentally disordered prisoners

    (b)   the date on and time at which the person was so removed;

    (c)   the address of the place of safety;

    (d)   if the person is removed to a police station, the reason why the person was removed there; and

    (e)   any other matter that the Scottish Ministers may, by regulations made by statutory instrument, prescribe.

(4)   The power conferred by subsection (3)(e) above may be exercised so as to make different provision for different cases or descriptions of case or for different purposes.

(5)   A statutory instrument containing regulations under subsection (3)(e) above shall be subject to annulment in pursuance of a resolution of the Scottish Parliament.".

Probation with a requirement of treatment

135   Amendment of 1995 Act: probation for treatment of mental disorder

In section 230 of the 1995 Act (probation orders requiring treatment for mental disorder)—

  (a) in subsection (1)—

     (i)   at the beginning there shall be inserted "Subject to subsection (3) below,"; and

    (ii)   the words ", not extending beyond 12 months from the date of the requirement," shall cease to have effect; and

  (b) for subsection (3) there shall be substituted—

  "(3) A court may make a probation order including a requirement under subsection (1) above only if it is satisfied—

    (a)   on the written or oral evidence of the registered medical practitioner or chartered psychologist by whom or under whose direction the treatment intended to be specified in the order is to be provided, that the treatment is appropriate; and

    (b)   that arrangements have been made for that treatment, including, where the offender is to be treated as a resident patient, arrangements for his reception in the hospital intended to be specified in the order.".

CHAPTER 3

MENTALLY DISORDERED PRISONERS

136   Transfer of prisoners for treatment for mental disorder

(1)   This section applies where a person (in this section referred to as the "prisoner") is serving a sentence of imprisonment.

(2)   If the Scottish Ministers are satisfied, on the written reports of an approved medical practitioner and a medical practitioner as to the matters mentioned in subsection (3) below, they may, subject to subsection (5) below, make a direction (referred to in this

Mental Health (Care and Treatment) (Scotland) Act 2003 (asp 13) 109
Part 8—Mentally disordered persons: criminal proceedings
Chapter 3—Mentally disordered prisoners

Act as a "transfer for treatment direction") authorising the measures mentioned in subsection (6) below.

(3) The matters referred to in subsection (2) above are—

(a) that the conditions mentioned in subsection (4) below are met in respect of the prisoner;

(b) that the prisoner could be admitted to the hospital to be specified in the direction before the expiry of the period of 7 days beginning with the day on which the direction is made; and

(c) that the hospital to be so specified is suitable for the purpose of giving medical treatment to the prisoner.

(4) The conditions referred to in subsection (3)(a) above are—

(a) that the prisoner has a mental disorder;

(b) that medical treatment which would be likely to—

(i) prevent the mental disorder worsening; or

(ii) alleviate any of the symptoms, or effects, of the disorder,

is available for the prisoner;

(c) that if the prisoner were not provided with such medical treatment there would be a significant risk—

(i) to the health, safety or welfare of the prisoner; or

(ii) to the safety of any other person; and

(d) that the making of a transfer for treatment direction in respect of the prisoner is necessary.

(5) A transfer for treatment direction may authorise detention in a state hospital only if, on the written reports of the approved medical practitioner and the medical practitioner mentioned in subsection (2) above, it appears to the Scottish Ministers—

(a) that the prisoner requires to be detained in hospital under conditions of special security; and

(b) that such conditions of special security can be provided only in a state hospital.

(6) The measures are—

(a) the removal, before the expiry of the period of 7 days beginning with the day on which the direction is made, of the prisoner to the specified hospital by—

(i) a constable;

(ii) a person employed in, or contracted to provide services in or to, the specified hospital who is authorised by the managers of that hospital to remove persons to hospital for the purposes of this section; or

(iii) a specified person;

(b) the detention of the prisoner in the specified hospital; and

(c) the giving to the prisoner, in accordance with Part 16 of this Act, of medical treatment.

110 *Mental Health (Care and Treatment) (Scotland) Act 2003 (asp 13)*
Part 9—Compulsion orders
Chapter 1—Duties following making of order

(7)   The Scottish Ministers shall be satisfied as to the condition mentioned in subsection (4)(a) above only if the descriptions of the prisoner's mental disorder by each of the medical practitioners mentioned in subsection (2) above specifies, by reference to the appropriate paragraph (or paragraphs) of the definition of "mental disorder" in section 328(1) of this Act, at least one type of mental disorder that the prisoner has that is also specified by the other.

(8)   A transfer for treatment direction—

(a)   shall specify, by reference to the appropriate paragraph (or paragraphs) of the definition of "mental disorder" in section 328(1) of this Act, the type (or types) of mental disorder that each of the medical practitioners mentioned in subsection (2) above specifies that the prisoner has that is also specified by the other; and

(b)   may include such directions as the Scottish Ministers think fit for the removal of the prisoner to, and the detention of the prisoner in, a place of safety pending the prisoner's admission to the specified hospital.

(9)   In subsection (1) above, the reference to a prisoner serving a sentence of imprisonment includes a reference—

(a)   to a prisoner detained in pursuance of any sentence or order for detention made by a court (other than an order under section 52D(2), 52M(2), 53(2), 54, 57(2), 57A(2), 118(5) or 190 of the 1995 Act); and

(b)   to a prisoner committed by a court to prison in default of payment of any fine to be paid on the prisoner's conviction.

(10)   In this section—

"place of safety" has the same meaning as in section 300 of this Act; and

"specified" means specified in the transfer for treatment direction.

PART 9

COMPULSION ORDERS

CHAPTER 1

DUTIES FOLLOWING MAKING OF ORDER

137   Part 9 care plan

(1)   This section applies where a compulsion order authorising the measures specified in it for the period mentioned in section 57A(2) of the 1995 Act (any such compulsion order being referred to in this Part of this Act as a "relevant compulsion order") is made in respect of a patient.

(2)   As soon as practicable after a patient's responsible medical officer is appointed under section 230 of this Act the responsible medical officer shall—

(a)   prepare a plan (any such plan being referred to in this Part of this Act as a "Part 9 care plan") relating to the patient; and

(b)   ensure that the patient's Part 9 care plan is included in the patient's medical records.

(3)   The Part 9 care plan shall record—

Mental Health (Care and Treatment) (Scotland) Act 2003 (asp 13).
Part 9—Compulsion orders
Chapter 2—Review of compulsion orders

111

    (a) the medical treatment—

        (i)   which it is proposed to give; and

        (ii) which is being given,

    to the patient while the patient is subject to the compulsion order; and

    (b) such other information relating to the care of the patient as may be prescribed by regulations.

(4)   Subject to subsection (5)(b) below, a patient's responsible medical officer may from time to time amend the patient's Part 9 care plan.

(5)   Regulations may prescribe—

    (a) circumstances in which a patient's responsible medical officer is required to amend the patient's Part 9 care plan;

    (b) information in a Part 9 care plan which may not be amended.

(6)   Where a patient's responsible medical officer amends the patient's Part 9 care plan—

    (a) the responsible medical officer shall secure that, as soon as practicable after it is amended, the amended Part 9 care plan is included in the patient's medical records; and

    (b) subsections (3) to (5) above and this subsection shall apply as if references to the Part 9 care plan were references to the amended Part 9 care plan.

138   Mental health officer's duty to identify named person

The mental health officer shall, as soon as practicable after a relevant compulsion order is made in respect of the patient, take such steps as are reasonably practicable to ascertain the name and address of the patient's named person.

CHAPTER 2

REVIEW OF COMPULSION ORDERS

Mandatory reviews by responsible medical officer

139   First review of compulsion order

(1)   This section applies where a relevant compulsion order is made in respect of a patient.

(2)   The patient's responsible medical officer shall, during the appropriate period, carry out a review in respect of the compulsion order (such review being referred to in this Part of this Act as the "first review") by complying with the requirements in subsection (3) below.

(3)   Those requirements are—

    (a) to—

        (i)   carry out a medical examination of the patient; or

        (ii) make arrangements for an approved medical practitioner to carry out such a medical examination;

    (b) to consider—

112   *Mental Health (Care and Treatment) (Scotland) Act 2003 (asp 13)*
Part 9—Compulsion orders
Chapter 2—Review of compulsion orders

      (i)   whether the conditions mentioned in subsection (4) below continue to apply in respect of the patient; and

      (ii)   whether it continues to be necessary for the patient to be subject to the compulsion order; and

  (c) to consult—

      (i)   the mental health officer;

      (ii)   such persons as are mentioned in subsection (5) below as the responsible medical officer considers appropriate; and

      (iii)   such other persons as the responsible medical officer considers appropriate.

(4)   Those conditions are—

  (a) that the patient has a mental disorder;

  (b) that medical treatment which would be likely to—

      (i)   prevent the mental disorder worsening; or

      (ii)   alleviate any of the symptoms, or effects, of the disorder,

    is available for the patient; and

  (c) that if the patient were not provided with such medical treatment there would be a significant risk—

      (i)   to the health, safety or welfare of the patient; or

      (ii)   to the safety of any other person.

(5)   The persons referred to in subsection (3)(c)(ii) above are—

  (a) persons who appear to the responsible medical officer to provide medical treatment of the kind that is recorded in the Part 9 care plan;

  (b) if any community care services or relevant services are set out in that plan, persons who appear to the responsible medical officer to provide services of that kind;

  (c) if any other treatment, care or service is set out in that plan, persons who appear to the responsible medical officer to provide treatment, care or a service of that kind.

(6)   In subsection (2) above, "appropriate period" means the period of 2 months ending with the day on which the relevant compulsion order ceases to authorise the measures specified in it.

140   Further reviews of compulsion order

(1)   This section applies where a relevant compulsion order is extended by virtue of an order under section 167 of this Act.

(2)   The patient's responsible medical officer shall, during the period mentioned in subsection (3) below, carry out a review in respect of the compulsion order (such review being referred to in this Part of this Act as a "further review") by complying with the requirements in section 139(3) of this Act.

(3)   The period referred to in subsection (2) above is the period of 2 months ending with the day on which the compulsion order, as extended by virtue of the order, ceases to authorise the measures specified in it.

Mental Health (Care and Treatment) (Scotland) Act 2003 (asp 13)   113
Part 9—Compulsion orders
Chapter 2—Review of compulsion orders

Revocation of order by responsible medical officer or Commission

141   **Responsible medical officer's duty to revoke compulsion order: mandatory reviews**

(1)   This section applies where a patient's responsible medical officer is carrying out—

      (a)   the first review of the relevant compulsion order to which the patient is subject; or

      (b)   a further review of that order.

(2)   If, having regard to any views expressed by persons consulted under section 139(3)(c) of this Act for the purpose of the review being carried out, the responsible medical officer is not satisfied—

      (a)   that the conditions mentioned in section 139(4) of this Act continue to apply in respect of the patient; or

      (b)   that it continues to be necessary for the patient to be subject to the compulsion order,

the responsible medical officer shall make a determination revoking the compulsion order.

(3)   A determination under this section shall be made as soon as practicable after the duty to make it arises.

142   **Revocation of compulsion order: responsible medical officer's duty to keep under review**

(1)   This section applies where a patient is subject to a relevant compulsion order.

(2)   Without prejudice to the duties imposed on the patient's responsible medical officer by sections 139(2), 140(2), 141(2) and 159(2) of this Act, the responsible medical officer shall from time to time consider—

      (a)   whether the conditions mentioned in section 139(4) of this Act continue to apply in respect of the patient; and

      (b)   whether it continues to be necessary for the patient to be subject to a compulsion order.

(3)   If, having considered the matters mentioned in paragraphs (a) and (b) of subsection (2) above, the responsible medical officer is not satisfied—

      (a)   that the conditions mentioned in section 139(4) of this Act continue to apply in respect of the patient; or

      (b)   that it continues to be necessary for the patient to be subject to a compulsion order,

the responsible medical officer shall make a determination revoking the compulsion order.

143   **Commission's power to revoke compulsion order**

(1)   This section applies where a patient is subject to a relevant compulsion order.

(2)   If the Commission is satisfied—

      (a)   that not all of the conditions mentioned in section 139(4) of this Act continue to apply in respect of the patient; or

114   *Mental Health (Care and Treatment) (Scotland) Act 2003 (asp 13)*
Part 9—Compulsion orders
Chapter 2—Review of compulsion orders

(b) that it does not continue to be necessary for the patient to be subject to a compulsion order,

it may make a determination revoking the compulsion order.

144   Revocation of compulsion order: notification

(1)   Where a patient's responsible medical officer makes a determination under section 141 or 142 of this Act, the responsible medical officer shall—

(a)   give notice of the determination; and

(b)   send a statement of the reasons for it,

to the Commission and to the persons mentioned in subsection (3) below.

(2)   Where the Commission makes a determination under section 143 of this Act it shall—

(a)   give notice of the determination; and

(b)   send a statement of the reasons for it,

to the patient's responsible medical officer and to the persons mentioned in subsection (3) below.

(3)   The persons referred to in subsections (1) and (2) above are—

(a)   the patient;

(b)   the patient's named person;

(c)   any guardian of the patient;

(d)   any welfare attorney of the patient;

(e)   the mental health officer; and

(f)   the Tribunal.

(4)   Notice under subsection (1) or (2) above—

(a)   to the persons mentioned in subsection (3)(a) to (d) above shall be given as soon as practicable after the determination is made and, in any event, before the expiry of the period of 7 days beginning with the day on which the determination is made; and

(b)   to—

(i)   the Commission;

(ii)   the patient's responsible medical officer; and

(iii) the persons mentioned in subsection (3)(e) and (f) above,

shall be given before the expiry of the period of 7 days beginning with the day on which the determination is made.

Further steps to be taken where order not revoked

145   Mandatory reviews: further steps to be taken where compulsion order not revoked

(1)   This section applies where a patient's responsible medical officer is carrying out—

(a)   the first review of the relevant compulsion order to which the patient is subject; or

Mental Health (Care and Treatment) (Scotland) Act 2003 (asp 13) 115
Part 9—Compulsion orders
Chapter 2—Review of compulsion orders

(b) a further review of that order.

(2) If, having regard to any views expressed by persons consulted under section 139(3)(c) of this Act for the purpose of the review being carried out, the patient's responsible medical officer is satisfied—

(a) that the conditions mentioned in section 139(4) of this Act continue to apply in respect of the patient; and

(b) that it continues to be necessary for the patient to be subject to a compulsion order,

the responsible medical officer shall comply with the requirements in subsection (3) below.

(3) Those requirements are—

(a) to consider whether it will continue to be necessary for the patient to be subject to a compulsion order after the day on which the order to which the patient is subject will cease (unless extended) to authorise the measures specified in it;

(b) to assess the needs of the patient for medical treatment;

(c) to consider—

(i) whether the compulsion order should be varied by modifying the measures specified in it;

(ii) if the order should be varied, what modification is appropriate; and

(d) to consider any views expressed on the matters mentioned in paragraphs (a) to (c) above by persons consulted under section 139(3)(c) of this Act.

Extension of order following first review

146 First review: responsible medical officer's duty where extension proposed

(1) This section applies where a patient's responsible medical officer is carrying out the first review of the relevant compulsion order to which the patient is subject.

(2) If, having regard to any views expressed by persons consulted under section 139(3)(c) of this Act, it appears to the responsible medical officer—

(a) that it will continue to be necessary for the patient to be subject to a compulsion order after the day on which the order will cease (unless extended) to authorise the measures specified in it; and

(b) that the compulsion order should not be varied by modifying the measures specified in it,

the responsible medical officer shall give notice to the mental health officer that the responsible medical officer is proposing to make an application under section 149 of this Act for an order under section 167 extending the compulsion order for the period of 6 months beginning with the day on which the compulsion order will cease (unless extended) to authorise the measures specified in it.

147 Proposed extension on first review: mental health officer's duties

(1) The mental health officer shall, as soon as practicable after receiving notice under section 146(2) of this Act, comply with the requirements in subsection (2) below.

116 *Mental Health (Care and Treatment) (Scotland) Act 2003 (asp 13)*
Part 9—Compulsion orders
Chapter 2—Review of compulsion orders

(2)   Those requirements are—

    (a) subject to subsection (3) below, to interview the patient;

    (b) to inform the patient—

        (i)   that the patient's responsible medical officer is proposing to make an application under section 149 of this Act for an order under section 167 of this Act;

        (ii) of the patient's rights in relation to such an application; and

        (iii) of the availability of independent advocacy services under section 259 of this Act;

    (c) to take appropriate steps to ensure that the patient has the opportunity of making use of those services; and

    (d) to inform the patient's responsible medical officer—

        (i)   as to whether the mental health officer agrees, or disagrees, that the proposed application should be made;

        (ii) if the mental health officer disagrees, of the reason why that is the case; and

        (iii) of any other matters that the mental health officer considers relevant.

(3)   If it is impracticable for the mental health officer to comply with the requirement in subsection (2)(a) above, the mental health officer need not do so.

148   First review: responsible medical officer's duty to apply for extension of compulsion order

(1)   This section applies where a patient's responsible medical officer is carrying out the first review of the relevant compulsion order to which the patient is subject.

(2)   If, having regard to—

    (a) any views expressed by persons consulted under section 139(3)(c) of this Act; and

    (b) any views expressed by the mental health officer under section 147(2)(d) of this Act,

the responsible medical officer is satisfied as to the matters mentioned in section 146(2)(a) and (b) of this Act, the responsible medical officer shall comply with the requirement mentioned in subsection (3) below.

(3)   The requirement referred to in subsection (2) above is to make an application to the Tribunal under section 149 of this Act for an order extending the compulsion order for the period of 6 months beginning with the day on which the order to which the patient is subject will cease (unless extended) to authorise the measures specified in it.

149   Application to Tribunal for extension of order following first review

An application under this section to the Tribunal by a patient's responsible medical officer—

    (a) shall state—

        (i)   the name and address of the patient;

        (ii) the name and address of the patient's named person; and

Mental Health (Care and Treatment) (Scotland) Act 2003 (asp 13)   117
Part 9—Compulsion orders
Chapter 2—Review of compulsion orders

         (iii) whether the mental health officer agrees, or disagrees, that the application should be made, or has failed to comply with the duty imposed by section 147(2)(d)(i) of this Act; and

    (b) shall be accompanied by such documents as may be prescribed by regulations.

Extension of order following further review

150   Further review: responsible medical officer's duty where extension proposed

(1) This section applies where a patient's responsible medical officer is carrying out a further review of the relevant compulsion order to which the patient is subject.

(2) If, having regard to any views expressed by persons consulted under section 139(3)(c) of this Act for the purpose of the review being carried out, it appears to the responsible medical officer—

    (a) that it will continue to be necessary for the patient to be subject to a compulsion order after the day on which the order will cease (unless extended) to authorise the measures specified in it; and

    (b) that the compulsion order should not be varied by modifying the measures specified in it,

the responsible medical officer shall give notice to the mental health officer that the responsible medical officer is proposing to make a determination under section 152 of this Act extending the order.

151   Proposed extension of order on further review: mental health officer's duties

(1) The mental health officer shall, as soon as practicable after receiving notice under section 150(2) of this Act, comply with the requirements in subsection (2) below.

(2) Those requirements are—

    (a) subject to subsection (3) below, to interview the patient;

    (b) to inform the patient—

         (i) that the patient's responsible medical officer is proposing to make a determination under section 152 of this Act extending the compulsion order to which the patient is subject for the period mentioned in section 152(3) of this Act that applies in the patient's case;

        (ii) of the patient's rights in relation to such a determination; and

        (iii) of the availability of independent advocacy services under section 259 of this Act;

    (c) to take appropriate steps to ensure that the patient has the opportunity of making use of those services; and

    (d) to inform the patient's responsible medical officer—

         (i) as to whether the mental health officer agrees, or disagrees, that the determination that is proposed should be made;

        (ii) if the mental health officer disagrees, of the reason why that is the case; and

        (iii) of any other matters that the mental health officer considers relevant.

118   *Mental Health (Care and Treatment) (Scotland) Act 2003 (asp 13)*
Part 9—Compulsion orders
Chapter 2—Review of compulsion orders

(3)   If it is impracticable for the mental health officer to comply with the requirement in subsection (2)(a) above, the mental health officer need not do so.

152   **Further review: responsible medical officer's duty to extend compulsion order**

(1)   This section applies where a patient's responsible medical officer is carrying out a further review of the relevant compulsion order to which the patient is subject.

(2)   If, having regard to—

    (a)   any views expressed by persons consulted under section 139(3)(c) of this Act for the purpose of the review being carried out; and

    (b)   any views expressed by the mental health officer under section 151(2)(d) of this Act for the purpose of that review,

the responsible medical officer is satisfied as to the matters mentioned in section 150(2)(a) and (b) of this Act, the responsible medical officer shall make a determination extending the compulsion order for the period mentioned in subsection (3) below.

(3)   The period referred to in subsection (2) above is—

    (a)   where a determination is made in respect of the first further review, the period of 12 months beginning with the expiry of the period for which the order is extended by virtue of an order under section 167 of this Act;

    (b)   where a determination is made in respect of a subsequent further review, the period of 12 months beginning with the expiry of the period of 12 months for which the order is extended as a result of the immediately preceding further review.

153   **Determination extending compulsion order: notification**

(1)   Where a patient's responsible medical officer makes a determination under section 152 of this Act, the responsible medical officer shall, as soon as practicable after the determination is made and, in any event, before the day on which the compulsion order will cease (unless extended) to authorise the measures specified in it, comply with the requirements in subsection (2) below.

(2)   Those requirements are—

    (a)   to prepare a record stating—

        (i)   the determination;

        (ii)   the reasons for it;

        (iii)   whether the mental health officer agrees, or disagrees, with the determination or has failed to comply with the duty imposed by section 151(2)(d)(i) of this Act;

        (iv)   if the mental health officer disagrees with the determination, the reasons for the disagreement;

        (v)   (by reference to the appropriate paragraph (or paragraphs) of the definition of "mental disorder" in section 328(1) of this Act) the type (or types) of mental disorder that the patient has; and if there is a difference between that type (or types) and the type (or types) of mental disorder recorded in the

Mental Health (Care and Treatment) (Scotland) Act 2003 (asp 13)   119
Part 9—Compulsion orders
Chapter 2—Review of compulsion orders

compulsion order in respect of which the determination is made, what that difference is; and

    (vi) such other matters as may be prescribed by regulations;

  (b) to submit the record to the Tribunal; and

  (c) at the same time as the responsible medical officer submits the record to the Tribunal, to give notice of the determination and send a copy of the record—

    (i) subject to subsection (3) below, to the patient;

    (ii) to the patient's named person;

    (iii) to the mental health officer; and

    (iv) to the Commission.

(3)   Where the responsible medical officer considers that there would be a risk of significant harm to the patient, or to others, if a copy of the record were sent to the patient, that officer need not send a copy to the patient.

(4)   At the same time as the responsible medical officer submits the record to the Tribunal the responsible medical officer shall send to the Tribunal, and to the persons mentioned in subsection (2)(c)(ii) to (iv) above, a statement of the matters mentioned in subsection (5) below.

(5)   Those matters are—

  (a) whether the responsible medical officer is sending a copy of the record to the patient; and

  (b) if the responsible medical officer is not sending a copy of the record to the patient, the reason for not doing so.

Extension and variation of order

154   **Responsible medical officer's duty where extension and variation proposed**

(1)   This section applies where a patient's responsible medical officer is carrying out—

  (a) the first review of the relevant compulsion order to which the patient is subject; or

  (b) a further review of that order.

(2)   If, having regard to any views expressed by persons consulted under section 139(3)(c) of this Act for the purpose of the review being carried out, it appears to the responsible medical officer—

  (a) that it will continue to be necessary for the patient to be subject to a compulsion order after the day on which the order will cease (unless extended) to authorise the measures specified in it; but

  (b) that the compulsion order should be varied by modifying the measures specified in it,

the responsible medical officer shall comply with the requirement in subsection (3) below.

(3)   The requirement is to give notice to the mental health officer—

120   *Mental Health (Care and Treatment) (Scotland) Act 2003 (asp 13)*
Part 9—Compulsion orders
Chapter 2—Review of compulsion orders

     (a)   that the responsible medical officer is proposing to make an application to the Tribunal under section 158 of this Act for an order under section 167 of this Act—

         (i)   extending the compulsion order for the period mentioned in subsection (4) below; and

         (ii)   varying the order by modifying the measures specified in it; and

     (b)   of the modification of the measures specified in that order that the responsible medical officer is proposing.

(4)   The period referred to in subsection (3)(a)(i) above is—

     (a)   where the application is made in respect of the first review, the period of 6 months beginning with the day on which the compulsion order will cease (unless extended) to authorise the measures specified in it;

     (b)   where the application is made in respect of the first further review, the period of 12 months beginning with the expiry of the period mentioned in paragraph (a) above;

     (c)   where the application is made in respect of a subsequent further review, the period of 12 months beginning with the expiry of the period of 12 months for which the order is extended as a result of the immediately preceding further review.

155   Mental health officer's duties: extension and variation of compulsion order

(1)   The mental health officer shall, as soon as practicable after receiving notice under section 154(3) of this Act, comply with the requirements in subsection (2) below.

(2)   Those requirements are—

     (a)   subject to subsection (3) below, to interview the patient;

     (b)   to inform the patient of the matters mentioned in subsection (4) below;

     (c)   to inform the patient of the availability of independent advocacy services under section 259 of this Act;

     (d)   to take appropriate steps to ensure that the patient has the opportunity of making use of those services; and

     (e)   to inform the patient's responsible medical officer—

         (i)   of whether the mental health officer agrees, or disagrees, that the application that is proposed should be made;

         (ii)   if the mental health officer disagrees, of the reason why that is the case; and

         (iii)   of any other matters that the mental health officer considers relevant.

(3)   If it is impracticable for the mental health officer to comply with the requirement in subsection (2)(a) above, the mental health officer need not do so.

(4)   The matters referred to in subsection (2)(b) above are—

     (a)   that the patient's responsible medical officer is proposing to make an application to the Tribunal under section 158 of this Act for an order—

         (i)   extending the compulsion order to which the patient is subject for the period mentioned in section 154(4) of this Act that applies in the patient's case; and

Mental Health (Care and Treatment) (Scotland) Act 2003 (asp 13)
Part 9—Compulsion orders
Chapter 2—Review of compulsion orders

121

      (ii) varying the compulsion order by modifying the measures specified in it;

  (b) the modification of the measures specified in that order that the responsible medical officer is proposing; and

  (c) the patient's rights in relation to such an application.

156   Responsible medical officer's duty to apply for extension and variation of compulsion order

(1) If, having regard to—

  (a) any views expressed by persons consulted under section 139(3)(c) of this Act for the purpose of the review being carried out; and

  (b) any views expressed by the mental health officer under section 155(2)(e) of this Act for the purpose of that review,

the responsible medical officer is satisfied as to the matters mentioned in section 154(2)(a) and (b) of this Act, the responsible medical officer shall comply with the requirement in subsection (2) below.

(2) That requirement is to make an application to the Tribunal under section 158 of this Act for an order—

  (a) extending the compulsion order for the period mentioned in section 154(4) of this Act that applies in the patient's case; and

  (b) varying that order by modifying the measures specified in it.

157   Application for extension and variation of compulsion order: notification

Where, by virtue of section 156(1) of this Act, an application is to be made under section 158 of this Act, the patient's responsible medical officer shall, as soon as practicable after the duty to make the application arises (and, in any event, before making the application), give notice that the application is to be made to—

  (a) the patient;

  (b) the patient's named person;

  (c) any guardian of the patient;

  (d) any welfare attorney of the patient;

  (e) the mental health officer; and

  (f) the Commission.

158   Application to Tribunal for extension and variation of compulsion order

An application under this section to the Tribunal by a patient's responsible medical officer for an order extending and varying a compulsion order—

  (a) shall state—

      (i) the name and address of the patient;

      (ii) the name and address of the patient's named person;

122   *Mental Health (Care and Treatment) (Scotland) Act 2003 (asp 13)*
Part 9—Compulsion orders
Chapter 2—Review of compulsion orders

      (iii) the modification of the measures authorised by the compulsion order that is proposed by the responsible medical officer;

      (iv) the reasons for seeking that modification; and

      (v) whether the mental health officer agrees, or disagrees, that the application should be made, or has failed to comply with the duty imposed by section 155(2)(e)(i) of this Act; and

  (b) shall be accompanied by such documents as may be prescribed by regulations.

Variation of order

159   Responsible medical officer's duties: variation of compulsion order

(1) This section applies where a patient is subject to a relevant compulsion order.

(2) Without prejudice to the duties imposed on the patient's responsible medical officer by sections 139(2), 140(2) and 145(2) of this Act, the responsible medical officer shall from time to time consider whether the compulsion order should be varied by modifying the measures specified in it.

(3) If it appears to the responsible medical officer that the compulsion order should be varied by modifying the measures specified in it, the responsible medical officer shall, as soon as practicable, comply with the requirements in subsection (4) below.

(4) Those requirements are—

  (a) to assess the needs of the patient for medical treatment;

  (b) to consider what modification, if any, of the measures specified in the compulsion order is appropriate; and

  (c) to consult—

      (i) the mental health officer; and

      (ii) such other persons as the responsible medical officer considers appropriate.

(5) If, having regard to any views expressed by persons consulted under subsection (4)(c) above, the responsible medical officer is satisfied that the compulsion order should be varied by modifying the measures specified in it, the responsible medical officer shall make an application to the Tribunal under section 161 of this Act for an order under section 167 of this Act varying the compulsion order in that way.

160   Application for variation of compulsion order: notification

Where, by virtue of section 159(5) of this Act, an application is to be made under section 161 of this Act, the patient's responsible medical officer shall, as soon as practicable after the duty to make the application arises (and, in any event, before making the application), give notice that the application is to be made to the persons mentioned in section 157(a) to (f) of this Act.

161   Application to Tribunal by responsible medical officer

An application under this section to the Tribunal by a patient's responsible medical officer for an order varying a compulsion order—

  (a) shall state the matters mentioned in section 158(a) of this Act; and

Mental Health (Care and Treatment) (Scotland) Act 2003 (asp 13)
Part 9—Compulsion orders
Chapter 2—Review of compulsion orders

123

   (b) shall be accompanied by such documents as may be prescribed by regulations.

Reference to Tribunal by Commission

162   Commission's power to make reference to Tribunal

(1)   This section applies where a patient is subject to a relevant compulsion order.

(2)   If it appears to the Commission that it is appropriate to do so, it may make a reference to the Tribunal in respect of the compulsion order to which the patient is subject.

(3)   Where a reference is to be made under subsection (2) above, the Commission shall, as soon as practicable, give notice that a reference is to be made to—

    (a) the patient's responsible medical officer; and

    (b) the persons mentioned in section 157(a) to (e) of this Act.

(4)   A reference under subsection (2) above shall state—

    (a) the name and address of the patient;

    (b) the name and address of the patient's named person; and

    (c) the reason for making the reference.

Applications to Tribunal by patient etc.

163   Application to Tribunal by patient etc. for revocation of determination extending compulsion order

(1)   Subject to subsection (2) below, where a patient's responsible medical officer makes a determination under section 152 of this Act—

    (a) the patient; or

    (b) the patient's named person,

may make an application under this section to the Tribunal for an order under section 167 of this Act revoking the determination.

(2)   Subsection (1) above does not apply where the Tribunal is required, by virtue of section 165 of this Act, to review the determination.

164   Application to Tribunal by patient etc. for revocation or variation of compulsion order

(1)   This section applies where a patient is subject to a relevant compulsion order.

(2)   Either of the persons mentioned in subsection (3) below may, subject to subsections (4) to (6) below, make an application under this section to the Tribunal for an order under section 167 of this Act—

    (a) revoking the compulsion order; or

    (b) varying that order by modifying the measures specified in it.

(3)   The persons referred to in subsection (2) above are—

    (a) the patient; and

    (b) the patient's named person.

124   *Mental Health (Care and Treatment) (Scotland) Act 2003 (asp 13)*
Part 9—Compulsion orders
Chapter 2—Review of compulsion orders

(4)   An application under this section may not be made—

    (a)   in respect of a compulsion order that has not been extended;

    (b)   during the period of 3 months beginning with the making of—

        (i)   an order in respect of the compulsion order made under section 166 of this Act; or

        (ii)   an order in respect of the compulsion order made, by virtue of section 149 or 158 of this Act, under section 167 of this Act.

(5)   If—

    (a)   an application under this section for revocation of a compulsion order is refused; or

    (b)   an application is made under this section for variation of a compulsion order,

the person who made the application shall not be entitled to make more than one further application under this section in respect of the compulsion order during the period mentioned in subsection (7) below.

(6)   If an application under section 163 of this Act for revocation of a determination under section 152 of this Act is refused, the person who made that application shall not be entitled to make more than one application under this section in respect of the compulsion order which is the subject of the determination during the period mentioned in subsection (7) below.

(7)   The period referred to in subsections (5) and (6) above is—

    (a)   where the application is made during the period of 6 months beginning with the expiry of the initial period, that period of 6 months; or

    (b)   any subsequent period of 12 months that begins with, or with an anniversary of, the expiry of the period of 6 months mentioned in paragraph (a) above.

(8)   In subsection (7)(a) above, "initial period" means the period of 6 months beginning with the day on which the compulsion order is made.

Review by Tribunal of determination extending order

165   Tribunal's duty to review determination under section 152

(1)   This section applies where a patient's responsible medical officer makes a determination under section 152 of this Act.

(2)   If—

    (a)   the record submitted to the Tribunal under section 153 of this Act states—

        (i)   that there is a difference between the type (or types) of mental disorder that the patient has and the type (or types) of mental disorder recorded in the compulsion order in respect of which the determination is made; or

        (ii)   that the mental health officer disagrees with the determination or has failed to comply with the duty imposed by section 151(2)(d)(i) of this Act; or

Mental Health (Care and Treatment) (Scotland) Act 2003 (asp 13)   125
Part 9—Compulsion orders
Chapter 2—Review of compulsion orders

(b) no decision has been made by the Tribunal under this section or section 167 of this Act in respect of the compulsion order to which the determination relates during the period of 2 years ending with the day on which the order, had it not been extended by the determination, would have ceased to authorise the measures specified in it,

the Tribunal shall review the determination.

Powers of Tribunal

166   Powers of Tribunal on review under section 165

(1) On the review of a determination under section 165 of this Act, the Tribunal may make an order under this section—

   (a) revoking the determination;

   (b) revoking both the determination and the compulsion order;

   (c) confirming the determination; or

   (d) confirming the determination and varying the compulsion order by modifying the measures specified in it.

(2) Before making a decision under subsection (1) above, the Tribunal shall allow the persons mentioned in subsection (3) below the opportunity—

   (a) of making representations (whether orally or in writing); and

   (b) of leading, or producing, evidence.

(3) Those persons are—

   (a) the patient;

   (b) the patient's named person;

   (c) any guardian of the patient;

   (d) any welfare attorney of the patient;

   (e) the mental health officer;

   (f) the patient's responsible medical officer;

   (g) the patient's primary carer;

   (h) any curator *ad litem* appointed in respect of the patient by the Tribunal; and

   (i) any other person appearing to the Tribunal to have an interest in the determination.

167   Powers of Tribunal on application under section 149, 158, 161, 163 or 164

(1) Where an application is made under section 149 of this Act, the Tribunal may make an order—

   (a) extending the compulsion order to which the application relates for the period mentioned in section 146(2) of this Act;

   (b) refusing the application; or

   (c) refusing the application and revoking the compulsion order.

126   *Mental Health (Care and Treatment) (Scotland) Act 2003 (asp 13)*
Part 9—Compulsion orders
Chapter 2—Review of compulsion orders

(2)   Where an application is made under section 158 of this Act, the Tribunal may make an order—

    (a)   extending the compulsion order to which the application relates for the period mentioned in section 154(4) of this Act and varying the compulsion order by modifying the measures specified in it;

    (b)   extending the compulsion order for that period;

    (c)   refusing the application; or

    (d)   refusing the application and revoking the compulsion order.

(3)   Where an application is made under section 163 of this Act, the Tribunal may make an order—

    (a)   revoking the determination to which the application relates;

    (b)   revoking—

        (i)   the determination; and

        (ii)   the compulsion order to which the determination relates;

    (c)   confirming the determination; or

    (d)   confirming the determination and varying the compulsion order by modifying the measures specified in it.

(4)   Where an application is made under section 164(2)(a) of this Act, the Tribunal may make an order—

    (a)   revoking the compulsion order to which the application relates;

    (b)   varying the compulsion order by modifying the measures specified in it; or

    (c)   refusing the application.

(5)   Where an application is made under section 161 or 164(2)(b) of this Act, the Tribunal may make an order—

    (a)   varying the compulsion order to which the application relates by modifying the measures specified in it;

    (b)   refusing the application; or

    (c)   refusing the application and revoking that order.

(6)   Before making a decision under any of subsections (1) to (5) above, the Tribunal shall afford the persons mentioned in subsection (7) below the opportunity—

    (a)   of making representations (whether orally or in writing); and

    (b)   of leading, or producing, evidence.

(7)   Those persons are—

    (a)   the persons mentioned in section 166(3) of this Act; and

    (b)   any other person appearing to the Tribunal to have an interest in the application.

168   Interim extension etc. of order: application under section 149

(1)   This section applies where an application is made under section 149 of this Act.

Mental Health (Care and Treatment) (Scotland) Act 2003 (asp 13)
Part 9—Compulsion orders
Chapter 2—Review of compulsion orders

127

(2)   Subject to section 170 of this Act, on the application of any person having an interest in the proceedings, or *ex proprio motu*, the Tribunal may, if it considers—

    (a)   that it will be unable to determine the application before the compulsion order to which the application relates ceases to authorise the measures specified in it; and

    (b)   that it is appropriate, pending its determining the application, to—

        (i)   extend the order; or

        (ii)   extend and vary the order by modifying the measures specified in it,

make an interim order extending, or extending and varying, the compulsion order for such period not exceeding 28 days as may be specified in the order of the Tribunal.

169   Interim variation of order following application, reference or review under Chapter

(1)   This section applies where—

    (a)   an application is made under section 149, 158, 161, 163 or 164 of this Act;

    (b)   a reference is made under section 162 of this Act; or

    (c)   the Tribunal is reviewing a determination under section 165 of this Act.

(2)   Subject to section 170 of this Act, on the application of any person having an interest in the proceedings, or *ex proprio motu*, the Tribunal may, if it considers that it is appropriate to do so pending its—

    (a)   determining the application or reference; or

    (b)   making its decision on the review,

make an interim order varying the compulsion order by modifying the measures specified in it for such period not exceeding 28 days as may be specified in the order of the Tribunal.

170   Limit on power of Tribunal to make interim order

The Tribunal may not make an interim order under section 168 or 169 of this Act if the effect of making the order would be that interim orders under either, or both, of those sections would be in force for a continuous period of more than 56 days.

171   Powers of Tribunal on reference under section 162

(1)   Where a reference is made under section 162 of this Act, the Tribunal may make an order—

    (a)   varying the compulsion order in respect of which the reference is made by modifying the measures specified in it; or

    (b)   revoking the compulsion order.

(2)   Before making an order under subsection (1) above, the Tribunal shall allow the persons mentioned in subsection (3) below the opportunity—

    (a)   of making representations (whether orally or in writing); and

    (b)   of leading, or producing, evidence.

128   *Mental Health (Care and Treatment) (Scotland) Act 2003 (asp 13)*
Part 9—Compulsion orders
Chapter 2—Review of compulsion orders

(3)   Those persons are—

    (a)   the persons mentioned in section 166(3) of this Act; and

    (b)   any other person appearing to the Tribunal to have an interest in the reference.

172   Tribunal's order varying compulsion order

Subject to subsection (2) below, where the Tribunal makes an order under section 166, 167 or 171 of this Act varying a compulsion order, the Tribunal—

    (a)   shall specify in its order the modifications made by its order to the measures specified in the compulsion order; and

    (b)   may specify in its order measures other than those set out in the application to which its order relates.

173   Applications to Tribunal: ancillary powers

(1)   This section applies where—

    (a)   an application is made to the Tribunal under section 149, 158, 161, 163 or 164 of this Act; or

    (b)   the Tribunal is, under section 165 of this Act, reviewing a determination.

(2)   Regulations may prescribe circumstances in which the Tribunal may require—

    (a)   the patient's responsible medical officer; or

    (b)   the mental health officer,

to prepare and submit to the Tribunal reports on such matters as may be prescribed.

Effect of interim orders: calculation of time periods in Chapter

174   Effect of interim orders: calculation of time periods in Chapter

(1)   Subject to subsection (2) below, in calculating, for the purpose of this Chapter of this Act, the day on which a relevant compulsion order—

    (a)   ceases;

    (b)   will cease; or

    (c)   would have ceased,

to authorise the measures specified in it, there shall be left out of account any period for which the order is extended (or extended and varied) by an interim order under section 168 of this Act.

(2)   Subsection (1) above does not apply as respects calculating that day for the purpose of that section.

Meaning of "modify"

175   Meaning of "modify"

In this Chapter any reference to modifying measures specified in a relevant compulsion order includes a reference to—

Mental Health (Care and Treatment) (Scotland) Act 2003 (asp 13)   129
Part 9—Compulsion orders
Chapter 3—Application of Chapters 5 to 7 of Part 7

    (a) amending those measures;

    (b) removing from the order any measure;

    (c) adding to the order any measure.

CHAPTER 3

APPLICATION OF CHAPTERS 5 TO 7 OF PART 7

Breach of order

176   Medical treatment: failure to attend

(1) Section 112 of this Act shall apply in relation to a patient subject to a relevant compulsion order as that section applies in relation to a patient subject to a compulsory treatment order; but subject to the modifications in subsection (2) below.

(2) Those modifications are—

    (a) in subsection (1)(a) of that section, the reference to section 66(1)(c) of this Act shall be read as a reference to section 57A(8)(c) of the 1995 Act; and

    (b) in subsection (4)(a) of that section, the reference to section 66(1)(b) of this Act shall be read as a reference to section 57A(8)(b) of the 1995 Act.

177   Non-compliance generally with compulsion order

(1) Section 113 of this Act shall apply in relation to a patient subject to a relevant compulsion order as that section applies in relation to a patient subject to a compulsory treatment order.

(2) Section 114 of this Act shall apply in relation to a patient subject to a relevant compulsion order as that section applies in relation to a patient subject to a compulsory treatment order; but subject to the modifications that references in that section to section 93(2) and (5) of this Act shall be read as references to section 159(2) and (5) of this Act respectively.

(3) Sections 116, 117, 119, 120, 121 and 122 shall apply in relation to a certificate granted by virtue of subsection (2) above as those sections apply in relation to a certificate granted under section 114(2) of this Act; but subject to the modifications that—

    (a) any references in those sections to section 93(2) of this Act shall be read as references to section 159(2) of this Act; and

    (b) any references to section 66(1)(b) of this Act shall be read as references to section 57A(8)(b) of the 1995 Act.

Transfers

178   Transfers

Sections 124 to 126 of this Act shall apply in relation to a patient whose detention in hospital is authorised by a relevant compulsion order as those sections apply in relation to a patient whose detention in hospital is authorised by a compulsory treatment order.

130   *Mental Health (Care and Treatment) (Scotland) Act 2003 (asp 13)*
Part 10—Compulsion orders and restriction orders
Chapter 1—Preliminary

Suspension of measures

179   Suspension of measures

(1)   Section 127 of this Act shall apply in relation to a patient subject to a relevant compulsion order as that section applies in relation to a patient subject to a compulsory treatment order; but subject to the modification that references in that section to section 66(1)(a) of this Act shall be read as references to section 57A(8)(a) of the 1995 Act.

(2)   Section 128 of this Act shall apply in relation to a patient subject to a relevant compulsion order as that section applies in relation to a patient subject to a compulsory treatment order; but subject to the modification that references in that section to section 66(1)(b) to (h) of this Act shall be read as references to section 57A(8)(b) to (h) of the 1995 Act.

(3)   Section 129 of this Act shall apply in relation to a patient subject to a relevant compulsion order as that section applies in relation to a patient subject to a compulsory treatment order.

CHAPTER 4

INTERPRETATION OF PART

180   Interpretation of Part

In this Part of this Act "relevant compulsion order" has the meaning given by section 137(1) of this Act.

PART 10

COMPULSION ORDERS AND RESTRICTION ORDERS

CHAPTER 1

PRELIMINARY

181   Mental health officer's duty to identify named person

(1)   This section applies where a compulsion order and a restriction order are made in respect of a patient.

(2)   The mental health officer shall, as soon as practicable after the compulsion order is made, take such steps as are reasonably practicable to ascertain the name and address of the patient's named person.

CHAPTER 2

REVIEW OF ORDERS

Annual review of orders

182   Review of compulsion order and restriction order

(1)   This section applies where a patient is subject to a compulsion order and a restriction order.

Mental Health (Care and Treatment) (Scotland) Act 2003 (asp 13)   131
Part 10—Compulsion orders and restriction orders
Chapter 2—Review of orders

(2)   The patient's responsible medical officer shall, during the period of 2 months ending with the relevant day, carry out a review in respect of both the compulsion order and restriction order by complying with the requirements set out in subsection (3) below.

(3)   Those requirements are—

     (a)   to—

         (i)   carry out a medical examination of the patient; or

         (ii)   make arrangements for an approved medical practitioner to carry out such a medical examination;

     (b)   to consider—

         (i)   whether the conditions mentioned in subsection (4) below continue to apply in respect of the patient;

         (ii)   whether, as a result of the patient's mental disorder, it is necessary, in order to protect any other person from serious harm, for the patient to be detained in hospital, whether or not for medical treatment;

         (iii)   whether it continues to be necessary for the patient to be subject to the compulsion order; and

         (iv)   whether it continues to be necessary for the patient to be subject to the restriction order; and

     (c)   to consult the mental health officer.

(4)   Those conditions are—

     (a)   that the patient has a mental disorder;

     (b)   that medical treatment which would be likely to—

         (i)   prevent the mental disorder worsening; or

         (ii)   alleviate any of the symptoms, or effects, of the disorder,

       is available for the patient; and

     (c)   that if the patient were not provided with such medical treatment there would be a significant risk—

         (i)   to the health, safety or welfare of the patient; or

         (ii)   to the safety of any other person.

(5)   In subsection (2) above, the "relevant day" means—

     (a)   the day which falls 12 months after the day on which the compulsion order is made; or

     (b)   where that relevant day has passed, the day falling on the same day in every year thereafter.

Consequences of annual review

183   **Responsible medical officer's report and recommendation following review of compulsion order and restriction order**

(1)   This section applies where a patient's responsible medical officer carries out a review under section 182(2) of this Act.

132　　　　　　　　*Mental Health (Care and Treatment) (Scotland) Act 2003 (asp 13)*
Part 10—Compulsion orders and restriction orders
Chapter 2—Review of orders

(2)　　The responsible medical officer shall, as soon as practicable after carrying out that review, submit a report in accordance with subsection (3) below to the Scottish Ministers.

(3)　　That report shall record the responsible medical officer's views as to—

　　(a)　whether the conditions mentioned in section 182(4) of this Act continue to apply in respect of the patient;

　　(b)　whether, as a result of the patient's mental disorder, it is necessary, in order to protect any other person from serious harm, for the patient to be detained in hospital, whether or not for medical treatment;

　　(c)　whether it continues to be necessary for the patient to be subject to the compulsion order; and

　　(d)　whether it continues to be necessary for the patient to be subject to the restriction order.

(4)　　If, after having regard to any views expressed by the mental health officer, the responsible medical officer is not satisfied that the patient has a mental disorder, the responsible medical officer shall include in the report submitted to the Scottish Ministers under subsection (2) above a recommendation that the compulsion order be revoked.

(5)　　If, after having regard to any views expressed by the mental health officer, the responsible medical officer—

　　(a)　is satisfied that the patient has a mental disorder; but

　　(b)　is not satisfied—

　　　　(i)　that, as a result of the patient's mental disorder, it is necessary, in order to protect any other person from serious harm, for the patient to be detained in hospital, whether or not for medical treatment; and

　　　　(ii)　that the conditions mentioned in paragraphs (b) and (c) of section 182(4) of this Act continue to apply in respect of the patient,

the responsible medical officer shall include in the report submitted under subsection (2) above a recommendation that the compulsion order be revoked.

(6)　　If, after having regard to any views expressed by the mental health officer, the responsible medical officer—

　　(a)　is satisfied—

　　　　(i)　that the conditions mentioned in section 182(4) of this Act continue to apply in respect of the patient; and

　　　　(ii)　that it continues to be necessary for the patient to be subject to the compulsion order; but

　　(b)　is not satisfied—

　　　　(i)　that, as a result of the patient's mental disorder, it is necessary, in order to protect any other person from serious harm, for the patient to be detained in hospital, whether or not for medical treatment; and

　　　　(ii)　that it continues to be necessary for the patient to be subject to the restriction order,

Mental Health (Care and Treatment) (Scotland) Act 2003 (asp 13)
Part 10—Compulsion orders and restriction orders
Chapter 2—Review of orders

133

the responsible medical officer shall include in the report submitted to the Scottish Ministers under subsection (2) above a recommendation that the restriction order be revoked.

(7) If, after having regard to any views expressed by the mental health officer, the responsible medical officer—

    (a) is satisfied—

        (i) that the conditions mentioned in section 182(4) of this Act continue to apply in respect of the patient; and

        (ii) that it continues to be necessary for the patient to be subject to the compulsion order and the restriction order; but

    (b) is not satisfied that, as a result of the patient's mental disorder, it is necessary, in order to protect any other person from serious harm, for the patient to be detained in hospital, whether or not for medical treatment,

the responsible medical officer may include in the report submitted to the Scottish Ministers under subsection (2) above a recommendation that the patient be conditionally discharged.

(8) Where the responsible medical officer—

    (a) submits a report under subsection (2) above that includes a recommendation under subsection (6) above; and

    (b) is satisfied that the compulsion order should be varied by modifying the measures specified in it,

the responsible medical officer shall include in the report a recommendation that the compulsion order be varied in that way.

Responsible medical officer's duty to keep orders under review

184 Responsible medical officer's duty to keep compulsion order and restriction order under review

(1) This section applies where a patient is subject to a compulsion order and a restriction order.

(2) Without prejudice to the duty imposed on the patient's responsible medical officer by section 182(2) of this Act, the responsible medical officer shall from time to time consider—

    (a) whether the conditions mentioned in section 182(4) of this Act continue to apply in respect of the patient;

    (b) whether, as a result of the patient's mental disorder, it is necessary, in order to protect any other person from serious harm, for the patient to be detained in hospital, whether or not for medical treatment;

    (c) whether it continues to be necessary for the patient to be subject to the compulsion order; and

    (d) whether it continues to be necessary for the patient to be subject to the restriction order.

134   *Mental Health (Care and Treatment) (Scotland) Act 2003 (asp 13)*
Part 10—Compulsion orders and restriction orders
Chapter 2—Review of orders

(3)   If, having considered the matters mentioned in paragraphs (a) to (d) of subsection (2) above, the responsible medical officer is not satisfied that the patient has a mental disorder, the responsible medical officer shall, as soon as practicable after considering those matters, submit to the Scottish Ministers a report complying with the requirements set out in section 183(3) of this Act and including a recommendation that the compulsion order be revoked.

(4)   If, having considered the matters mentioned in paragraphs (a) to (d) of subsection (2) above, the responsible medical officer—

    (a) is satisfied that the patient has a mental disorder; but

    (b) is not satisfied—

        (i)   that, as a result of the patient's mental disorder, it is necessary, in order to protect any other person from serious harm, for the patient to be detained in hospital, whether or not for medical treatment; and

        (ii)   that the conditions mentioned in paragraphs (b) and (c) of section 182(4) of this Act continue to apply in respect of the patient,

the responsible medical officer shall, as soon as practicable after considering those matters, submit to the Scottish Ministers a report complying with the requirements set out in section 183(3) of this Act and including a recommendation that the compulsion order be revoked.

(5)   If, having considered the matters mentioned in paragraphs (a) to (d) of subsection (2) above, the responsible medical officer—

    (a) is satisfied—

        (i)   that the conditions mentioned in section 182(4) of this Act continue to apply in respect of the patient; and

        (ii)   that it continues to be necessary for the patient to be subject to the compulsion order; but

    (b) is not satisfied that—

        (i)   that, as a result of the patient's mental disorder, it is necessary, in order to protect any other person from serious harm, for the patient to be detained in hospital, whether or not for medical treatment; and

        (ii)   that it continues to be necessary for the patient to be subject to the restriction order,

the responsible medical officer shall, as soon as practicable after considering those matters, submit to the Scottish Ministers a report complying with the requirements set out in section 183(3) of this Act and including a recommendation that the restriction order be revoked.

(6)   If, having considered the matters mentioned in paragraphs (a) to (d) of subsection (2) above, the responsible medical officer—

    (a) is satisfied—

        (i)   that the conditions mentioned in section 182(4) of this Act continue to apply in respect of the patient; and

        (ii)   that it continues to be necessary for the patient to be subject to the compulsion order and the restriction order; but

Mental Health (Care and Treatment) (Scotland) Act 2003 (asp 13)   135
Part 10—Compulsion orders and restriction orders
Chapter 2—Review of orders

(b) is not satisfied that, as a result of the patient's mental disorder, it is necessary, in order to protect any other person from serious harm, for the patient to be detained in hospital, whether or not for medical treatment,

the responsible medical officer may submit to the Scottish Ministers a report complying with the requirements set out in section 183(3) of this Act and including a recommendation that the patient be conditionally discharged.

(7) Where the responsible medical officer—

(a) submits a report under subsection (5) above; and

(b) is satisfied that the compulsion order should be varied by modifying the measures specified in it,

the responsible medical officer shall include in the report a recommendation that the compulsion order be varied in that way.

Reference to Tribunal by Scottish Ministers

185   Duty of Scottish Ministers on receiving report from responsible medical officer

(1) Where a patient's responsible medical officer submits to the Scottish Ministers—

(a) a report under section 183(2) of this Act that includes a recommendation; or

(b) a report under section 184 of this Act,

the Scottish Ministers shall make a reference to the Tribunal in respect of the compulsion order and restriction order to which the patient is subject.

(2) Where a reference is made under subsection (1) above, the Scottish Ministers shall, as soon as practicable, give notice that a reference is to be made to—

(a) the patient;

(b) the patient's named person;

(c) any guardian of the patient;

(d) any welfare attorney of the patient;

(e) the patient's responsible medical officer;

(f) the mental health officer; and

(g) the Commission.

(3) A reference under subsection (1) above shall state—

(a) the name and address of the patient;

(b) the name and address of the patient's named person; and

(c) the recommendation included in the report submitted by the responsible medical officer.

186   Commission's power to require Scottish Ministers to make reference to Tribunal

(1) This section applies where a patient is subject to a compulsion order and a restriction order.

136   *Mental Health (Care and Treatment) (Scotland) Act 2003 (asp 13)*
Part 10—Compulsion orders and restriction orders
Chapter 2—Review of orders

(2)   If it appears to the Commission that it is appropriate to do so, it may, by notice in writing to the Scottish Ministers, require them to make a reference to the Tribunal in respect of the compulsion order and the restriction order to which the patient is subject.

(3)   Where, under subsection (2), the Commission gives notice to the Scottish Ministers, the Commission shall include in that notice its reasons for requiring the Scottish Ministers to make the reference.

187   **Notice under section 186(2): reference to Tribunal**

(1)   This section applies where, under section 186(2) of this Act, the Commission gives notice to the Scottish Ministers.

(2)   The Scottish Ministers shall, as soon as practicable after receiving notice under section 186(2) of this Act, make a reference to the Tribunal in respect of the compulsion order and restriction order to which the patient is subject.

(3)   Where a reference is made under subsection (2) above, the Scottish Ministers shall, as soon as practicable, give notice that the reference is to be or, as the case may be, has been made to the persons mentioned in paragraphs (a) to (g) of section 185(2) of this Act.

(4)   A reference under subsection (2) above shall state—

     (a)   the name and address of the patient;

     (b)   the name and address of the patient's named person; and

     (c)   the reason given by the Commission in the notice under section 186(2) of this Act for requiring the Scottish Ministers to make the reference.

Scottish Ministers' duty to keep orders under review

188   **Duty of Scottish Ministers to keep compulsion order and restriction order under review**

(1)   This section applies where a patient is subject to a compulsion order and a restriction order.

(2)   Without prejudice to the duties imposed on the Scottish Ministers by sections 185(1), 187(2) and 189(2) of this Act, the Scottish Ministers shall from time to time consider—

     (a)   whether the conditions mentioned in section 182(4) of this Act continue to apply in respect of the patient;

     (b)   whether, as a result of the patient's mental disorder, it is necessary, in order to protect any other person from serious harm, for the patient to be detained in hospital, whether or not for medical treatment;

     (c)   whether it continues to be necessary for the patient to be subject to the compulsion order; and

     (d)   whether it continues to be necessary for the patient to be subject to the restriction order.

(3)   If, having considered the matters mentioned in paragraphs (a) to (d) of subsection (2) above, the Scottish Ministers are not satisfied that the patient has a mental disorder, they shall apply to the Tribunal under section 191 of this Act for an order under section 193 of this Act revoking the compulsion order.

Mental Health (Care and Treatment) (Scotland) Act 2003 (asp 13)
Part 10—Compulsion orders and restriction orders
Chapter 2—Review of orders

137

(4) If, having considered the matters mentioned in paragraphs (a) to (d) of subsection (2) above, the Scottish Ministers—

    (a). are satisfied that the patient has a mental disorder; but

    (b) are not satisfied—

        (i) that, as a result of the patient's mental disorder, it is necessary, in order to protect any other person from serious harm, for the patient to be detained in hospital, whether or not for medical treatment; and

        (ii) that the conditions mentioned in paragraphs (b) and (c) of section 182(4) of this Act continue to apply in respect of the patient,

they shall, as soon as practicable after considering those matters, apply to the Tribunal under section 191 of this Act for an order under section 193 of this Act revoking the compulsion order.

(5) If, having considered the matters mentioned in paragraphs (a) to (d) of subsection (2) above, the Scottish Ministers—

    (a) are satisfied—

        (i) that the conditions mentioned in section 182(4) of this Act continue to apply in respect of the patient; and

        (ii) that it continues to be necessary for the patient to be subject to the compulsion order; but

    (b) are not satisfied—

        (i) that, as a result of the patient's mental disorder, it is necessary, in order to protect any other person from serious harm, for the patient to be detained in hospital, whether or not for medical treatment; and

        (ii) that it continues to be necessary for the patient to be subject to the restriction order,

they shall apply to the Tribunal under section 191 of this Act for an order under section 193 of this Act revoking the restriction order.

(6) Where the Scottish Ministers—

    (a) apply, by virtue of subsection (5) above, for an order revoking the restriction order; and

    (b) are satisfied that the compulsion order should be varied by modifying the measures specified in it,

they shall apply to the Tribunal under section 191 of this Act for an order under section 193 of this Act varying the compulsion order in that way.

(7) If, having considered the matters mentioned in paragraphs (a) to (d) of subsection (2) above, the Scottish Ministers—

    (a) are satisfied—

        (i) that the conditions mentioned in section 182(4) of this Act continue to apply in respect of the patient; and

        (ii) that it continues to be necessary for the patient to be subject to the compulsion order and the restriction order; but

138   *Mental Health (Care and Treatment) (Scotland) Act 2003 (asp 13)*
Part 10—Compulsion orders and restriction orders
Chapter 2—Review of orders

(b)   are not satisfied that, as a result of the patient's mental disorder, it is necessary, in order to protect any other person from serious harm, for the patient to be detained in hospital, whether or not for medical treatment,

they may apply to the Tribunal under section 191 of this Act for an order under section 193 of this Act conditionally discharging the patient.

189   Reference to Tribunal by Scottish Ministers

(1)   This section applies where a patient is subject to a compulsion order and a restriction order.

(2)   If—

     (a)   during the period of 2 years ending with the relevant day—

         (i)   no reference under section 185(1) or 187(2) of this Act has been made to the Tribunal; and

         (ii)   no application under section 191 or 192(2) of this Act has been made to the Tribunal; and

     (b)   during each period of 2 years ending with the anniversary, in every year thereafter, of the relevant day—

         (i)   no reference such as is mentioned in paragraph (a)(i) above or, subject to subsection (3) below, under this subsection has been made to the Tribunal; and

         (ii)   no application such as is mentioned in paragraph (a)(ii) above has been made to the Tribunal,

the Scottish Ministers shall make a reference to the Tribunal in respect of the compulsion order and restriction order to which the patient is subject.

(3)   The Scottish Ministers shall, in considering, under subsection (2)(b)(i) above, whether a reference has been made to the Tribunal during any 2 year period, leave out of account any reference made under subsection (2) above during the first year of that 2 year period.

(4)   Where a reference is made under subsection (2) above, the Scottish Ministers shall, as soon as practicable, give notice that a reference is to be or, as the case may be, has been made to the persons mentioned in paragraphs (a) to (g) of section 185(2) of this Act.

(5)   A reference under subsection (2) above shall state—

     (a)   the name and address of the patient;

     (b)   the name and address of the patient's named person; and

     (c)   the reason for making the reference.

(6)   In subsection (2) above, the "relevant day" means the day which falls 2 years after the day on which the compulsion order is made.

Mental Health (Care and Treatment) (Scotland) Act 2003 (asp 13) 139
Part 10—Compulsion orders and restriction orders
Chapter 2—Review of orders

190   Application by Scottish Ministers: notification

Where, by virtue of section 188 of this Act, an application is to be made under section 191 of this Act, the Scottish Ministers shall, as soon as practicable after the duty to make the application arises, give notice to the persons mentioned in paragraphs (a) to (g) of section 185(2) of this Act that the application is to be or, as the case may be, has been made.

191   Application to Tribunal

An application under this section to the Tribunal by the Scottish Ministers for an order under section 193 of this Act—

(a)   shall state—

    (i)   the name and address of the patient;

    (ii)   the name and address of the patient's named person;

    (iii)   the order (or orders) sought;

    (iv)   the modification of the measures specified in the compulsion order that is proposed by the Scottish Ministers; and

    (v)   the reasons for seeking that modification; and

(b)   shall be accompanied by such documents as may be prescribed by regulations.

Application by patient etc.

192   Application to Tribunal by patient and named person

(1)   This section applies where a patient is subject to a compulsion order and a restriction order.

(2)   Each of the persons mentioned in subsection (3) below may, subject to subsections (4) and (5) below, make an application under this section to the Tribunal for an order under section 193 of this Act—

(a)   conditionally discharging the patient;

(b)   revoking the restriction order to which the patient is subject;

(c)   revoking the restriction order and varying the compulsion order by modifying the measures specified in it; or

(d)   revoking the compulsion order to which the patient is subject.

(3)   Those persons are—

(a)   the patient; and

(b)   the patient's named person.

(4)   An application under this section may not be made—

(a)   during the period of 6 months beginning with the making of the compulsion order;

(b)   during the period of 3 months beginning with—

    (i)   the making of an order in respect of the compulsion order made under section 193 of this Act; or

140   *Mental Health (Care and Treatment) (Scotland) Act 2003 (asp 13)*
Part 10—Compulsion orders and restriction orders
Chapter 2—Review of orders

     (ii)   the making, under section 193 of this Act, by the Tribunal of a decision to make no order under that section.

(5)   Neither of the persons mentioned in subsection (3) above may make more than one application under this section during—

    (a)   the period of 12 months beginning with the day on which the compulsion order was made; or

    (b)   any subsequent period of 12 months that begins with or with an anniversary of the expiry of the period of 12 months mentioned in paragraph (a) above.

(6)   Where a patient's named person makes an application under subsection (2) above, the named person shall give notice to the patient of the making of the application.

Proceedings before Tribunal

193   Powers of Tribunal on reference under section 185(1), 187(2) or 189(2) or application under section 191 or 192(2)

(1)   This section applies where—

    (a)   an application is made under section 191 or 192(2) of this Act; or

    (b)   a reference is made under section 185(1), 187(2) or 189(2) of this Act.

(2)   If the Tribunal is satisfied—

    (a)   that the patient has a mental disorder; and

    (b)   that, as a result of the patient's mental disorder, it is necessary, in order to protect any other person from serious harm, for the patient to be detained in hospital, whether or not for medical treatment,

it shall make no order under this section.

(3)   If the Tribunal is not satisfied that the patient has a mental disorder, the Tribunal shall make an order revoking the compulsion order.

(4)   If the Tribunal—

    (a)   is satisfied that the patient has a mental disorder; but

    (b)   is not satisfied—

     (i)   that, as a result of the patient's mental disorder, it is necessary, in order to protect any other person from serious harm, for the patient to be detained in hospital, whether or not for medical treatment; and

     (ii)   that the conditions mentioned in paragraphs (b) and (c) of section 182(4) of this Act continue to apply in respect of the patient,

it shall make an order revoking the compulsion order.

(5)   If the Tribunal—

    (a)   is satisfied—

     (i)   that the conditions mentioned in section 182(4) of this Act continue to apply in respect of the patient; and

     (ii)   that it continues to be necessary for the patient to be subject to the compulsion order; but

Mental Health (Care and Treatment) (Scotland) Act 2003 (asp 13)   141
Part 10—Compulsion orders and restriction orders
Chapter 2—Review of orders

   (b) is not satisfied—

      (i) that, as a result of the patient's mental disorder, it is necessary, in order to protect any other person from serious harm, for the patient to be detained in hospital, whether or not for medical treatment; and

      (ii) that it continues to be necessary for the patient to be subject to the restriction order,

it shall make an order revoking the restriction order.

(6) If the Tribunal—

   (a) makes an order, under subsection (5) above, revoking the restriction order; and

   (b) is satisfied that the compulsion order should be varied by modifying the measures specified in it,

it shall make an order varying the compulsion order in that way.

(7) If the Tribunal—

   (a) is satisfied—

      (i) that the conditions mentioned in section 182(4) of this Act continue to apply in respect of the patient; and

      (ii) that it continues to be necessary for the patient to be subject to the compulsion order and the restriction order; but

   (b) is not satisfied—

      (i) that, as a result of the patient's mental disorder, it is necessary, in order to protect any other person from serious harm, for the patient to be detained in hospital, whether or not for medical treatment; and

      (ii) that it is necessary for the patient to be detained in hospital,

the Tribunal may make an order that the patient be conditionally discharged and impose such conditions on that discharge as it thinks fit.

(8) Before making a decision under this section the Tribunal shall—

   (a) afford the persons mentioned in subsection (9) below the opportunity—

      (i) of making representations (whether orally or in writing); and

      (ii) of leading, or producing, evidence; and

   (b) whether or not any such representations are made, hold a hearing.

(9) Those persons are—

   (a) the patient;

   (b) the patient's named person;

   (c) the patient's primary carer;

   (d) any guardian of the patient;

   (e) any welfare attorney of the patient;

   (f) any curator *ad litem* appointed by the Tribunal in respect of the patient;

   (g) the Scottish Ministers;

142   *Mental Health (Care and Treatment) (Scotland) Act 2003 (asp 13)*
                           Part 10—Compulsion orders and restriction orders
                                                       Chapter 2—Review of orders

(h)   the patient's responsible medical officer;

(i)   the mental health officer; and

(j)   any other person appearing to the Tribunal to have an interest.

(10)   Nothing in section 102 (state hospitals) of the National Health Service (Scotland) Act 1978 (c.29) prevents or restricts the detention of a patient in a state hospital as a result of a decision of the Tribunal not to make any order under this section.

194   Tribunal's powers etc. when varying compulsion order

Where the Tribunal makes an order under section 193(6) of this Act varying a compulsion order, the Tribunal shall specify in its order the modifications made by its order to the measures specified in the compulsion order.

195   Deferral of conditional discharge

Where the Tribunal makes an order under section 193(7) of this Act conditionally discharging a patient, it may defer that discharge until such arrangements as appear to the Tribunal to be necessary for that purpose have been made.

Effect of modification or revocation of orders

196   General effect of orders under section 193

(1)   Where the Tribunal makes an order under section 193 of this Act—

(a)   revoking a compulsion order;

(b)   revoking a restriction order;

(c)   conditionally discharging a patient; or

(d)   varying a compulsion order by modifying the measures specified in it,

the order shall not have effect until the occurrence of the first to occur of the events mentioned in subsection (2) below.

(2)   Those events are—

(a)   the expiry of the appeal period, no appeal having been lodged within that period; and

(b)   where an appeal has been lodged within the appeal period—

(i)   the receipt by both the Court of Session and the managers of the hospital specified in the compulsion order of notice from the Scottish Ministers that they do not intend to move the Court of Session to make an order under section 323 of this Act;

(ii)   the refusal by the Court of Session to make such an order; and

(iii) the recall of any such order or the expiry of its effect.

(3)   In subsection (2) above—

"appeal" means an appeal under section 322 of this Act; and

Mental Health (Care and Treatment) (Scotland) Act 2003 (asp 13)
Part 10—Compulsion orders and restriction orders
Chapter 3—Conditional discharge

143

"appeal period" means, in relation to an appeal, the period, prescribed by regulations made under section 324(7) of this Act, within which the appeal has to be lodged in order to be competent.

197 Effect of revocation of compulsion order

Where the Tribunal makes an order under section 193(3) or (4) of this Act revoking a compulsion order, the restriction order to which the patient is subject shall cease to have effect.

198 Effect of revocation of restriction order

(1) This section applies where the Tribunal—

    (a) makes an order under subsection (5) of section 193 of this Act revoking the restriction order to which the patient is subject; but

    (b) does not make an order under subsection (3) or (4) of that section revoking the compulsion order to which the patient is subject.

(2) Part 9 of this Act shall apply to the patient as if the compulsion order to which the patient is subject were a relevant compulsion order made on the day on which the Tribunal revoked the restriction order.

(3) In this section, "relevant compulsion order" has the meaning given by section 137(1) of this Act.

Meaning of "modify"

199 Meaning of "modify"

In this Chapter, any reference to modifying the measures specified in a compulsion order includes a reference to—

    (a) amending those measures;

    (b) removing from the order any measure; or

    (c) adding to the order any measure.

CHAPTER 3

CONDITIONAL DISCHARGE

200 Variation of conditions imposed on conditional discharge

(1) This section applies where—

    (a) a patient has been conditionally discharged by the Tribunal under section 193(7) of this Act; and

    (b) the Tribunal imposed conditions on that discharge under that section.

(2) The Scottish Ministers may, if satisfied that it is necessary, vary such of the conditions imposed by the Tribunal under section 193(7) of this Act as they think fit.

(3) Where the Scottish Ministers vary, under subsection (2) above, conditions imposed by the Tribunal under section 193(7) of this Act, the Scottish Ministers shall, as soon as practicable, give notice of that variation to—

144   *Mental Health (Care and Treatment) (Scotland) Act 2003 (asp 13)*
Part 10—Compulsion orders and restriction orders
Chapter 3—Conditional discharge

(a) the patient;

(b) the patient's named person;

(c) the patient's responsible medical officer; and

(d) the mental health officer.

201   Appeal to Tribunal against variation of conditions imposed on conditional discharge

(1)   Where the Scottish Ministers vary, under section 200(2) of this Act, conditions imposed by the Tribunal under section 193(7) of this Act on a patient who has been conditionally discharged under that section, the persons mentioned in subsection (2) below may, before the expiry of the period of 28 days beginning with the day on which notice is given under section 200(3) of this Act, appeal against the variation of those conditions to the Tribunal.

(2)   Those persons are—

    (a) the patient; and

    (b) the patient's named person.

(3)   Where an appeal is made to the Tribunal under subsection (1) above, section 193 of this Act shall apply as if the patient had applied under section 192 of this Act for an order conditionally discharging the patient.

202   Recall of patients from conditional discharge

(1)   This section applies to a patient conditionally discharged by the Tribunal under section 193(7) of this Act.

(2)   If the Scottish Ministers are satisfied that it is necessary for the patient to be detained in hospital, they may, by warrant, recall the patient to hospital.

203   Effect of recall from conditional discharge

Where the Scottish Ministers recall a patient to hospital under section 202 of this Act, if the hospital specified in the warrant is not the hospital specified in the compulsion order to which the patient is subject, that order shall have effect as if the hospital specified in the warrant were the hospital specified in the order.

204   Appeal to Tribunal against recall from conditional discharge

(1)   Where a patient has been recalled to hospital under section 202 of this Act, each of the persons mentioned in subsection (2) below may, before the expiry of the period of 28 days beginning with the day on which the patient returns or is returned to hospital, appeal against that recall to the Tribunal.

(2)   Those persons are—

    (a) the patient; and

    (b) the patient's named person.

Mental Health (Care and Treatment) (Scotland) Act 2003 (asp 13)
Part 11—Hospital directions and transfer for treatment directions

145

(3) Where an appeal is made to the Tribunal under subsection (1) above, section 193 of this Act shall apply as if the patient had applied under section 192 of this Act for an order conditionally discharging the patient.

PART 11

HOSPITAL DIRECTIONS AND TRANSFER FOR TREATMENT DIRECTIONS

Preliminary

205   Mental health officer's duty to identify named person

(1) This section applies where—

　(a) a hospital direction; or

　(b) a transfer for treatment direction,

is made in respect of a patient.

(2) The mental health officer shall, as soon as practicable after the direction is made, take such steps as are reasonably practicable to ascertain the name and address of the patient's named person.

Review of directions

206   Review of hospital direction and transfer for treatment direction

(1) This section applies where a patient is subject to—

　(a) a hospital direction; or

　(b) a transfer for treatment direction.

(2) The patient's responsible medical officer shall, during the period of 2 months ending with the relevant day, carry out a review in respect of the direction by complying with the requirements set out in subsection (3) below.

(3) Those requirements are—

　(a) to—

　　(i) carry out a medical examination of the patient; or

　　(ii) make arrangements for an approved medical practitioner to carry out such a medical examination;

　(b) to consider—

　　(i) whether the conditions mentioned in subsection (4) below continue to apply in respect of the patient;

　　(ii) whether, as a result of the patient's mental disorder, it is necessary, in order to protect any other person from serious harm, for the patient to be detained in hospital, whether or not for medical treatment; and

　　(iii) whether it continues to be necessary for the patient to be subject to the direction; and

　(c) to consult—

　　(i) the mental health officer; and

          (ii)   such other persons as the responsible medical officer considers appropriate.

(4)   Those conditions are—

    (a)   that the patient has a mental disorder;

    (b)   that medical treatment which would be likely to—

        (i)   prevent the mental disorder worsening; or

        (ii)   alleviate any of the symptoms, or effects, of the disorder,

    is available for the patient; and

    (c)   that if the patient were not provided with such medical treatment there would be a significant risk—

        (i)   to the health, safety or welfare of the patient; or

        (ii)   to the safety of any other person.

(5)   In subsection (2) above, the "relevant day" means—

    (a)   the day which falls 12 months after the day on which the direction is made; or

    (b)   where that relevant day has passed, the day falling on the same day in every year thereafter.

Consequences of review

207   Responsible medical officer's report following review of direction

(1)   This section applies where a patient's responsible medical officer carries out a review under section 206(2) of this Act.

(2)   The responsible medical officer shall, as soon as practicable after carrying out that review, submit a report in accordance with subsection (3) below to the Scottish Ministers.

(3)   That report shall record the responsible medical officer's views as to—

    (a)   whether the conditions mentioned in section 206(4) of this Act continue to apply in respect of the patient;

    (b)   whether, as a result of the patient's mental disorder, it is necessary, in order to protect any other person from serious harm, for the patient to be detained in hospital, whether or not for medical treatment; and

    (c)   whether it continues to be necessary for the patient to be subject to the direction.

(4)   If, after having regard to any views expressed by persons consulted under section 206(3)(c) of this Act, the responsible medical officer is not satisfied that the patient has a mental disorder, the responsible medical officer shall include in the report submitted to the Scottish Ministers under subsection (2) above a recommendation that the direction be revoked.

(5)   If, after having regard to any views expressed by persons consulted under section 206(3)(c) of this Act, the responsible medical officer—

    (a)   is satisfied that the patient has a mental disorder; but

    (b)   is not satisfied—

Mental Health (Care and Treatment) (Scotland) Act 2003 (asp 13)
Part 11—Hospital directions and transfer for treatment directions

147

(i)   that, as a result of the patient's mental disorder, it is necessary, in order to protect any other person from serious harm, for the patient to be detained in hospital, whether or not for medical treatment; and

(ii) that the conditions mentioned in paragraphs (b) and (c) of section 206(4) of this Act continue to apply in respect of the patient,

the responsible medical officer shall include in the report submitted to the Scottish Ministers under subsection (2) above a recommendation that the direction be revoked.

Responsible medical officer's duty to keep directions under review

208   Responsible medical officer's duty to keep directions under review

(1) This section applies where a patient is subject to—

(a) a hospital direction; or

(b) a transfer for treatment direction.

(2) Without prejudice to the duty imposed on the patient's responsible medical officer by section 206(2) of this Act, the responsible medical officer shall from time to time consider—

(a) whether the conditions mentioned in section 206(4) of this Act continue to apply in respect of the patient;

(b) whether, as a result of the patient's mental disorder, it is necessary, in order to protect any other person from serious harm, for the patient to be detained in hospital, whether or not for medical treatment; and

(c) whether it continues to be necessary for the patient to be subject to the direction.

(3) If, having considered the matters mentioned in paragraphs (a) to (c) of subsection (2) above, the responsible medical officer is not satisfied that the patient has a mental disorder, the responsible medical officer shall, as soon as practicable after considering those matters, submit to the Scottish Ministers a report complying with the requirements set out in section 207(3) of this Act and including a recommendation that the direction be revoked.

(4) If, having considered the matters mentioned in paragraphs (a) to (c) of subsection (2) above, the responsible medical officer—

(a) is satisfied that the patient has a mental disorder; but

(b) is not satisfied—

(i)   that, as a result of the patient's mental disorder, it is necessary, in order to protect any other person from serious harm, for the patient to be detained in hospital, whether or not for medical treatment; and

(ii) that the conditions mentioned in paragraphs (b) and (c) of section 206(4) of this Act continue to apply in respect of the patient,

the responsible medical officer shall, as soon as practicable after considering those matters, submit to the Scottish Ministers a report complying with the requirements set out in section 207(3) of this Act and including a recommendation that the direction be revoked.

Reference to Tribunal by Scottish Ministers

209 **Commission's power to require Scottish Ministers to make reference to Tribunal**

(1) This section applies where a patient is subject to—

    (a) a hospital direction; or

    (b) a transfer for treatment direction.

(2) If it appears to the Commission that it is appropriate to do so, it may, by notice in writing to the Scottish Ministers, require them to make a reference to the Tribunal in respect of the direction to which the patient is subject.

(3) Where, under subsection (2), the Commission gives notice to the Scottish Ministers, the Commission shall include in that notice its reasons for requiring the Scottish Ministers to make the reference.

210 **Duty of Scottish Ministers on receiving report from responsible medical officer**

(1) This section applies where a patient's responsible medical officer submits to the Scottish Ministers—

    (a) a report under section 207(2) of this Act that includes a recommendation; or

    (b) a report under section 208(3) or (4) of this Act.

(2) If, having considered the matters mentioned in paragraphs (a) to (c) of section 212(2) of this Act, the Scottish Ministers—

    (a) are not satisfied that the patient has a mental disorder; or

    (b) are so satisfied but are not satisfied—

        (i) that, as a result of the patient's mental disorder, it is necessary, in order to protect any other person from serious harm, for the patient to be detained in hospital, whether or not for medical treatment; and

        (ii) that the conditions mentioned in paragraphs (b) and (c) of section 206(4) of this Act continue to apply in respect of the patient,

the Scottish Ministers shall revoke the direction to which the patient is subject.

(3) Where the Scottish Ministers do not, under subsection (2) above, revoke the direction to which the patient is subject, they shall make a reference to the Tribunal in respect of the direction.

(4) Where a reference is made under subsection (3) above, the Scottish Ministers shall, as soon as practicable, give notice that a reference is to be made to—

    (a) the patient;

    (b) the patient's named person;

    (c) any guardian of the patient;

    (d) any welfare attorney of the patient;

    (e) the patient's responsible medical officer;

    (f) the mental health officer; and

    (g) the Commission.

(5) A reference under subsection (3) above shall state—

    (a) the name and address of the patient;

    (b) the name and address of the patient's named person; and

    (c) the recommendation made by the responsible medical officer.

(6)   Nothing in section 102 (state hospitals) of the National Health Service (Scotland) Act 1978 (c.29) prevents or restricts the detention of a patient in a state hospital as a result of a decision under this section by the Scottish Ministers not to revoke the direction to which the patient is subject.

211   Notice under section 209(2): reference to Tribunal

(1)   This section applies where, under section 209(2) of this Act, the Commission gives notice to the Scottish Ministers.

(2)   The Scottish Ministers shall, as soon as practicable after receiving notice under section 209(2) of this Act, make a reference to the Tribunal in respect of the direction to which the patient is subject.

(3)   Where a reference is made under subsection (2) above, the Scottish Ministers shall, as soon as practicable, give notice that a reference is to be made to the persons mentioned in paragraphs (a) to (g) of section 210(4) of this Act.

(4)   A reference under subsection (2) above shall state—

    (a) the name and address of the patient;

    (b) the name and address of the patient's named person; and

    (c) the reason given by the Commission in the notice under section 209(2) of this Act for requiring the Scottish Ministers to make the reference.

Scottish Ministers' duty to keep directions under review

212   Duty of Scottish Ministers to keep directions under review

(1)   This section applies where a patient is subject to—

    (a) a hospital direction; or

    (b) a transfer for treatment direction.

(2)   Without prejudice to the duties imposed on the Scottish Ministers by sections 210(2) and (3), 211(2) and 213(2) of this Act, the Scottish Ministers shall from time to time consider—

    (a) whether the conditions mentioned in section 206(4) of this Act continue to apply in respect of the patient;

    (b) whether, as a result of the patient's mental disorder, it is necessary, in order to protect any other person from serious harm, for the patient to be detained in hospital, whether or not for medical treatment; and

    (c) whether it continues to be necessary for the patient to be subject to the direction.

(3)   If, having considered the matters mentioned in paragraphs (a) to (c) of subsection (2) above, the Scottish Ministers are not satisfied that the patient has a mental disorder, they shall revoke the direction.

(4)   If, having considered the matters mentioned in paragraphs (a) to (c) of subsection (2) above, the Scottish Ministers—

(a)   are satisfied that the patient has a mental disorder; but

(b)   are not satisfied—

      (i)   that, as a result of the patient's mental disorder, it is necessary, in order to protect any other person from serious harm, for the patient to be detained in hospital, whether or not for medical treatment; and

      (ii)   that the conditions mentioned in paragraphs (b) and (c) of section 206(4) of this Act continue to apply in respect of the patient,

they shall revoke the direction.

(5)   Nothing in section 102 (state hospitals) of the National Health Service (Scotland) Act 1978 (c.29) prevents or restricts the detention of a patient in a state hospital as a result of a decision under this section by the Scottish Ministers not to revoke the direction to which the patient is subject.

213   Reference to Tribunal by Scottish Ministers

(1)   This section applies where a patient is subject to—

    (a)   a hospital direction; or

    (b)   a transfer for treatment direction.

(2)   If—

    (a)   during the period of 2 years ending with the relevant day—

      (i)   no reference under section 210(3) or 211(2) of this Act has been made to the Tribunal; and

      (ii)   no application under section 214(2) of this Act has been made to the Tribunal; and

    (b)   during each period of 2 years ending with the anniversary, in every year thereafter, of the relevant day—

      (i)   no reference such as is mentioned in paragraph (a)(i) above or, subject to subsection (3) below, under this subsection has been made to the Tribunal; and

      (ii)   no application such as is mentioned in paragraph (a)(ii) above has been made to the Tribunal,

the Scottish Ministers shall make a reference to the Tribunal in respect of the direction to which the patient is subject.

(3)   The Scottish Ministers shall, in considering, under subsection (2)(b)(i) above, whether a reference has been made to the Tribunal during any 2 year period, leave out of account any reference made under subsection (2) above during the first year of that 2 year period.

(4)   Where a reference is made under subsection (2) above, the Scottish Ministers shall, as soon as practicable, give notice that a reference is to be made to the persons mentioned in paragraphs (a) to (g) of section 210(4) of this Act.

(5)   A reference under subsection (2) above shall state—

    (a)   the name and address of the patient;

    (b)   the name and address of the patient's named person; and

Mental Health (Care and Treatment) (Scotland) Act 2003 (asp 13)
Part 11—Hospital directions and transfer for treatment directions

151

    (c) the reason for making the reference.

(6) In subsection (2) above, the "relevant day" means the day which falls 2 years after the day on which the direction is made.

Application by patient etc.

214   **Application to Tribunal by patient and named person**

(1) This section applies where a patient is subject to—

    (a) a hospital direction; or

    (b) a transfer for treatment direction.

(2) Each of the persons mentioned in subsection (3) below may, subject to subsections (4) to (6) below, make an application under this section to the Tribunal for the revocation of the direction to which the patient is subject.

(3) Those persons are—

    (a) the patient; and

    (b) the patient's named person.

(4) Where a patient is subject to a hospital direction, an application under this section may not be made before the expiry of the period of 6 months beginning with the day on which the direction was made.

(5) Where a patient is subject to a transfer for treatment direction, an application under this section—

    (a) may be made during the period of 12 weeks beginning with the day on which the direction is made; but

    (b) otherwise may not be made before the expiry of the period of 6 months beginning with the day on which the direction was made.

(6) Neither of the persons mentioned in subsection (3) above may make more than one application under this section during—

    (a) the period of 12 months beginning with the day on which the direction was made; or

    (b) any subsequent period of 12 months that begins with or with an anniversary of the expiry of the period of 12 months mentioned in paragraph (a) above.

(7) Where a patient's named person makes an application under subsection (2) above, the named person shall give notice to the patient of the making of the application.

Proceedings before Tribunal

215   **Powers of Tribunal on reference under section 210(3), 211(2) or 213(2) or on application under section 214(2)**

(1) This section applies where—

    (a) a reference is made under section 210(3), 211(2) or 213(2) of this Act; or

    (b) an application is made under section 214(2) of this Act.

(2) If the Tribunal is satisfied—

(a) that the patient has a mental disorder; and

(b) that, as a result of the patient's mental disorder, it is necessary, in order to protect any other person from serious harm, for the patient to be detained in hospital, whether or not for medical treatment,

it shall make no direction to the Scottish Ministers under this section.

(3) If the Tribunal is not satisfied that the patient has a mental disorder, it shall direct the Scottish Ministers to revoke the direction to which the patient is subject.

(4) If the Tribunal—

(a) is satisfied that the patient has a mental disorder; but

(b) is not satisfied—

(i)   that, as a result of the patient's mental disorder, it is necessary, in order to protect any other person from serious harm, for the patient to be detained in hospital, whether or not for medical treatment; and

(ii) that the conditions mentioned in paragraphs (b) and (c) of section 206(4) of this Act continue to apply in respect of the patient,

the Tribunal shall direct the Scottish Ministers to revoke the direction to which the patient is subject.

(5) The Scottish Ministers shall, if directed to do so by the Tribunal under subsection (3) or (4) above, revoke the direction to which the patient is subject.

(6) Before making a decision under this section, the Tribunal shall—

(a) afford the persons mentioned in subsection (7) below the opportunity—

(i)   of making representations (whether orally or in writing); and

(ii) of leading, or producing, evidence; and

(b) whether or not any such representations are made, hold a hearing.

(7) Those persons are—

(a) the patient;

(b) the patient's named person;

(c) the patient's primary carer;

(d) any guardian of the patient;

(e) any welfare attorney of the patient;

(f) any curator *ad litem* appointed in respect of the patient by the Tribunal;

(g) the Scottish Ministers;

(h) the patient's responsible medical officer;

(i) the mental health officer; and

(j) any other person appearing to the Tribunal to have an interest.

(8) Nothing in section 102 (state hospitals) of the National Health Service (Scotland) Act 1978 (c.29) prevents or restricts the detention of a patient in a state hospital as a result of a decision under this section by the Tribunal not to direct the Scottish Ministers to revoke the direction to which the patient is subject.

Effect of revocation of direction

216   Effect of revocation of direction

(1)   This section applies where, under section 210(2), 212(3) or (4) or 215(5) of this Act, the Scottish Ministers revoke—

    (a)   a hospital direction; or

    (b)   a transfer for treatment direction.

(2)   Where the Scottish Ministers revoke a direction they shall direct that the patient be admitted to a prison, institution or other place in which the patient might have been detained had the patient not been detained in hospital by virtue of the direction.

(3)   The direction shall cease to have effect on the patient's admission to the prison, institution or place to which the patient is admitted by virtue of the direction under subsection (2) above.

Termination of direction on release of patient

217   Termination of hospital direction on release of patient

(1)   This section applies where a patient is subject to—

    (a)   a hospital direction; or

    (b)   a transfer for treatment direction.

(2)   Where a patient is released under Part 1 of the Prisoners and Criminal Proceedings (Scotland) Act 1993 (c.9) or otherwise the direction to which the patient is subject shall cease to have effect.

PART 12

PARTS 10 AND 11: TRANSFERS

218   Transfer of patients between hospitals

(1)   This section applies where a patient is subject to—

    (a)   a compulsion order and a restriction order;

    (b)   a hospital direction; or

    (c)   a transfer for treatment direction.

(2)   The managers of the hospital in which the patient is detained may, where the conditions mentioned in subsection (3) below are satisfied, transfer the patient to another hospital.

(3)   Those conditions are—

    (a)   that the managers of the hospital to which it is proposed to transfer the patient; and

    (b)   the Scottish Ministers,

consent to the transfer.

(4)   Where the managers of a hospital propose to transfer a patient under subsection (2) above, they shall, subject to subsections (5) and (7) below, give the persons mentioned in subsection (8) below at least 7 days' notice of the transfer.

(5) The managers of a hospital need not give notice under subsection (4) above where it is necessary that the patient be transferred urgently.

(6) Where, by virtue of subsection (5) above, no notice is given under subsection (4) above, the managers of the hospital shall, subject to subsection (7) below, give the persons mentioned in subsection (8) below notice—

    (a) where the proposed transfer has not taken place, of the proposed transfer; or

    (b) where the transfer has taken place, of the transfer,

as soon as practicable before, on or, as the case may be, after the transfer.

(7) The managers of the hospital need not give notice under subsection (4) or (6) above to the patient where the patient consents to the transfer.

(8) The persons referred to in subsections (4) and (6) above and (10)(b) below are—

    (a) the patient; and

    (b) the patient's named person.

(9) Where—

    (a) notice is given under subsection (4) or (6)(a) above of a proposed transfer under subsection (2) above; and

    (b) the proposed transfer does not take place before the end of the period of 3 months beginning with the day on which notice is given,

the managers of the hospital may transfer the patient as proposed only if subsection (10) below applies.

(10) This subsection applies where—

    (a) the conditions mentioned in subsection (3) above continue to be satisfied; and

    (b) the persons mentioned in subsection (8) above are given at least 7 days' notice of the proposed transfer.

(11) Subsections (5) to (7) above shall apply to the giving of notice under subsection (10)(b) above as they apply to the giving of notice under subsection (4) above.

(12) Where the patient is transferred under subsection (2) above, the managers of the hospital from which the patient is transferred shall, before the expiry of the period of 7 days beginning with the transfer, give notice to the Commission of the matters mentioned in subsection (13) below.

(13) Those matters are—

    (a) the date on which the patient was transferred;

    (b) the hospital to which the patient was transferred;

    (c) that—

        (i) notice was given under subsection (4) above; or

        (ii) if no such notice was given, the reasons why it was necessary that the patient be transferred urgently; and

    (d) whether notice was given under subsection (6) or (10)(b) above.

(14) Where a patient is transferred under subsection (2) above, the compulsion order, hospital direction or, as the case may be, transfer for treatment direction to which the patient is subject shall, for the purposes of this Act (other than sections 219 and 220), be taken to specify the hospital to which the patient is transferred.

219   Appeal to Tribunal against transfer under section 218 to hospital other than state hospital

(1)   This section applies where—

    (a) a patient—

        (i)   receives notice under subsection (4), (6)(a) or (10)(b) of section 218 of this Act that it is proposed to transfer the patient; or

        (ii) is transferred under subsection (2) of that section,

    to any hospital other than a state hospital; and

    (b) the hospital to which the patient is, or is proposed to be, transferred is not specified in the compulsion order, hospital direction or, as the case may be, transfer for treatment direction to which the patient is subject.

(2)   The patient, or the patient's named person, may, during the period mentioned in subsection (3) below, appeal to the Tribunal against the proposed transfer or, as the case may be, the transfer.

(3)   That period is—

    (a) in the case of the patient—

        (i)   where notice is given to the patient before the proposed transfer, the period beginning with the day on which notice is given and ending 28 days after the transfer;

        (ii) where notice is given to the patient on or after the transfer, the period beginning with the day on which the patient is transferred and ending 28 days after the day on which notice is given; or

        (iii) where notice is not given to the patient, the period of 28 days beginning with the day on which the patient is transferred;

    (b) in the case of the patient's named person—

        (i)   where notice is given to the patient's named person before the proposed transfer, the period beginning with the day on which notice is given and ending 28 days after the transfer; or

        (ii) where notice is given to the patient's named person on or after the transfer, the period of 28 days beginning with the day on which notice is given.

(4)   If, when an appeal under subsection (2) above against a proposed transfer is made to the Tribunal, the proposed transfer has not taken place—

    (a) the managers of the hospital shall not transfer the patient as proposed; but

    (b) the Tribunal may, if satisfied that, pending the determination of the appeal, the patient should be transferred as proposed, make an order that the patient be so transferred.

(5)   On an appeal under subsection (2) above, the Tribunal may make an order that the proposed transfer not take place or, as the case may be, that the patient be returned to the hospital from which the patient was transferred.

220   Appeal to Tribunal against transfer under section 218 to state hospital

(1)   This section applies where—

    (a)   a patient—

        (i)   receives notice under subsection (4), (6)(a) or (10)(b) of section 218 of this Act that it is proposed to transfer the patient; or

        (ii)   is transferred under subsection (2) of that section,

    to a state hospital; and

    (b)   the state hospital to which the patient is, or is proposed to be, transferred is not specified in the compulsion order, hospital direction or, as the case may be, transfer for treatment direction to which the patient is subject.

(2)   The patient, or the patient's named person, may, during the period mentioned in subsection (3) below, appeal to the Tribunal against the proposed transfer or, as the case may be, the transfer.

(3)   That period is—

    (a)   in the case of the patient—

        (i)   where notice is given to the patient before the proposed transfer, the period beginning with the day on which notice is given and ending 12 weeks after the transfer;

        (ii)   where notice is given to the patient on or after the transfer, the period beginning with the day on which the patient is transferred and ending 12 weeks after the day on which notice is given; or

        (iii)   where notice is not given to the patient, the period of 12 weeks beginning with the day on which the patient is transferred;

    (b)   in the case of the patient's named person—

        (i)   where notice is given to the patient's named person before the proposed transfer, the period beginning with the day on which notice is given and ending 12 weeks after the transfer; or

        (ii)   where notice is given to the patient's named person on or after the transfer, the period of 12 weeks beginning with the day on which notice is given.

(4)   If, when an appeal under subsection (2) above against a proposed transfer is made to the Tribunal, the proposed transfer has not taken place—

    (a)   the managers of the hospital shall not transfer the patient as proposed; but

    (b)   the Tribunal may, if satisfied that, pending determination of the appeal, the patient should be transferred as proposed, make an order that the patient be so transferred.

(5)   On an appeal under subsection (2) above, the Tribunal may, if not satisfied as to the matter mentioned in subsection (6) below, make an order that the proposed transfer not take place or, as the case may be, that the patient be returned to the hospital from which the patient was transferred.

(6)   That matter is—

    (a)   that the patient requires to be detained in hospital under conditions of special security; and

    (b)   that those conditions of special security can be provided only in a state hospital.

PART 13

PARTS 8, 10 AND 11: SUSPENSION

Assessment orders

221   Assessment order: suspension of measure authorising detention

(1)   This section applies where a patient is subject to an assessment order.

(2)   Subject to subsection (3) below, where the patient's responsible medical officer grants a certificate specifying a period during which the assessment order to which the patient is subject shall not authorise the detention of the patient in hospital, the order does not authorise that detention during that period.

(3)   The patient's responsible medical officer may grant a certificate under subsection (2) above only with the consent of the Scottish Ministers.

(4)   A period specified in a certificate under subsection (2) above may be expressed as—

    (a)   the duration of—

        (i)   an event; or

        (ii)   a series of events; or

    (b)   the duration of—

        (i)   an event; or

        (ii)   a series of events,

    and any associated travel.

(5)   If the responsible medical officer considers that it is necessary—

    (a)   in the interests of the patient; or

    (b)   for the protection of any other person,

a certificate under subsection (2) above may include conditions such as are mentioned in subsection (6) below; and any such conditions shall have effect.

(6)   Those conditions are—

    (a)   that, during the period specified in the certificate, the patient be kept in the charge of a person authorised in writing for the purpose by the patient's responsible medical officer; and

    (b)   such other conditions as may be specified by the patient's responsible medical officer.

222   Certificate under section 221: revocation by responsible medical officer

(1)   Subsection (2) below applies where a certificate is granted under section 221(2) of this Act.

(2)   If the patient's responsible medical officer is satisfied that it is necessary—

    (a) in the interests of the patient; or

    (b) for the protection of any other person,

that the certificate be revoked, the responsible medical officer may revoke the certificate.

(3)   Where, under subsection (2) above, the responsible medical officer revokes a certificate, the responsible medical officer shall, as soon as practicable after the revocation, give notice of it to—

    (a) the patient;

    (b) where a person is authorised for the purposes of section 221(6)(a) of this Act, that person; and

    (c) the Scottish Ministers.

223   Certificate under section 221: revocation by Scottish Ministers

(1)   Subsection (2) below applies where a certificate is granted under section 221(2) of this Act.

(2)   If the Scottish Ministers are satisfied that it is necessary—

    (a) in the interests of the patient; or

    (b) for the protection of any other person,

that the certificate be revoked, the Scottish Ministers may revoke the certificate.

(3)   Where, under subsection (2) above, the Scottish Ministers revoke a certificate, they shall, as soon as practicable after the revocation, give notice of it to—

    (a) the patient;

    (b) the patient's responsible medical officer; and

    (c) where a person is authorised for the purposes of section 221(6)(a) of this Act, that person.

Certain other orders and directions

224   Patients subject to certain other orders and directions: suspension of measure authorising detention

(1)   This section applies where a patient is subject to—

    (a) a treatment order;

    (b) an interim compulsion order;

    (c) a compulsion order and a restriction order;

    (d) a hospital direction; or

    (e) a transfer for treatment direction.

(2)   Subject to subsections (3) and (4) below, where the patient's responsible medical officer grants a certificate specifying a period not exceeding 3 months during which the order or direction to which the patient is subject shall not authorise the detention of the patient in hospital, the order or direction does not authorise that detention during that period.

(3) The patient's responsible medical officer may grant a certificate under subsection (2) above only with the consent of the Scottish Ministers.

(4) If the sum of—

    (a) the period that the responsible medical officer proposes to specify in a certificate under subsection (2) above; and

    (b) the period specified in any other certificate granted under that subsection in respect of the same patient,

would exceed 9 months in the period of 12 months ending with the expiry of the period mentioned in paragraph (a) above, the responsible medical officer may not grant a certificate under that subsection.

(5) A period specified in a certificate under subsection (2) above may be expressed as—

    (a) the duration of—

        (i) an event; or

        (ii) a series of events; or

    (b) the duration of—

        (i) an event; or

        (ii) a series of events,

    and any associated travel.

(6) If the responsible medical officer considers that it is necessary—

    (a) in the interests of the patient; or

    (b) for the protection of any other person,

a certificate under subsection (2) above may include conditions such as are mentioned in subsection (7) below; and any such conditions shall have effect.

(7) Those conditions are—

    (a) that, during the period specified in the certificate, the patient be kept in the charge of a person authorised in writing for the purpose by the patient's responsible medical officer; and

    (b) such other conditions as may be specified by the patient's responsible medical officer.

(8) Where a patient's responsible medical officer proposes to grant a certificate under subsection (2) above specifying—

    (a) a period of more than 28 days; or

    (b) a period which, when taken together with the period specified in any other certificate granted under that subsection, would exceed 28 days,

the responsible medical officer shall, before granting such a certificate, give notice of the proposal to the persons mentioned in subsection (9) below.

(9) Those persons are—

    (a) the patient;

    (b) the patient's named person;

    (c) the patient's general medical practitioner; and

      (d) the mental health officer.

(10) Where a certificate is granted under subsection (2) above specifying a period of more than 28 days, the patient's responsible medical officer shall, before the expiry of the period of 14 days beginning with the day on which the certificate is granted, give notice of the granting of the certificate to the Commission.

225   Certificate under section 224: revocation by responsible medical officer

(1) Subsection (2) below applies where a certificate is granted under 224(2) of this Act.

(2) If the patient's responsible medical officer is satisfied that it is necessary—

      (a) in the interests of the patient; or

      (b) for the protection of any other person,

that the certificate be revoked, the responsible medical officer may revoke the certificate.

(3) Where, under subsection (2) above, the responsible medical officer revokes a certificate, the responsible medical officer shall, as soon as practicable after the revocation, give notice of it to—

      (a) the patient;

      (b) the patient's named person;

      (c) in a case where the certificate specified a period of more than 28 days, the patient's general medical practitioner;

      (d) where a person is authorised for the purposes of section 224(7)(a) of this Act, that person;

      (e) the mental health officer; and

      (f) the Scottish Ministers.

(4) Where, under subsection (2) above, the responsible medical officer revokes a certificate granted under section 224(2) of this Act that specified a period of more than 28 days, the responsible medical officer shall, before the expiry of the period of 14 days beginning with the day on which the certificate is revoked, give notice of the revocation to the Commission.

226   Certificate under section 224: revocation by Scottish Ministers

(1) Subsection (2) below applies where a certificate is granted under section 224(2) of this Act.

(2) If the Scottish Ministers are satisfied that it is necessary—

      (a) in the interests of the patient; or

      (b) for the protection of any other person,

that the certificate be revoked, the Scottish Ministers may revoke the certificate.

(3) Where, under subsection (2) above, the Scottish Ministers revoke a certificate, they shall, as soon as practicable after the revocation, give notice of it to—

      (a) the patient;

      (b) the patient's named person;

(c) in a case where the certificate specified a period of more than 28 days, the patient's general medical practitioner;

(d) the patient's responsible medical officer;

(e) the mental health officer; and

(f) where a person is authorised for the purposes of section 224(7)(a) of this Act, that person.

(4) Where, under subsection (2) above, the Scottish Ministers revoke a certificate granted under section 224(2) of this Act that specified a period of more than 28 days, they shall, before the expiry of the period of 14 days beginning with the day on which the certificate is revoked, give notice of the revocation to the Commission.

PART 14

ASSESSMENT OF NEEDS

227   Assessment of needs for community care services etc.

(1) Where—

(a) a patient is a person for whom a local authority are under a duty or have a power to provide, or secure the provision of, community care services;

(b) it appears to the mental health officer that, for the purposes of this Act or the 1995 Act, the patient should be assessed under subsection (1)(a) of section 12A of the Social Work (Scotland) Act 1968 (c.49); and

(c) the mental health officer notifies the local authority that the patient may be in need of community care services,

the patient shall for the purposes of that section be deemed to appear to the local authority to be a person who may be in need of any such services.

(2) In section 23(3) of the Children (Scotland) Act 1995 (c.36) (local authority's duty to carry out, in response to request by parent or guardian, assessment of needs of child)—

(a) after "by", where it first occurs, there shall be inserted "—

(a)"; and

(b) after "guardian", there shall be inserted "; or

(b) a mental health officer (as defined in section 329 of the Mental Health (Care and Treatment) (Scotland) Act 2003 (asp 13)) who—

(i) has responsibility under that Act or the Criminal Procedure (Scotland) Act 1995 (c.46) for a child's case; and

(ii) makes the request for the purposes of either of those Acts,".

228   Request for assessment of needs: duty on local authorities and Health Boards

(1) Where—

(a) a—

(i) local authority receive a request in writing for the needs of a person to be assessed under section 12A(1)(a) of the Social Work (Scotland) Act 1968 (c.49); or

      (ii)   Health Board receives a request in writing for the needs of a person for services which are provided by Health Boards in respect of mentally disordered persons to be assessed; and

    (b) any of the circumstances mentioned in paragraphs (a) to (c) of subsection (2) below apply,

the authority or, as the case may be, the Board shall comply with the requirement in subsection (3) below.

(2)   The circumstances referred to in subsection (1)(b) above are—

    (a) that the request bears—

      (i)   to be made by a mentally disordered person; and

      (ii)   to be a request for the needs of that person to be assessed;

    (b) that the request bears—

      (i)   to be made by the primary carer, or named person, of a mentally disordered person; and

      (ii)   to be a request for the needs of the mentally disordered person to be assessed; and

    (c) though the request does not bear to be made as mentioned in paragraph (a) or (b) above, it appears to the local authority or, as the case may be, the Health Board that the request—

      (i)   is a request for the needs of a mentally disordered person to be assessed; and

      (ii)   is made by that person, or by that person's primary carer or named person.

(3)   The requirement referred to in subsection (1) above is to give notice, before the expiry of the period of 14 days beginning with the day on which the request is received, to the person who made the request—

    (a) of whether—

      (i)   the local authority intend; or

      (ii)   the Health Board intends,

    to undertake the assessment; and

    (b) if the intention is not to undertake the assessment, of the reason why that is the case.

PART 15

PRELIMINARY DUTIES ON MAKING OF ORDERS ETC.

Designation of mental health officer

229   Designation of mental health officer responsible for patient's case

(1)   The relevant local authority—

    (a) shall, as soon as is reasonably practicable after a relevant event occurs in respect of a patient, ensure that a mental health officer is designated as the mental health officer having responsibility for the patient's case; and

(b) shall ensure that, so long as the patient is subject to a certificate, order or direction mentioned in section 232 of this Act, a mental health officer is designated as such mental health officer.

(2) The relevant local authority having responsibility under subsection (1) above may at any time designate—

    (a) for all purposes; or

    (b) for a particular purpose or for particular circumstances,

a mental health officer in place of the mental health officer designated under that subsection.

(3) In this section, "relevant local authority" means—

    (a) as respects the making of an order mentioned in section 232 of this Act which does not authorise the detention of the patient in hospital, the local authority for the area in which the patient resides;

    (b) as respects the granting of a certificate or the making of a direction mentioned in that section, or the making of an order mentioned in that section which authorises the detention of the patient in hospital—

        (i) the local authority for the area in which the patient was resident immediately before the relevant event occurred; or

        (ii) where the patient was not resident in Scotland immediately before the relevant event occurred, the local authority for the area in which the hospital is situated.

Patient's responsible medical officer

230 Appointment of patient's responsible medical officer

(1) As soon as is reasonably practicable after the occurrence of an appropriate act in relation to a patient, the relevant managers shall appoint an approved medical practitioner to be the patient's responsible medical officer.

(2) Where, immediately before the occurrence of an appropriate act, a patient has a responsible medical officer, the person appointed under subsection (1) above may be that person.

(3) The relevant managers having responsibility under subsection (1) above may at any time—

    (a) appoint an approved medical practitioner to be the patient's responsible medical officer in place of the existing responsible medical officer;

    (b) authorise an approved medical practitioner to act (whether for a particular purpose or in particular circumstances) in place of the patient's responsible medical officer.

(4) In this section—

    "appropriate act" means—

        (a) a relevant event;

        (b) the granting of an emergency detention certificate;

(c)   the making of a temporary compulsion order under section 54(1)(c) of the 1995 Act;

(d)   the variation of—

     (i)   a compulsory treatment order; or

     (ii)   a compulsion order;

(e)   transfer to another hospital under section 124(2), 125(4)(b), 126(4), 218(2), 219(4)(b) or 220(4)(b) of this Act;

(f)   return to a hospital under section 125(5), 126(5), 219(5) or 220(5) of this Act; and

"relevant managers" means—

(a)   in a case where the appropriate act falls within any of paragraphs (a) to (c) of the definition of that expression above, the managers of the hospital in which the patient is detained or, as the case may be, which is specified in the order;

(b)   in a case where the appropriate act falls within paragraph (d) of that definition, the managers of the hospital specified in the order following modification under section 102, 103, 104, 106, 166, 167, 169, 171 or, as the case may be, 193(6) of this Act;

(c)   in a case where the appropriate act falls within paragraph (e) of that definition, the managers of the hospital to which the patient is transferred under any of the provisions mentioned in that paragraph; and

(d)   in a case where the appropriate act falls within paragraph (f) of that definition, the managers of the hospital to which the patient is returned under any of the provisions mentioned in that paragraph.

Social circumstances reports

231   Social circumstances report: mental health officer's duties

(1)   Subject to subsection (2) below, where a relevant event occurs in respect of a patient, the mental health officer shall, before the expiry of the period of 21 days beginning with the day on which the event occurs—

(a)   prepare in respect of the patient a social circumstances report; and

(b)   send a copy of the report to—

     (i)   the patient's responsible medical officer; and

     (ii)   the Commission.

(2)   If in any case the mental health officer considers that a social circumstances report would serve little, or no, practical purpose, the mental health officer—

(a)   need not comply with subsection (1) above; but

(b)   shall, before the expiry of the period mentioned in that subsection—

     (i)   record the reasons for deciding that any such report would serve little, or no, practical purpose; and

     (ii)   send a statement of those reasons to the patient's responsible medical officer and to the Commission.

(3) In this section, "social circumstances report" means a report setting out such information as may be prescribed by regulations.

Meaning of "relevant event"

232 Meaning of "relevant event"

In this Part of this Act, "relevant event" means—

(a) the granting of a short-term detention certificate;

(b) the making of—

    (i) an interim compulsory treatment order;

    (ii) a compulsory treatment order;

    (iii) an assessment order;

    (iv) a treatment order;

    (v) an interim compulsion order;

    (vi) a compulsion order;

    (vii) a hospital direction; or

    (viii) a transfer for treatment direction.

PART 16

MEDICAL TREATMENT

Designated medical practitioners

233 Designated medical practitioners

(1) The Commission shall compile and maintain a list of medical practitioners who appear to the Commission to have such—

(a) qualifications; and

(b) experience,

as the Commission considers appropriate for the purposes of discharging the functions conferred on designated medical practitioners by virtue of this Part of this Act.

(2) A medical practitioner included for the time being in the list mentioned in subsection (1) above is referred to in this Act as a "designated medical practitioner".

(3) The Commission shall ensure that the list mentioned in subsection (1) above includes child specialists.

(4) A designated medical practitioner may, for the purposes of discharging any functions conferred by virtue of this Part of this Act—

(a) interview a patient at any reasonable time and require any such interview to be conducted in private;

(b) carry out a medical examination of a patient in private at any reasonable time; and

(c) require any person holding medical records of a patient to produce such records for inspection by the designated medical practitioner.

(5)   A designated medical practitioner shall undertake such training as the Commission may require.

(6)   The Commission shall pay to designated medical practitioners for or in connection with the discharge of the functions conferred on them by virtue of this Part of this Act such fees, expenses and allowances as may be prescribed by regulations.

Safeguards for certain surgical operations etc.

234   **Certain surgical operations etc.**

(1)   The types of medical treatment mentioned in subsection (2) below may be given to a patient only in accordance with section 235 or 236 of this Act.

(2)   The types of medical treatment referred to in subsection (1) above are—

       (a)   any surgical operation for destroying—

            (i)   brain tissue; or

            (ii)   the functioning of brain tissue; and

       (b)   such other types of medical treatment as may be specified in regulations for the purposes of this section.

(3)   Before making regulations under subsection (2)(b) above the Scottish Ministers shall consult such persons as they consider appropriate.

235   **Treatment mentioned in section 234(2): patients capable of consenting**

(1)   Medical treatment mentioned in section 234(2) of this Act is given to a patient in accordance with this section if the requirements set out in subsections (2) and (3) below are satisfied.

(2)   Subject to subsection (6) below, the first requirement is that a designated medical practitioner who is not the patient's responsible medical officer certifies in writing that—

       (a)   the patient is capable of consenting to the treatment;

       (b)   the patient consents in writing to the treatment; and

       (c)   having regard to the likelihood of its alleviating, or preventing a deterioration in, the patient's condition, it is in the patient's best interests that the treatment should be given to the patient.

(3)   The second requirement is that two other persons (not being medical practitioners) appointed by the Commission for the purposes of this subsection certify in writing that—

       (a)   the patient is capable of consenting to the treatment; and

       (b)   the patient consents in writing to the treatment.

(4)   A person appointed for the purposes of subsection (3) above may—

       (a)   interview the patient at any reasonable time; and

       (b)   require any such interview to be conducted in private.

(5)   If the patient withdraws consent to the treatment (in writing or otherwise) at any time before its completion, this section shall then apply as if the remainder of the treatment were a separate treatment.

(6)   Where—

         (a)   the patient is a child; and

         (b)   the patient's responsible medical officer is not a child specialist,

the first requirement is that the matters mentioned in paragraphs (a) to (c) of subsection (2) above are certified in writing by a designated medical practitioner who is a child specialist.

(7)   References in subsections (2) and (6)(b) above to a patient's responsible medical officer include, in any case where a patient does not have a responsible medical officer, references to the medical practitioner primarily responsible for treating the patient.

236   Treatment mentioned in section 234(2): patients incapable of consenting

(1)   Medical treatment mentioned in section 234(2) of this Act is given to a patient in accordance with this section if—

         (a)   the requirements set out in subsections (2) to (4) below are satisfied; and

         (b)   the patient does not resist or object to the treatment.

(2)   Subject to subsection (6) below, the first requirement is that a designated medical practitioner who is not the patient's responsible medical officer certifies in writing that—

         (a)   the patient is incapable of consenting to the treatment;

         (b)   the patient does not object to the treatment; and

         (c)   having regard to the likelihood of its alleviating, or preventing a deterioration in, the patient's condition, it is in the patient's best interests that the treatment should be given to the patient.

(3)   The second requirement is that two persons (not being medical practitioners) appointed by the Commission for the purposes of this subsection certify in writing that—

         (a)   the patient is incapable of consenting to the treatment; and

         (b)   the patient does not object to the treatment.

(4)   The third requirement is that on the application of the patient's responsible medical officer, the Court of Session has made an order declaring that the treatment may lawfully be given.

(5)   The Court of Session may make an order such as is mentioned in subsection (4) above only if it is satisfied that—

         (a)   having regard to the likelihood of its alleviating, or preventing a deterioration in, the patient's condition, it is in the patient's best interests that the treatment should be given to the patient; and

         (b)   the patient does not object to the treatment.

(6)   Where the patient is a child, the first requirement is that the matters mentioned in paragraphs (a) to (c) of subsection (2) above are certified—

    (a) where the patient's responsible medical officer is a child specialist, by a medical practitioner approved for the purposes of this subsection by the Commission;

    (b) where the patient's responsible medical officer is not a child specialist, by a child specialist who is on the list maintained under section 233(1) of this Act.

(7) References in subsections (2), (4) and (6) above to a patient's responsible medical officer include, in any case where a patient does not have a responsible medical officer, references to the medical practitioner primarily responsible for treating the patient.

Safeguards for other medical treatment

237   **Electro-convulsive therapy etc.**

(1) This section applies where the giving of medical treatment to a patient is authorised by virtue of this Act or the 1995 Act.

(2) Subject to section 243 of this Act, the types of medical treatment mentioned in subsection (3) below may be given to the patient only in accordance with section 238 or 239 of this Act.

(3) The types of medical treatment referred to in subsection (2) above are—

    (a) electro-convulsive therapy; and

    (b) such other types of medical treatment as may be specified in regulations for the purposes of this section.

(4) Before making regulations under subsection (3)(b) above the Scottish Ministers shall consult such persons as they consider appropriate.

238   **Treatment mentioned in sections 237(3) and 240(3): patients capable of consenting and not refusing consent**

(1) Subject to subsection (3) below, medical treatment mentioned in section 237(3) or 240(3) of this Act is given to a patient in accordance with this section if the patient's responsible medical officer or a designated medical practitioner certifies in writing that—

    (a) the patient is capable of consenting to the treatment;

    (b) the patient consents in writing to the treatment;

    (c) the giving of medical treatment to the patient is authorised by virtue of this Act or the 1995 Act; and

    (d) having regard to the likelihood of its alleviating, or preventing a deterioration in, the patient's condition, it is in the patient's best interests that the treatment should be given.

(2) If the patient withdraws consent to the treatment (in writing or otherwise) at any time before its completion, this section shall then apply as if the remainder of the treatment were a separate treatment.

(3) Where the patient is a child, any certificate under subsection (1) above shall be given by a child specialist.

239   Treatment mentioned in section 237(3): patients incapable of consenting

(1)   Subject to subsections (2) to (4) below, medical treatment mentioned in section 237(3) of this Act is given to a patient in accordance with this section if a designated medical practitioner who is not the patient's responsible medical officer certifies in writing that—

   (a)   the patient is incapable of understanding the nature, purpose and likely effects of the treatment;

   (b)   the giving of medical treatment to the patient is authorised by virtue of this Act or the 1995 Act; and

   (c)   having regard to the likelihood of its alleviating, or preventing a deterioration in, the patient's condition, it is in the patient's best interests that the treatment should be given.

(2)   Where the patient resists or objects to the treatment, certification under subsection (1) above is effective only if, instead of certifying the matter mentioned in paragraph (c) of that subsection, the designated medical practitioner certifies that—

   (a)   the patient resists or objects to the treatment; but

   (b)   it is necessary to give the treatment to the patient for a purpose mentioned in any of paragraphs (a) to (c) of section 243(3) of this Act and specified in the certificate.

(3)   Where the patient is a child, certification under subsection (1) above is effective only if done—

   (a)   where the patient's responsible medical officer is a child specialist, by a medical practitioner approved for the purposes of this subsection by the Commission;

   (b)   where the patient's responsible medical officer is not a child specialist, by a child specialist who is on the list maintained under section 233(1) of this Act.

(4)   Where the patient is not in hospital, subsection (1) above does not authorise the giving of medical treatment by force to the patient.

240   Treatments given over period of time etc.

(1)   This section applies where the giving of medical treatment to a patient is authorised by virtue of this Act or the 1995 Act.

(2)   Subject to subsection (4) below and to section 243 of this Act, the types of treatment mentioned in subsection (3) below, when given as treatment for mental disorder or in consequence of the patient having a mental disorder, may be given to the patient only in accordance with section 238 or 241 of this Act.

(3)   The types of treatment referred to in subsection (2) above are—

   (a)   any medicine (other than the surgical implantation of hormones) given for the purpose of reducing sex drive;

   (b)   any other medicine;

   (c)   provision, without the consent of the patient and by artificial means, of nutrition to the patient; and

   (d)   such other types of treatment as may be specified in regulations for the purposes of this section.

(4) Subsection (2) above does not apply to the giving of medicine in a relevant period until 2 months have passed since the patient was first in the relevant period given any medicine that was not, when given, a treatment specified under subsection (3)(d) above or section 234(2)(b) or 237(3)(b) of this Act.

(5) The Scottish Ministers may by order amend subsection (4) above for the purpose of substituting a period specified in the order for (as the case may be)—

  (a) the period of 2 months mentioned in that subsection; or

  (b) the period that is for the time being mentioned in that subsection in place of that period of 2 months.

(6) For the purposes of subsection (4) above—

  "medicine" does not include medicine such as is mentioned in paragraph (a) of subsection (3) above or any treatment specified in regulations under paragraph (d) of that subsection; and

  "relevant period", in relation to a patient, means any period during which the giving of medical treatment to the patient is authorised by virtue of this Act or the 1995 Act.

(7) Before making regulations under subsection (3)(d) above the Scottish Ministers shall consult such persons as they consider appropriate.

241 **Treatment mentioned in section 240(3): patients refusing consent or incapable of consenting**

(1) Subject to subsections (3) and (4) below, medical treatment mentioned in section 240(3) of this Act is given in accordance with this section if a designated medical practitioner who is not the patient's responsible medical officer certifies in writing that—

  (a) the patient—

    (i) does not consent to the treatment; or

    (ii) is incapable of consenting to the treatment;

  (b) the giving of medical treatment to the patient is authorised by virtue of this Act or the 1995 Act; and

  (c) having regard to the likelihood of its alleviating, or preventing a deterioration in, the patient's condition, it is in the patient's best interests that the treatment should be given.

(2) If the condition mentioned in subsection (1)(a)(i) above applies, the designated medical practitioner shall—

  (a) if the reason for refusal of consent is known, have regard to the reason for the refusal; and

  (b) if the designated medical practitioner is of the opinion that the treatment should be given, include in any certificate under subsection (1) above a statement of the reason for that opinion.

(3) Where the patient is a child, the certification of the matters mentioned in paragraphs (a) to (c) of subsection (1) above is effective only if done—

  (a) where the patient's responsible medical officer is a child specialist, by a medical practitioner approved for the purposes of this subsection by the Commission;

(b) where the patient's responsible medical officer is not a child specialist, by a child specialist who is on the list maintained under section 233(1) of this Act.

(4) Where the patient is not in hospital, subsection (1) above does not authorise the giving of medical treatment by force to the patient.

242 **Treatment not mentioned in section 234(2), 237(3) or 240(3)**

(1) This section applies where the giving of medical treatment to a patient is authorised by virtue of this Act or the 1995 Act.

(2) Subject to subsection (6) below and to sections 234(1), 237(2), 240(2) and 243 of this Act, medical treatment may be given to the patient only in accordance with subsection (3) or (4) below.

(3) If the patient—

(a) is capable of consenting to the treatment; and

(b) consents in writing to the treatment,

medical treatment is given to the patient in accordance with this subsection if the treatment is given by, or under the direction of, the patient's responsible medical officer.

(4) If the patient—

(a) is capable of consenting to the treatment but—

(i) does not consent; or

(ii) consents otherwise than in writing; or

(b) is incapable of consenting to the treatment,

medical treatment is given to the patient in accordance with this subsection if the requirements in subsection (5) below are satisfied.

(5) Those requirements are—

(a) after having regard—

(i) in a case where subsection (4)(a)(i) above applies, to the reason for not consenting (if it has been disclosed to the patient's responsible medical officer);

(ii) to any views expressed by the patient;

(iii) to any views expressed by the patient's named person;

(iv) to any advance statement made by the patient; and

(v) to the likelihood of the treatment's alleviating, or preventing a deterioration in, the patient's condition,

the responsible medical officer determines that it is in the patient's best interests that the treatment be given;

(b) in the case of a patient subject to an assessment order, an approved medical practitioner who is not the patient's responsible medical officer determines, after having regard to the matters mentioned in sub-paragraphs (i) to (v) of paragraph (a) above, that it is in the patient's best interests that the treatment be given;

(c) the treatment is given by, or under the direction of, the patient's responsible medical officer;

(d) the patient's responsible medical officer records in writing the reasons for giving the treatment; and

(e) in the case of a patient subject to an assessment order, the approved medical practitioner who makes the determination referred to in paragraph (b) above records in writing the reasons for that determination.

(6) Where the patient is not in hospital, subsection (4) above does not authorise the giving of medical treatment by force to the patient.

Urgent medical treatment where patient detained in hospital

243   Urgent medical treatment

(1) This section applies where the detention in hospital of a patient is authorised by virtue of—

(a) this Act; or

(b) the 1995 Act.

(2) Where it is necessary as a matter of urgency for medical treatment to be given to the patient for any of the purposes mentioned in subsection (3) below, the treatment may, subject to subsections (4) and (5) below, be given notwithstanding that the patient—

(a) does not consent; or

(b) is incapable of consenting,

to the treatment.

(3) The purposes are—

(a) saving the patient's life;

(b) preventing serious deterioration in the patient's condition;

(c) alleviating serious suffering on the part of the patient; and

(d) preventing the patient from—

(i) behaving violently; or

(ii) being a danger to the patient or to others.

(4) Subsection (2) above authorises the giving of medical treatment—

(a) for a purpose mentioned in any of paragraphs (b) to (d) of subsection (3) above only if the treatment is not likely to entail unfavourable, and irreversible, physical or psychological consequences;

(b) for a purpose mentioned in paragraph (c) or (d) of that subsection only if the treatment does not entail significant physical hazard to the patient.

(5) Subsection (2) above does not authorise the giving of electro-convulsive therapy if the patient is capable of consenting but does not consent to the treatment.

(6) Where the patient is given medical treatment by virtue of subsection (2) above, the patient's responsible medical officer shall, before the expiry of the period of 7 days beginning with the day on which such treatment is given (or first given), give notice to the Commission of—

(a) the type of treatment given; and

(b) the purpose mentioned in subsection (3) above for which it was given.

Additional safeguards for certain informal patients

244   Scottish Ministers' power to make provision in relation to treatment for certain informal patients

Regulations may prescribe conditions that must be satisfied before types of medical treatment specified in the regulations may be given to patients—

(a) who are under 16 years of age; and

(b) in respect of whom the giving of medical treatment is not authorised by virtue of this Act or the 1995 Act.

Supplementary

245   Certificates under sections 235, 236, 239 and 241

(1) This section applies to certificates under sections 235, 236, 239 and 241 of this Act.

(2) A certificate shall contain such particulars as may be prescribed by regulations.

(3) Before giving a certificate, the person giving it shall consult—

(a) subject to subsection (4) below—

(i)   the patient; and

(ii) the patient's named person; and

(b) such person or persons as appear to the person giving the certificate to be principally concerned with the patient's medical treatment.

(4) The person giving a certificate need not consult any person such as is mentioned in paragraph (a) of subsection (3) above in any case where it is impracticable to do so.

(5) A person who gives a certificate shall, before the expiry of the period of 7 days beginning with the day on which the certificate is given, send a copy of it to the Commission.

246   Certificates under section 238

A certificate under section 238 of this Act shall contain such particulars as may be prescribed by regulations.

247   Scope of consent or certificate under sections 235, 236, 238, 239 and 241

Any—

(a) consent; or

(b) certificate,

given under section 235, 236, 238, 239 or 241 of this Act may relate to a plan of treatment under which (whether during a specified period or otherwise) one or more of the types of treatment to which the consent or certificate relates is to be given to the patient.

174   *Mental Health (Care and Treatment) (Scotland) Act 2003 (asp 13)*
Part 17—Patient representation etc.
Chapter 1—Named person

248   Sections 235, 236, 238, 239 and 241: review of treatment etc.

(1)   Where medical treatment is given to a patient by virtue of section 235, 236, 239 or 241 of this Act, the patient's responsible medical officer shall—

     (a)   on the next occasion after the giving of the treatment on which the patient's responsible medical officer submits a record to the Tribunal under section 87(2)(b) of this Act or, as the case may be, makes an application to the Tribunal under section 92 of this Act; or

     (b)   at such other time as the patient's responsible medical officer is required to do so by the Commission,

submit to the Commission a report as to the treatment given and the patient's condition.

(2)   The Commission may at any time by notice to the patient's responsible medical officer revoke, with effect from such time as may be specified in the notice, a certificate given under section 235(2) or (3), 236(2) or (3), 238(1), 239 or 241(1) of this Act.

(3)   A time specified in a notice under subsection (2) above may not be earlier than the time of the notice.

Interpretation of Part

249   Interpretation of Part

In this Part—

     "child" means a person who has not attained the age of 18 years; and

     "child specialist" means a medical practitioner who has such qualifications or experience in relation to children as the Commission may determine from time to time.

PART 17

PATIENT REPRESENTATION ETC.

CHAPTER 1

NAMED PERSON

Meaning of "named person"

250   Nomination of named person

(1)   Where a person who has attained the age of 16 years (a "nominator") nominates in accordance with subsection (2) below another person who has attained that age to be the nominator's named person, that person is, subject to subsections (3) and (6) below, the nominator's named person.

(2)   A person is nominated in accordance with this subsection if—

     (a)   the nomination is signed by the nominator;

     (b)   the nominator's signature is witnessed by a prescribed person;

     (c)   the prescribed person certifies that, in the opinion of the prescribed person, the nominator—

Mental Health (Care and Treatment) (Scotland) Act 2003 (asp 13)
Part 17—Patient representation etc.
Chapter 1—Named person

175

        (i)   understands the effect of nominating a person to be the nominator's named person; and

        (ii)   has not been subjected to any undue influence in making the nomination.

(3)   A nomination under subsection (1) above may be revoked by the nominator in accordance with subsection (4) below.

(4)   The nomination of a named person is revoked in accordance with this subsection if—

    (a) the revocation is signed by the nominator;

    (b) the nominator's signature is witnessed by a prescribed person;

    (c) the prescribed person certifies that, in the opinion of the prescribed person, the nominator—

        (i)   understands the effect of revoking the appointment of a person as named person; and

        (ii)   has not been subjected to any undue influence in making the revocation.

(5)   The nomination of a named person shall be effective notwithstanding the nominator's becoming, after making the nomination, incapable.

(6)   A person nominated under subsection (1) above may decline to be the nominator's named person by giving notice to—

    (a) the nominator; and

    (b) the local authority for the area in which the nominator resides,

to that effect.

(7)   In this section—

"incapable" means incapable by reason of mental disorder or of inability to communicate because of physical disability; but a person shall not fall within this definition by reason only of a lack or deficiency in a faculty of communication if that lack or deficiency can be made good by human or mechanical aid (whether of an interpretative nature or otherwise); and

"prescribed person" means a person of a class prescribed by regulations.

251   **Named person where no person nominated or nominated person declines to act**

(1)   Subject to subsections (2) to (5) below, where, in the case of a person who has attained the age of 16 years, there is no person who is by virtue of section 250 of this Act the person's named person, the person's primary carer shall, unless the person's primary carer has not attained the age of 16 years, be the person's named person.

(2)   Where a person's primary carer has not attained the age of 16 years, but the person has a carer who has attained that age, that carer shall be the person's named person.

(3)   Where—

    (a) a person does not have a primary carer; or

    (b) a person's primary carer has not attained the age of 16 years,

but the person has two or more carers who have attained the age of 16 years, those carers may agree which of them is to be the named person of the person.

176   *Mental Health (Care and Treatment) (Scotland) Act 2003 (asp 13)*
Part 17—Patient representation etc.
Chapter 1—Named person

(4)   Where, by virtue of subsection (2) or (3) above, a carer is a person's named person, the references in subsections (5) and (6) below to a person's primary carer shall be construed as references to that carer.

(5)   If—

    (a)   the person has no primary carer; or

    (b)   the person's primary carer declines in accordance with subsection (6) below to be the person's named person,

the person's nearest relative shall be the person's named person.

(6)   A person's primary carer declines in accordance with this subsection to be the person's named person by giving notice to—

    (a)   the person; and

    (b)   the local authority for the area in which the person resides,

to that effect.

252   Named person in relation to child

(1)   The named person of a person who has not attained the age of 16 years ("the child") shall be—

    (a)   subject to subsection (2) below, in a case where a person who has attained the age of 16 years has parental rights and parental responsibilities in relation to the child, that person;

    (b)   in a case where the child is in the care of a local authority by virtue of a care order made under section 31 of the Children Act 1989 (c.41), that authority; or

    (c)   in any other case, where the child's primary carer has attained the age of 16 years, that person.

(2)   Subject to subsection (3) below, where two or more persons who have attained the age of 16 years have parental rights and parental responsibilities in relation to the child, the named person of the child shall be—

    (a)   if those persons agree that one of them is to be the named person of the child, that person; or

    (b)   if those persons do not so agree, the one of them—

        (i)   who provides, on a regular basis, all, or most, of the care for, and support to, the child;

        (ii)   in a case where the child is in hospital, who provided all, or most, of that care for, and support to, the child before the child was admitted to hospital.

(3)   If—

    (a)   one of the persons who has parental rights and parental responsibilities in relation to the child is a local authority; and

    (b)   the local authority has those rights and responsibilities by virtue of an order under section 86(1) of the Children (Scotland) Act 1995 (c.36) (orders transferring parental rights and parental responsibilities),

the local authority shall be the child's named person.

Mental Health (Care and Treatment) (Scotland) Act 2003 (asp 13)
Part 17—Patient representation etc.
Chapter 1—Named person

177

(4) In this section—

"parental responsibilities", in relation to a child, has the meaning given by section 1(3) of the Children (Scotland) Act 1995 (c.36); and

"parental rights", in relation to a child, has the meaning given by section 2(4) of that Act.

253 Declaration in relation to named person

(1) Subject to subsection (4) below and to section 257 of this Act, where a person who has attained the age of 16 years ("the declarer") makes a declaration in writing in accordance with subsection (2) below stating that a person specified in the declaration shall not be the declarer's named person, that person shall not be the declarer's named person.

(2) A declaration is made in accordance with this subsection if—

   (a) signed by the declarer; and

   (b) witnessed by a prescribed person who certifies that, in the opinion of the prescribed person, the declarer—

      (i) understands the effect of making the declaration; and

      (ii) has not been subjected to any undue influence in making the declaration.

(3) A declaration under this section shall be effective notwithstanding the individual's becoming, after making the declaration, incapable.

(4) A declaration under subsection (1) above may be revoked by the declarer in accordance with subsection (5) below.

(5) A declaration is revoked in accordance with this subsection if the revocation is—

   (a) signed by the declarer; and

   (b) witnessed by a prescribed person who shall certify that, in the opinion of the prescribed person, the declarer—

      (i) understands the effect of revoking the declaration; and

      (ii) has not been subjected to any undue influence in making the revocation.

(6) In this section, "incapable" and "prescribed person" have the same meaning as in section 250 of this Act.

254 Meaning of "nearest relative"

(1) In this Act, "nearest relative", in relation to a person (the "relevant person"), means—

   (a) subject to subsection (3) below, in a case where only one person falls within the list set out in subsection (2) below, that person;

   (b) subject to subsections (3) and (4) below, in a case where two or more persons fall within that list, the person falling within the paragraph first appearing in the list set out in subsection (2) below.

(2) The list mentioned in subsection (1) above is—

   (a) the relevant person's spouse;

178   *Mental Health (Care and Treatment) (Scotland) Act 2003 (asp 13)*
Part 17—Patient representation etc.
Chapter 1—Named person

(b) a person such as is mentioned in subsection (7) below;

(c) the relevant person's child;

(d) the relevant person's parent;

(e) the relevant person's brother or sister;

(f) the relevant person's grandparent;

(g) the relevant person's grandchild;

(h) the relevant person's uncle or aunt;

(i) the relevant person's niece or nephew;

(j) the person mentioned in subsection (8) below.

(3)   If the relevant person's spouse—

(a) is permanently separated (either by agreement or under an order of a court) from the relevant person; or

(b) has deserted, or has been deserted by, the relevant person and the desertion continues,

subsection (2)(a) above shall be disregarded for the purposes of subsection (1) above.

(4)   Where two or more persons fall within the paragraph first appearing on the list set out in subsection (2) above, the nearest relative shall be—

(a) if those persons agree that one of them should be the nearest relative, that person; or

(b) if those persons do not so agree, the person determined in accordance with the following rules—

(i)   brothers and sisters of the whole blood shall be preferred over brothers and sisters of the half-blood; and

(ii) the elder or eldest, as the case may be, shall be preferred.

(5)   A relevant person's nearest relative may decline to be the named person of the relevant person by giving notice to—

(a) the relevant person; and

(b) the local authority for the area in which the relevant person resides,

to that effect.

(6)   For the purposes of subsection (2) above—

(a) a relationship of the half-blood shall, subject to subsection (4)(b)(i) above, be treated as a relationship of the whole blood;

(b) the stepchild of a person shall be treated as the child of that person;

(c) if the relevant person is ordinarily resident in the United Kingdom, the Channel Islands or the Isle of Man, any person who is not so resident shall be disregarded; and

(d) any person who is under 16 years of age shall be disregarded.

(7)   The person referred to in subsection (2)(b) above is a person who—

Mental Health (Care and Treatment) (Scotland) Act 2003 (asp 13)   179
Part 17—Patient representation etc.
Chapter 1—Named person

     (a) is living with the relevant person—

        (i)   as husband and wife; or

        (ii) in a relationship which has the characteristics of the relationship between husband and wife except that the person and the relevant person are of the same sex; and

     (b) has been living with the relevant person for a period of at least 6 months or, if the relevant person is for the time being in hospital, had been living with the relevant person for such period when the relevant person was admitted to hospital.

(8)   The person referred to in subsection (2)(j) above is a person who—

     (a) is living with the relevant person and has been living with the relevant person for a period of at least 5 years; or

     (b) if the relevant person is in hospital, had been living with the relevant person for such period when the relevant person was admitted to hospital.

Mental health officer's duties etc.

255   Named person: mental health officer's duties etc.

(1)   Subsection (2) below applies where—

     (a) a mental health officer is discharging any function by virtue of this Act or the 1995 Act in relation to a patient; and

     (b) it is necessary for the purposes of the discharge of the function to establish whether the patient has a named person.

(2)   The mental health officer shall take such steps as are reasonably practicable—

     (a) to establish whether the patient has a named person; and

     (b) if so, to ascertain who that person is.

(3)   Subsection (4) below applies where the mental health officer—

     (a) establishes that the patient does not have a named person; or

     (b) is unable to establish whether the patient has a named person.

(4)   The mental health officer—

     (a) shall make a record of the steps taken under subsection (2)(a) above; and

     (b) may apply to the Tribunal for an order under section 257 of this Act.

(5)   Where the mental health officer makes a record under subsection (4)(a) above, the mental health officer shall, as soon as practicable, give a copy of the record to—

     (a) the Tribunal; and

     (b) the Commission.

(6)   Where by virtue of subsection (2) above—

     (a) the mental health officer—

        (i)   establishes that the patient has a named person; and

        (ii) ascertains the name of that person ("the apparent named person"); but

180   *Mental Health (Care and Treatment) (Scotland) Act 2003 (asp 13)*
Part 17—Patient representation etc.
Chapter 1—Named person

    (b) the mental health officer considers that it is inappropriate for the apparent named person to be the patient's named person,

the mental health officer shall apply to the Tribunal for an order under section 257 of this Act.

(7)   Where—

    (a) a mental health officer is discharging any function by virtue of this Act in relation to a patient; and

    (b) it appears to the mental health officer—

        (i)   that the patient does not have a named person; or

        (ii) that the patient has a named person ("the apparent named person") but the mental health officer considers that it is inappropriate for the apparent named person to be the patient's named person,

the mental health officer may apply to the Tribunal for an order under section 257 of this Act.

Applications to Tribunal by patient etc.

256   **Named person: application by patient etc.**

(1)   Where—

    (a) it appears to a person mentioned in subsection (2) below (any such person being referred to in this section as "the applicant") that a patient does not have a named person;

    (b) the applicant considers that though the patient has a named person it is inappropriate that that person be the patient's named person; or

    (c) circumstances of such description as may be prescribed by regulations exist,

the applicant may apply to the Tribunal for an order under section 257 of this Act in relation to the patient.

(2)   Those persons are—

    (a) the patient;

    (b) the patient's responsible medical officer;

    (c) if the patient is a child, any person who has parental responsibilities in relation to the patient;

    (d) if the patient is in hospital, the managers of the hospital;

    (e) any welfare attorney of the patient;

    (f) any guardian of the patient;

    (g) any relative of the patient; and

    (h) any other person having an interest in the welfare of the patient.

(3)   In subsection (2)(c) above, "child" and "parental responsibilities" have the same meanings as they have in Part I of the Children (Scotland) Act 1995 (c.36).

Mental Health (Care and Treatment) (Scotland) Act 2003 (asp 13)
Part 17—Patient representation etc.
Chapter 2—Advocacy etc.

181

Tribunal's powers

257   Named person: Tribunal's powers

(1)   Where—

    (a) an application is made under section 255(4)(b) or (7)(b)(i) or 256(1)(a) of this Act; and

    (b) the Tribunal is satisfied that the patient does not have a named person,

the Tribunal may, subject to subsection (4) below, make an order appointing the person specified in the order to be the patient's named person.

(2)   Where—

    (a) an application is made under section 255(6) or (7)(b)(ii) or 256(1)(b) of this Act; and

    (b) the Tribunal is satisfied that it is inappropriate for the named person ("the acting named person") to be the patient's named person,

the Tribunal may, subject to subsection (4) below, make an order declaring that the acting named person is not the named person or appointing the person specified in the order to be the patient's named person in place of the acting named person.

(3)   Where an application is made under section 256(1)(c) of this Act, the Tribunal may, subject to subsection (4) below, make such order as it thinks fit.

(4)   It shall not be competent for the Tribunal to make an order under this section appointing a person who has not attained the age of 16 years to be a patient's named person.

Interpretation of Chapter

258   Interpretation of Chapter

In this Chapter, other than section 252, "person" means a natural person.

CHAPTER 2

ADVOCACY ETC.

Advocacy

259   Advocacy

(1)   Every person with a mental disorder shall have a right of access to independent advocacy; and accordingly it is the duty of—

    (a) each local authority, in collaboration with the (or each) relevant Health Board; and

    (b) each Health Board, in collaboration with the (or each) relevant local authority,

to secure the availability, to persons in its area who have a mental disorder, of independent advocacy services and to take appropriate steps to ensure that those persons have the opportunity of making use of those services.

(2)   Each relevant Health Board and local authority shall, for the purposes of subsection (1) above, collaborate with the local authority or, as the case may be, Health Board in relation to which it is the relevant Board or authority.

182 *Mental Health (Care and Treatment) (Scotland) Act 2003 (asp 13)*
Part 17—Patient representation etc.
Chapter 2—Advocacy etc.

(3)   For the purposes of subsections (1) and (2) above—

  (a)   a Health Board is, in relation to a local authority, a "relevant" Health Board if its area or part of its area is the same as or is included in the area of the local authority; and

  (b)   a local authority is, in relation to a Health Board, a "relevant" local authority if its area or part of its area is the same as or is included in the area of the Health Board.

(4)   In subsection (1) above, "advocacy services" are services of support and representation made available for the purpose of enabling the person to whom they are available to have as much control of, or capacity to influence, that person's care and welfare as is, in the circumstances, appropriate.

(5)   For the purposes of subsection (1) above, advocacy services are "independent" if they are to be provided by a person who is none of the following—

  (a)   a local authority;

  (b)   a Health Board;

  (c)   a National Health Service trust;

  (d)   a member of—

    (i)   the local authority;

    (ii)   the Health Board;

    (iii) a National Health Service trust,

  in the area of which the person to whom those services are made available is to be provided with them;

  (e)   a person who—

    (i)   in pursuance of arrangements made between that person and a Health Board, is giving medical treatment to;

    (ii)   in pursuance of those arrangements, is providing, under the National Health Service (Scotland) Act 1978 (c.29), treatment, care or services for; or

    (iii) in pursuance of arrangements made between that person and a local authority, is providing, under Part II of the Social Work (Scotland) Act 1968 (c.49) (promotion of social welfare) or any of the enactments specified in section 5(1B) of that Act, services for,

  the person to whom the advocacy services are made available;

  (f)   in relation to a patient detained in a state hospital or a person who (by virtue of any of the means specified in subsection (11)(b) below) is no longer detained there, the State Hospitals Board for Scotland or a member of that Board.

(6)   In subsection (5)(d) above the reference to the area of a National Health Service trust is a reference to the Health Board area in which the trust discharges its functions.

(7)   It is the duty of the State Hospitals Board for Scotland (the "State Hospitals Board") to secure the availability to persons who are patients detained in a state hospital of the services referred to in subsection (1) above and, in relation to those persons, to take the steps there referred to.

(8)   It is the duty of—

Mental Health (Care and Treatment) (Scotland) Act 2003 (asp 13)
Part 17—Patient representation etc.
Chapter 2—Advocacy etc.

183

(a) the State Hospitals Board, in collaboration with each relevant local authority and Health Board; and

(b) each relevant local authority and Health Board, in collaboration with the State Hospitals Board,

to secure the availability to relevant persons of the services referred to in subsection (1) above, and, in relation to those persons, to take the steps there referred to.

(9) Each relevant local authority and Health Board shall, for the purposes of subsection (8)(a) above, collaborate with the State Hospitals Board and with each other.

(10) The State Hospitals Board shall, for the purposes of subsection (8)(b) above, collaborate with each relevant local authority and Health Board.

(11) For the purposes of subsections (8) to (10) above—

(a) a local authority or Health Board is a relevant local authority or, as the case may be, Health Board if there is residing in its area a relevant person;

(b) a relevant person is a person with a mental disorder who, having been detained as a patient in a state hospital, is (by virtue of section 127 or 193(7) of this Act) no longer detained there.

Information

260   Provision of information to patient

(1) This section applies where a patient—

(a) is detained in hospital by virtue of—

(i)   this Act; or

(ii)   the 1995 Act; or

(b) though not detained in hospital, is subject to—

(i)   an emergency detention certificate;

(ii)   a short-term detention certificate;

(iii)   a compulsory treatment order;

(iv)   an interim compulsory treatment order;

(v)   an assessment order;

(vi)   a treatment order;

(vii) a hospital direction;

(viii) a transfer for treatment direction;

(ix)   an interim compulsion order; or

(x)   a compulsion order.

(2) The appropriate person shall—

(a) take all reasonable steps—

(i)   to ensure that the patient understands the relevant matters at each of the times mentioned in subsection (3) below;

184   *Mental Health (Care and Treatment) (Scotland) Act 2003 (asp 13)*
Part 17—Patient representation etc.
Chapter 2—Advocacy etc.

     (ii) to ensure that the patient is supplied with material appropriate to the patient's needs (and in a form that is appropriate to those needs and permanent) from which the patient may refresh the patient's understanding of those matters; and

     (iii) to inform the patient of the availability under section 259 of this Act of independent advocacy services at each of those times; and

   (b) take appropriate steps to ensure that the patient has the opportunity of making use of those services.

(3) Those times are—

   (a) as soon as practicable after—

     (i) where the patient is detained in hospital, the beginning of such detention; or

     (ii) where the patient is not so detained, the making of the order;

   (b) as soon as practicable after any occasion on which the patient reasonably requests to be informed of those matters; and

   (c) such other times as may be prescribed by regulations.

(4) Where material is supplied to the patient under subsection (2)(a)(ii) above, the appropriate person shall, as soon as practicable after such material is supplied, take all reasonable steps to ensure that the patient's named person is supplied with a copy of such material in a form that is appropriate to the person's needs.

(5) In this section—

   "the appropriate person" means—

   (a) where the patient is detained in hospital, the managers of the hospital;

   (b) where by virtue of a certificate granted under any provision of this Act, the authorisation to detain the patient in a hospital is suspended, the managers of the hospital in which, but for the certificate, the patient would be authorised to be detained;

   (c) in any other case, the managers of the hospital specified in the order; and

   "the relevant matters" means—

   (a) the provision of this Act or the 1995 Act by virtue of which—

     (i) the patient is being detained; or

     (ii) the order has effect;

   (b) the consequences of the operation of that provision;

   (c) the powers that the patient's responsible medical officer and the Tribunal each has in relation to revoking that provision;

   (d) any right to make an application, or appeal, to the Tribunal that the patient has by virtue of that provision;

   (e) the powers exercisable by the Tribunal in the event of any such right being exercised;

   (f) how the patient may exercise any such right;

Mental Health (Care and Treatment) (Scotland) Act 2003 (asp 13)
Part 17—Patient representation etc.
Chapter 2—Advocacy etc.

185

(g) the functions that the Commission has that appear to be relevant to the patient's case;

(h) how the patient may obtain legal assistance as respects any such right.

261   Provision of assistance to patient with communication difficulties

(1) This section applies where—

(a) a patient is detained in hospital by virtue of—

(i) this Act; or

(ii) the 1995 Act; or

(b) though not detained in hospital, a patient is subject to—

(i) an emergency detention certificate;

(ii) a short-term detention certificate;

(iii) a compulsory treatment order;

(iv) an interim compulsory treatment order;

(v) an assessment order;

(vi) a treatment order;

(vii) a hospital direction;

(viii) a transfer for treatment direction;

(ix) an interim compulsion order; or

(x) a compulsion order,

and the patient has difficulty in communicating or generally communicates in a language other than English.

(2) The appropriate person shall take all reasonable steps to secure that, for the purpose of enabling the patient to communicate during each of the events mentioned in subsection (3) below—

(a) arrangements appropriate to the patient's needs are made; or

(b) the patient is provided with assistance, or material, appropriate to the patient's needs.

(3) Those events are—

(a) any medical examination of the patient carried out for the purpose of assessing the patient's mental disorder;

(b) any review under this Act or the 1995 Act of the patient's detention; or

(c) any proceedings before the Tribunal relating to the patient.

(4) As soon as practicable after taking any steps under subsection (2) above, the appropriate person shall make a written record of the steps.

(5) In this section "the appropriate person" has the meaning given by section 260(5) of this Act.

186   *Mental Health (Care and Treatment) (Scotland) Act 2003 (asp 13)*
Part 17—Patient representation etc.
Chapter 2—Advocacy etc.

Access to medical practitioner

262   Access to medical practitioner for purposes of medical examination

(1)   This section applies where a patient is detained in hospital by virtue of—

    (a)   this Act; or

    (b)   the 1995 Act.

(2)   A duly authorised medical practitioner may, for any of the purposes mentioned in subsection (3) below, visit the patient at any reasonable hour and carry out a medical examination of the patient in private.

(3)   Those purposes are—

    (a)   advising the patient or, as the case may be, the patient's named person about the making of applications to the Tribunal in respect of the patient under this Act; and

    (b)   providing to the patient or, as the case may be, the patient's named person information as respects the condition of the patient for the purpose of—

        (i)   any such application (or proposed application); or

        (ii)   any other proceedings before the Tribunal in respect of the patient in which the patient or, as the case may be, the patient's named person is taking part (or considering whether to take part).

(4)   For the purposes of subsection (2) above and subject to subsection (5) below, a medical practitioner is duly authorised if authorised for the purposes of this section by—

    (a)   the patient; or

    (b)   the patient's named person.

(5)   Authorisation given for the purposes of this section by the patient's named person may be rescinded by the patient at any time when the patient is not incapable.

(6)   In subsection (5) above, "incapable" has the same meaning as in section 250(7) of this Act.

263   Inspection of records by medical practitioner

(1)   A duly authorised medical practitioner may, for any of the purposes mentioned in subsection (3) below, require any person holding records relating to—

    (a)   the detention of; or

    (b)   medical treatment given at any time to,

a patient whose detention in hospital is authorised by virtue of this Act or the 1995 Act to produce them for inspection by the medical practitioner.

(2)   A duly authorised medical practitioner may, for any of the purposes mentioned in subsection (3) below, require any person holding records relating to medical treatment given at any time to a patient who is subject to—

    (a)   a compulsory treatment order; or

    (b)   a compulsion order,

that does not authorise the detention of the patient in hospital to produce them for inspection by the medical practitioner.

Mental Health (Care and Treatment) (Scotland) Act 2003 (asp 13)
Part 17—Patient representation etc.
Chapter 3—Detention in conditions of excessive security

187

(3) Those purposes are—

    (a) advising the patient or, as the case may be, the patient's named person about the making of applications to the Tribunal in respect of the patient under this Act;

    (b) providing to the patient or, as the case may be, the patient's named person information as respects the condition of the patient for the purpose of—

        (i) any such application (or proposed application); or

        (ii) any other proceedings before the Tribunal in respect of the patient in which the patient or, as the case may be, the patient's named person is taking part (or considering whether to take part).

(4) For the purposes of subsections (1) and (2) above and subject to subsection (5) below, a medical practitioner is duly authorised if authorised for the purposes of this section by—

    (a) the patient; or

    (b) the patient's named person.

(5) Authorisation given for the purposes of this section by the patient's named person may be rescinded by the patient at any time when the patient is not incapable.

(6) In subsection (5) above, "incapable" has the same meaning as in section 250(7) of this Act.

CHAPTER 3

DETENTION IN CONDITIONS OF EXCESSIVE SECURITY

State hospitals

264 Detention in conditions of excessive security: state hospitals

(1) This section applies where a patient's detention in a state hospital is authorised by—

    (a) a compulsory treatment order;

    (b) a compulsion order;

    (c) a hospital direction; or

    (d) a transfer for treatment direction;

and whether or not a certificate under section 127(1) (either as enacted or as applied by section 179(1) of this Act) or 224(2) of this Act has effect in relation to the patient.

(2) On the application of any of the persons mentioned in subsection (6) below, the Tribunal may, if satisfied that the patient does not require to be detained under conditions of special security that can be provided only in a state hospital, make an order—

    (a) declaring that the patient is being detained in conditions of excessive security; and

    (b) specifying a period, not exceeding 3 months and beginning with the making of the order, during which the duties under subsections (3) to (5) below shall be performed.

(3) Where the Tribunal makes an order under subsection (2) above in respect of a relevant patient, the relevant Health Board shall identify a hospital—

    (a) which is not a state hospital;

188   *Mental Health (Care and Treatment) (Scotland) Act 2003 (asp 13)*
Part 17—Patient representation etc.
Chapter 3—Detention in conditions of excessive security

      (b)   which the Board and the Scottish Ministers, and its managers if they are not the Board, agree is a hospital in which the patient could be detained in appropriate conditions; and

      (c)   in which accommodation is available for the patient.

(4)   Where the Tribunal makes an order under subsection (2) above in respect of a patient who is not a relevant patient, the relevant Health Board shall identify a hospital—

      (a)   which is not a state hospital;

      (b)   which the Board considers, and its managers if they are not the Board agree, is a hospital in which the patient could be detained in appropriate conditions; and

      (c)   in which accommodation is available for the patient.

(5)   Where the Tribunal makes an order under subsection (2) above in respect of a patient, the relevant Health Board shall, as soon as practicable after identifying a hospital under subsection (3) or, as the case may be, (4) above, give notice to the managers of the state hospital of the name of the hospital so identified.

(6)   The persons referred to in subsection (2) above are—

      (a)   the patient;

      (b)   the patient's named person;

      (c)   any guardian of the patient;

      (d)   any welfare attorney of the patient; and

      (e)   the Commission.

(7)   An application may not be made under subsection (2) above—

      (a)   if the compulsory treatment order that authorises the patient's detention in hospital has not been extended;

      (b)   during the period of 6 months beginning with the making of the compulsion order that authorises the patient's detention in hospital; or

      (c)   before the expiry of the period of 6 months beginning with the making of—

          (i)   the hospital direction; or

          (ii)   the transfer for treatment direction,

      that authorises the patient's detention in hospital.

(8)   No more than one application may be made under subsection (2) above in respect of the same patient—

      (a)   during the period of 12 months beginning with the day on which the order, or direction, authorising the patient's detention in hospital is made;

      (b)   during any subsequent period of 12 months that begins with, or with an anniversary of, the expiry of the period mentioned in paragraph (a) above.

(9)   Before determining an application under subsection (2) above, the Tribunal shall—

      (a)   afford the persons mentioned in subsection (10) below the opportunity—

          (i)   of making representations (whether orally or in writing); and

          (ii)   of leading, or producing, evidence; and

Mental Health (Care and Treatment) (Scotland) Act 2003 (asp 13)
Part 17—Patient representation etc.
Chapter 3—Detention in conditions of excessive security

189

(b) whether or not any such representations are made, hold a hearing.

(10) Those persons are—

(a) the patient;

(b) the patient's named person;

(c) the relevant Health Board;

(d) the patient's responsible medical officer;

(e) the managers of the state hospital in which the patient is detained;

(f) the mental health officer;

(g) any guardian of the patient;

(h) any welfare attorney of the patient;

(i) any curator *ad litem* appointed by the Tribunal in respect of the patient;

(j) the Commission;

(k) in the case of a relevant patient, the Scottish Ministers; and

(l) any other person appearing to the Tribunal to have an interest in the application.

265   Order under section 264: further provision

(1) This section applies where—

(a) an order is made under section 264(2) of this Act in respect of a patient; and

(b) the order is not recalled under section 267 of this Act;

and whether or not a certificate under section 127(1) (either as enacted or as applied by section 179(1) of this Act) or 224(2) of this Act has effect in relation to the patient.

(2) If the relevant Health Board fails, during the period specified in the order, to give notice to the Tribunal that the patient has been transferred to another hospital, there shall be a hearing before the Tribunal.

(3) Where such a hearing is held, the Tribunal may, if satisfied that the patient does not require to be detained under conditions of special security that can be provided only in a state hospital, make an order—

(a) declaring that the patient is being detained in conditions of excessive security; and

(b) specifying—

(i) a period of 28 days; or

(ii) such longer period not exceeding 3 months as the Tribunal thinks fit,

beginning with the day on which the order is made during which the duties under subsections (4) to (6) below shall be performed.

(4) Where the Tribunal makes an order under subsection (3) above in respect of a relevant patient, the relevant Health Board shall identify a hospital—

(a) which is not a state hospital;

190   *Mental Health (Care and Treatment) (Scotland) Act 2003 (asp 13)*
Part 17—Patient representation etc.
Chapter 3—Detention in conditions of excessive security

(b) which the Board and the Scottish Ministers, and its managers if they are not the Board, agree is a hospital in which the patient could be detained in appropriate conditions; and

(c) in which accommodation is available for the patient.

(5) Where the Tribunal makes an order under subsection (3) above in respect of a patient who is not a relevant patient, the relevant Health Board shall identify a hospital—

(a) which is not a state hospital;

(b) which the Board considers, and its managers if they are not the Board agree, is a hospital in which the patient could be detained in appropriate conditions; and

(c) in which accommodation is available for the patient.

(6) Where the Tribunal makes an order under subsection (3) above in respect of a patient, the relevant Health Board shall, as soon as practicable after identifying a hospital under subsection (4) or, as the case may be, (5) above, give notice to the managers of the state hospital of the name of the hospital so identified.

(7) Before making an order under subsection (3) above, the Tribunal shall afford the persons mentioned in section 264(10) of this Act the opportunity—

(a) of making representations (whether orally or in writing); and

(b) of leading, or producing, evidence.

266   Order under section 265: further provision

(1) This section applies where—

(a) an order is made under subsection (3) of section 265 of this Act in respect of a patient;

(b) the order specifies the period mentioned in paragraph (b)(ii) of that subsection; and

(c) the order is not recalled under section 267 of this Act;

and whether or not a certificate under section 127(1) (either as enacted or as applied by section 179(1) of this Act) or 224(2) of this Act has effect in relation to the patient.

(2) If the relevant Health Board fails, during the period specified in the order, to give notice to the Tribunal that the patient has been transferred to another hospital, there shall be a hearing before the Tribunal.

(3) Where such a hearing is held, the Tribunal may, if satisfied that the patient does not require to be detained under conditions of special security that can be provided only in a state hospital, make an order—

(a) declaring that the patient is being detained in conditions of excessive security; and

(b) specifying the period of 28 days beginning with the day on which the order is made during which the duties under subsections (4) to (6) below shall be performed.

(4) Where the Tribunal makes an order under subsection (3) above in respect of a relevant patient, the relevant Health Board shall identify a hospital—

(a) which is not a state hospital;

Mental Health (Care and Treatment) (Scotland) Act 2003 (asp 13)
Part 17—Patient representation etc.
Chapter 3—Detention in conditions of excessive security

191

   (b) which the Board and the Scottish Ministers, and its managers if they are not the Board, agree is a hospital in which the patient could be detained in appropriate conditions; and

   (c) in which accommodation is available for the patient.

(5) Where the Tribunal makes an order under subsection (3) above in respect of a patient who is not a relevant patient, the relevant Health Board shall identify a hospital—

   (a) which is not a state hospital;

   (b) which the Board considers, and its managers if they are not the Board agree, is a hospital in which the patient could be detained in appropriate conditions; and

   (c) in which accommodation is available for the patient.

(6) Where the Tribunal makes an order under subsection (3) above in respect of a patient, the relevant Health Board shall, as soon as practicable after identifying a hospital under subsection (4) or, as the case may be, (5) above, give notice to the managers of the state hospital of the name of the hospital so identified.

(7) Before making an order under subsection (3) above, the Tribunal shall afford the persons mentioned in section 264(10) of this Act the opportunity—

   (a) of making representations (whether orally or in writing); and

   (b) of leading, or producing, evidence.

267 Orders under sections 264 to 266: recall

(1) This section applies where an order is made under section 264(2), 265(3) or 266(3) of this Act in respect of a patient.

(2) On the application of any of the persons mentioned in subsection (4) below, the Tribunal—

   (a) shall, if satisfied that the patient requires to be detained under conditions of special security that can be provided only in a state hospital, recall the order;

   (b) may, on any other grounds, recall the order.

(3) Where the order is recalled, the relevant Health Board ceases to be subject to the duties under section 264(3) to (5), 265(4) to (6) or 266(4) to (6) to which it became subject by virtue of the making of the order.

(4) The persons referred to in subsection (2) above are—

   (a) the relevant Health Board;

   (b) in the case of a relevant patient, the Scottish Ministers;

   (c) in the case of a patient who is not a relevant patient, the patient's responsible medical officer.

(5) Before determining an application under subsection (2) above, the Tribunal shall—

   (a) afford the persons mentioned in section 264(10) of this Act the opportunity—

      (i) of making representations (whether orally or in writing); and

      (ii) of leading, or producing, evidence; and

   (b) whether or not any such representations are made, hold a hearing.

192   *Mental Health (Care and Treatment) (Scotland) Act 2003 (asp 13)*
Part 17—Patient representation etc.
Chapter 3—Detention in conditions of excessive security

Other hospitals

268   Detention in conditions of excessive security: hospitals other than state hospitals

(1) This section applies where a qualifying patient's detention in a qualifying hospital is authorised by—

    (a) a compulsory treatment order;

    (b) a compulsion order;

    (c) a hospital direction; or

    (d) a transfer for treatment direction;

and whether or not a certificate under section 127(1) (either as enacted or as applied by section 179(1) of this Act) or 224(2) of this Act has effect in relation to the patient.

(2) On the application of any of the persons mentioned in subsection (6) below, the Tribunal may, if satisfied that detention of the qualifying patient in the qualifying hospital involves the patient being subject to a level of security that is excessive in the patient's case, make an order—

    (a) declaring that the patient is being detained in conditions of excessive security; and

    (b) specifying a period, not exceeding 3 months and beginning with the making of the order, during which the duties under subsections (3) to (5) below shall be performed.

(3) Where the Tribunal makes an order under subsection (2) above in respect of a relevant patient, the relevant Health Board shall identify a hospital—

    (a) which is not a state hospital;

    (b) which the Board and the Scottish Ministers, and its managers if they are not the Board, agree is a hospital in which the patient could be detained in conditions that would not involve the patient being subject to a level of security that is excessive in the patient's case; and

    (c) in which accommodation is available for the patient.

(4) Where the Tribunal makes an order under subsection (2) above in respect of a patient who is not a relevant patient, the relevant Health Board shall identify a hospital—

    (a) which is not a state hospital;

    (b) which the Board considers, and its managers if they are not the Board agree, is a hospital in which the patient could be detained in conditions that would not involve the patient being subject to a level of security that is excessive in the patient's case; and

    (c) in which accommodation is available for the patient.

(5) Where the Tribunal makes an order under subsection (2) above in respect of a patient, the relevant Health Board shall, as soon as practicable after identifying a hospital under subsection (3) or, as the case may be, (4) above, give notice to the managers of the qualifying hospital of the name of the hospital so identified.

(6) The persons referred to in subsection (2) above are—

    (a) the qualifying patient;

    (b) the qualifying patient's named person;

Mental Health (Care and Treatment) (Scotland) Act 2003 (asp 13) 193
Part 17—Patient representation etc.
Chapter 3—Detention in conditions of excessive security

      (c)   any guardian of the qualifying patient;

      (d)   any welfare attorney of the qualifying patient; and

      (e)   the Commission.

(7)   An application may not be made under subsection (2) above—

      (a)   if the compulsory treatment order that authorises the patient's detention in hospital has not been extended;

      (b)   during the period of 6 months beginning with the making of the compulsion order that authorises the patient's detention in hospital; or

      (c)   before the expiry of the period of 6 months beginning with the making of—

           (i)   the hospital direction; or

           (ii)   the transfer for treatment direction,

      that authorises the patient's detention in hospital.

(8)   No more than one application may be made under subsection (2) above in respect of the same patient—

      (a)   during the period of 12 months beginning with the day on which the order, or direction, authorising the patient's detention in hospital is made;

      (b)   during any subsequent period of 12 months that begins with, or with an anniversary of, the expiry of the period mentioned in paragraph (a) above.

(9)   Before determining an application under subsection (2) above, the Tribunal shall—

      (a)   afford the persons mentioned in subsection (10) below the opportunity—

           (i)   of making representations (whether orally or in writing); and

           (ii)   of leading, or producing, evidence; and

      (b)   whether or not any such representations are made, hold a hearing.

(10)   Those persons are—

      (a)   the qualifying patient;

      (b)   the qualifying patient's named person;

      (c)   the relevant Health Board;

      (d)   the qualifying patient's responsible medical officer;

      (e)   the managers of the qualifying hospital;

      (f)   the mental health officer;

      (g)   any guardian of the qualifying patient;

      (h)   any welfare attorney of the qualifying patient;

      (i)   any curator *ad litem* appointed by the Tribunal in respect of the qualifying patient;

      (j)   the Commission;

      (k)   in the case of a relevant patient, the Scottish Ministers; and

      (l)   any other person appearing to the Tribunal to have an interest in the application.

194   *Mental Health (Care and Treatment) (Scotland) Act 2003 (asp 13)*
Part 17—Patient representation etc.
Chapter 3—Detention in conditions of excessive security

(11)   A patient is a "qualifying patient" for the purposes of this section and sections 269 to 271 of this Act if the patient is of a description specified in regulations.

(12)   A hospital is a "qualifying hospital" for the purposes of this section and sections 269 to 271 of this Act if—

      (a) it is not a state hospital; and

      (b) it is specified, or of a description specified, in regulations.

(13)   Regulations under subsection (11) or (12) above may in particular have the effect—

      (a) that "qualifying patient" means a patient;

      (b) that "qualifying hospital" means—

          (i)   a hospital other than a state hospital; or

          (ii)   a part of a hospital.

(14)   Regulations may make provision as to when for the purposes of this section and sections 269 to 271 of this Act a patient's detention in a hospital is to be taken as involving the patient being subject to a level of security that is excessive in the patient's case.

269   Order under section 268: further provision

(1)   This section applies where—

      (a) an order is made under section 268(2) of this Act in respect of a qualifying patient; and

      (b) the order is not recalled under section 271 of this Act;

    and whether or not a certificate under section 127(1) (either as enacted or as applied by section 179(1) of this Act) or 224(2) of this Act has effect in relation to the patient.

(2)   If the relevant Health Board fails, during the period specified in the order, to give notice to the Tribunal that the qualifying patient has been transferred to another hospital, there shall be a hearing before the Tribunal.

(3)   Where such a hearing is held, the Tribunal may, if satisfied that detention of the patient in the qualifying hospital involves the patient being subject to a level of security that is excessive in the patient's case, make an order—

      (a) declaring that the patient is being detained in conditions of excessive security; and

      (b) specifying—

          (i)   a period of 28 days; or

          (ii)   such longer period not exceeding 3 months as the Tribunal thinks fit,

         beginning with the day on which the order is made during which the duties under subsections (4) to (6) below shall be performed.

(4)   Where the Tribunal makes an order under subsection (3) above in respect of a relevant patient, the relevant Health Board shall identify a hospital—

      (a) which is not a state hospital;

Mental Health (Care and Treatment) (Scotland) Act 2003 (asp 13)
Part 17—Patient representation etc.
Chapter 3—Detention in conditions of excessive security

195

(b) which the Board and the Scottish Ministers, and its managers if they are not the Board, agree is a hospital in which the patient could be detained in conditions that would not involve the patient being subject to a level of security that is excessive in the patient's case; and

(c) in which accommodation is available for the patient.

(5) Where the Tribunal makes an order under subsection (3) above in respect of a patient who is not a relevant patient, the relevant Health Board shall identify a hospital—

(a) which is not a state hospital;

(b) which the Board considers, and its managers if they are not the Board agree, is a hospital in which the patient could be detained in conditions that would not involve the patient being subject to a level of security that is excessive in the patient's case; and

(c) in which accommodation is available for the patient.

(6) Where the Tribunal makes an order under subsection (3) above in respect of a patient, the relevant Health Board shall, as soon as practicable after identifying a hospital under subsection (4) or, as the case may be, (5) above, give notice to the managers of the qualifying hospital of the name of the hospital so identified.

(7) Before making an order under subsection (3) above, the Tribunal shall afford the persons mentioned in section 268(10) of this Act the opportunity—

(a) of making representations (whether orally or in writing); and

(b) of leading, or producing, evidence.

270 Order under section 269: further provision

(1) This section applies where—

(a) an order is made under subsection (3) of section 269 of this Act in respect of a qualifying patient;

(b) the order specifies the period mentioned in paragraph (b)(ii) of that subsection; and

(c) the order is not recalled under section 271 of this Act;

and whether or not a certificate under section 127(1) (either as enacted or as applied by section 179(1) of this Act) or 224(2) of this Act has effect in relation to the patient.

(2) If the relevant Health Board fails, during the period specified in the order, to give notice to the Tribunal that the qualifying patient has been transferred to another hospital, there shall be a hearing before the Tribunal.

(3) Where such a hearing is held, the Tribunal may, if satisfied that detention of the patient in the qualifying hospital involves the patient being subject to a level of security that is excessive in the patient's case, make an order—

(a) declaring that the patient is being detained in conditions of excessive security; and

(b) specifying the period of 28 days beginning with the day on which the order is made during which the duties under subsections (4) to (6) below shall be performed.

196   *Mental Health (Care and Treatment) (Scotland) Act 2003 (asp 13)*
Part 17—Patient representation etc.
Chapter 3—Detention in conditions of excessive security

(4)   Where the Tribunal makes an order under subsection (3) above in respect of a relevant patient, the relevant Health Board shall identify a hospital—

    (a)   which is not a state hospital;

    (b)   which the Board and the Scottish Ministers, and its managers if they are not the Board, agree is a hospital in which the patient could be detained in conditions that would not involve the patient being subject to a level of security that is excessive in the patient's case; and

    (c)   in which accommodation is available for the patient.

(5)   Where the Tribunal makes an order under subsection (3) above in respect of a patient who is not a relevant patient, the relevant Health Board shall identify a hospital—

    (a)   which is not a state hospital;

    (b)   which the Board considers, and its managers if they are not the Board agree, is a hospital in which the patient could be detained in conditions that would not involve the patient being subject to a level of security that is excessive in the patient's case; and

    (c)   in which accommodation is available for the patient.

(6)   Where the Tribunal makes an order under subsection (3) above in respect of a patient, the relevant Health Board shall, as soon as practicable after identifying a hospital under subsection (4) or, as the case may be, (5) above, give notice to the managers of the qualifying hospital of the name of the hospital so identified.

(7)   Before making an order under subsection (3) above, the Tribunal shall afford the persons mentioned in section 268(10) of this Act the opportunity—

    (a)   of making representations (whether orally or in writing); and

    (b)   of leading, or producing, evidence.

271   Orders under sections 268 to 270: recall

(1)   This section applies where an order is made under section 268(2), 269(3) or 270(3) of this Act in respect of a qualifying patient.

(2)   On the application of any of the persons mentioned in subsection (4) below, the Tribunal—

    (a)   shall, if satisfied that detention of the patient in the qualifying hospital does not involve the patient being subject to a level of security that is excessive in the patient's case, recall the order;

    (b)   may, on any other grounds, recall the order.

(3)   Where the order is recalled, the relevant Health Board ceases to be subject to the duties under section 268(3) to (5), 269(4) to (6) or 270(4) to (6) to which it became subject by virtue of the making of the order.

(4)   The persons referred to in subsection (2) above are—

    (a)   the relevant Health Board;

    (b)   in the case of a relevant patient, the Scottish Ministers;

Mental Health (Care and Treatment) (Scotland) Act 2003 (asp 13) 197
Part 17—Patient representation etc.
Chapter 3—Detention in conditions of excessive security

(c) in the case of a patient who is not a relevant patient, the patient's responsible medical officer.

(5) Before determining an application under subsection (2) above, the Tribunal shall—

(a) afford the persons mentioned in section 268(10) of this Act the opportunity—

(i) of making representations (whether orally or in writing); and

(ii) of leading, or producing, evidence; and

(b) whether or not any such representations are made, hold a hearing.

Enforcement: civil proceedings

272   Proceedings for specific performance of statutory duty

(1) The duties imposed by virtue of—

(a) an order under section 264(2) of this Act;

(b) an order under subsection (3) of section 265 of this Act which specifies the period mentioned in paragraph (b)(ii) of that subsection;

(c) an order under section 268(2) of this Act; or

(d) an order under subsection (3) of section 269 of this Act which specifies the period mentioned in paragraph (b)(ii) of that subsection,

shall not be enforceable by proceedings for specific performance of a statutory duty under section 45(b) of the Court of Session Act 1988 (c.36).

(2) Without prejudice to the rights of any other person, the duties imposed by virtue of—

(a) an order under subsection (3) of section 265 of this Act which specifies the period mentioned in paragraph (b)(i) of that subsection;

(b) an order under section 266(3) of this Act;

(c) an order under subsection (3) of section 269 of this Act which specifies the period mentioned in paragraph (b)(i) of that subsection; or

(d) an order under section 270(3) of this Act,

shall be enforceable by proceedings by the Commission for specific performance of a statutory duty under section 45(b) of that Act of 1988.

Interpretation of Chapter

273   Interpretation of Chapter

In this Chapter—

"relevant Health Board" means, in relation to a patient of such description as may be specified in regulations, the Health Board, or Special Health Board—

(a) of such description as may be so specified; or

(b) determined under such regulations; and

"relevant patient" means—

(a) in sections 264 to 267 of this Act—

      (i)   a patient whose detention in hospital is authorised by a compulsion order and who is also subject to a restriction order; or

      (ii)   a patient whose detention in hospital is authorised by a hospital direction or a transfer for treatment direction;

  (b)   in sections 268 to 271 of this Act—

      (i)   a qualifying patient whose detention in hospital is authorised by a compulsion order and who is also subject to a restriction order; or

      (ii)   a qualifying patient whose detention in hospital is authorised by a hospital direction or a transfer for treatment direction.

PART 18

MISCELLANEOUS

Code of practice

274   Code of practice

(1)   The Scottish Ministers shall, in accordance with this section, draw up, give effect to and publish a code of practice giving guidance to any person discharging functions by virtue of this Act as to—

  (a)   the discharge of such of those functions; and

  (b)   such matters arising in connection with the discharge of those functions,

as they think fit.

(2)   The Scottish Ministers shall, before giving effect to a code of practice drawn up under subsection (1) above—

  (a)   consult such persons as they think fit; and

  (b)   lay a draft of the code before the Scottish Parliament.

(3)   A code of practice drawn up under subsection (1) above shall be given effect by being—

  (a)   confirmed by order made; and

  (b)   brought into force on a day appointed,

by the Scottish Ministers.

(4)   Any person discharging functions by virtue of this Act shall have regard (so far as they are applicable to the discharge of those functions by that person) to the provisions of any code of practice published under subsection (1) above for the time being in force.

(5)   The references in subsections (1) and (4) above to a person discharging functions by virtue of this Act do not include references to—

  (a)   any court;

  (b)   the Tribunal; and

  (c)   the Commission.

(6)   The Scottish Ministers may, from time to time, revise the whole or part of any code of practice published under subsection (1) above; and if a code is so revised, the Scottish Ministers shall publish the revised code.

(7)   Subsections (2) to (6) above apply to a code of practice revised under subsection (6) above as they apply to a code of practice published under subsection (1) above.

Advance statements

275   Advance statements: making and withdrawal

(1)   An "advance statement" is a statement complying with subsection (2) below and specifying—

    (a)   the ways the person making it wishes to be treated for mental disorder;

    (b)   the ways the person wishes not to be so treated,

in the event of the person's becoming mentally disordered and the person's ability to make decisions about the matters referred to in paragraphs (a) and (b) above being, because of that, significantly impaired.

(2)   An advance statement complies with this subsection if—

    (a)   at the time of making it, the person has the capacity of properly intending the wishes specified in it;

    (b)   it is in writing;

    (c)   it is subscribed by the person making it;

    (d)   that person's subscription of it is witnessed by a person (the "witness") who is within the class of persons prescribed by regulations for the purposes of this paragraph and who signs the statement as a witness to that subscription; and

    (e)   the witness certifies in writing on the document which comprises the statement that, in the witness's opinion, the person making the statement has the capacity referred to in paragraph (a) above.

(3)   An advance statement may be withdrawn by the person who made it by a withdrawal complying with this subsection; and a withdrawal so complies if—

    (a)   at the time of making it the person has the capacity properly to intend to withdraw the statement; and

    (b)   it is made by means of a document which, were it an advance statement, would comply with paragraphs (b) to (e) of subsection (2) above.

276   Advance statements: effect

(1)   If the Tribunal is satisfied as to the matters set out in subsection (2) below, it shall, in making any decision in respect of a patient who is a person who has made and not withdrawn an advance statement, have regard to the wishes specified in the statement.

(2)   Those matters are—

    (a)   that, because of mental disorder, the ability of the person who made the advance statement to make decisions about the matters referred to in paragraphs (a) and (b) of subsection (1) of section 275 of this Act is significantly impaired;

    (b)   that the statement complies with subsection (2) of that section;

    (c) that any measures or treatment which might or will be authorised by virtue of the decision referred to in subsection (1) above or might or will, by virtue of that decision, no longer be authorised correspond to any wishes specified in the statement; and

    (d) that, since the person made the statement, there has been no change of circumstances which, were the person to have been considering making the statement at the time the Tribunal is making the decision referred to in subsection (1) above, would have been likely to cause the person not to make the statement or to make a substantially different one.

(3)   A person giving medical treatment authorised by virtue of this Act or the 1995 Act to a patient who is a person—

    (a) who has made and not withdrawn an advance statement; and

    (b) whose ability to make decisions about the matters referred to in paragraphs (a) and (b) of subsection (1) of section 275 of this Act is, because of mental disorder, significantly impaired,

shall have regard to the wishes specified in the advance statement.

(4)   Before making a decision under section 236(2)(c), 239(1)(c) or 241(1)(c) of this Act in relation to a patient who is a person who has made and not withdrawn an advance statement, a designated medical practitioner shall have regard to the wishes specified in the statement.

(5)   For the purposes of subsections (1) and (2) above and (in the case where medical treatment is to or might be given to a patient otherwise than by virtue of any such decision as is referred to in subsection (1) above or is to be given to the patient by virtue of such a decision which was made in ignorance of the existence or the withdrawal of an advance statement) of subsections (3) and (4) above—

    (a) an advance statement shall be taken to comply with subsection (2) of section 275 of this Act; and

    (b) a withdrawal of an advance statement shall be taken to comply with subsection (3) of that section,

unless the contrary appears.

(6)   For the purposes of subsections (3) and (4) above in the case where the medical treatment is authorised by virtue of a decision such as is referred to in subsection (1) above—

    (a) an advance statement shall be taken to comply with subsection (2) of section 275 of this Act; and

    (b) a withdrawal of an advance statement shall be taken to comply with subsection (3) of that section,

if the Tribunal was satisfied when making the decision that the statement or, as the case may be, the withdrawal so complies.

(7)   If, in respect of a patient who is a person who has made and not withdrawn an advance statement—

    (a) the Tribunal makes such a decision as is referred to in subsection (1) above authorising measures which conflict with the wishes specified in the statement;

(b) a person having functions under this Act gives medical treatment authorised by virtue of this Act or the 1995 Act to the person and that treatment conflicts with those wishes;

(c) a designated medical practitioner makes such a decision as is referred to in subsection (4) above and it conflicts with those wishes; or

(d) such measures, treatment or decision which could have been so authorised, given or, as the case may be, made are not so authorised or is not so given or made, with the consequence that there is a conflict with those wishes,

then the Tribunal, person having those functions or, as the case may be, designated medical practitioner shall comply with the requirements set out in subsection (8) below.

(8) Those requirements are—

(a) recording in writing the circumstances in which those measures were or treatment or decision was authorised, given or made or, as the case may be, not authorised, given or made, and the reasons why;

(b) supplying—

(i) the person who made the statement;

(ii) that person's named person;

(iii) that person's welfare attorney;

(iv) that person's guardian; and

(v) the Commission,

with a copy of that record; and

(c) placing a copy of that record with that person's medical records.

Education

277   Education of persons who have mental disorder

(1) The Education (Scotland) Act 1980 (c.44) shall be amended as follows.

(2) In section 14(1) (education for children unable to attend school by reason of extraordinary circumstances or prolonged ill-health), in paragraph (b) after "ill-health" there is inserted "or a pupil's being subject to any measures authorised by virtue of the Mental Health (Care and Treatment) (Scotland) Act 2003 (asp 13) or authorised, in consequence of the pupil's mental disorder, by virtue of the Criminal Procedure (Scotland) Act 1995 (c.46)".

(3) In section 131(2) (persons to whom duties and powers under the Act do not extend), in paragraph (a) after "court" there is inserted "(other than an order so made under the Mental Health (Care and Treatment) (Scotland) Act 2003 (asp 13))".

Parental relations

278   Duty to mitigate adverse effect of compulsory measures on parental relations

(1) Subsection (2) below applies—

(a) where—

        (i)   a child is subject to any measures authorised by virtue of this Act or authorised, in consequence of the child's mental disorder, by virtue of the 1995 Act; and

        (ii)   the measures will or will be likely to impair the personal relations or diminish direct contact between the child and any person with parental responsibilities in relation to the child; or

    (b) where—

        (i)   a person with parental responsibilities in relation to a child is subject to any measures authorised by virtue of this Act or authorised, in consequence of the person's mental disorder, by virtue of the 1995 Act; and

        (ii)   the measures will or will be likely to impair the personal relations or diminish direct contact between that person and the child.

(2)   Every person having functions by virtue of this Act which include responsibility for the administration of any of the measures mentioned in subsection (1) above shall take such steps as are practicable and appropriate to mitigate the impairment or diminution referred to in that subsection or, as the case may be, the likelihood of that impairment or diminution.

(3)   In this section, "child" and "parental responsibilities" have the same meanings as they have in Part I of the Children (Scotland) Act 1995 (c.36).

Research

279   Information for research

(1)   A person having functions by virtue of this Act shall, on being required to do so by the Scottish Ministers—

    (a) provide them or any other person specified in the requirement with such relevant information as is so specified; and

    (b) do so in any such form as may be so specified.

(2)   The Scottish Ministers may, under subsection (1) above, require the provision of relevant information only if, in their opinion, it is needed by them (or, as the case may be, the other person specified in the requirement) for research purposes within the meaning given by section 33 of the Data Protection Act 1998 (c.29) (research, history and statistics).

(3)   Information need not be provided under this section if, were it evidence which might be given in proceedings in any court in Scotland, the person having that evidence could not be compelled to give it in such proceedings.

(4)   Where information required under subsection (1) above—

    (a) is, or refers to, information about a natural person and would identify or enable the identification of the person; and

    (b) can reasonably be provided under subsection (1) above so as not to identify or enable the identification of the person,

it shall be so provided.

(5)   Where—

(a) the person required under subsection (1) above to provide the information is under a duty of confidentiality in respect of that information; and

(b) the person cannot provide the information without breaching the duty,

the information shall not be provided unless the person to whom the duty is owed has consented to its provision.

(6) On receipt of information provided under this section, the Scottish Ministers (or any other person provided under this section with the information) may, for the purposes referred to in subsection (2) above, do any, or all, of the following—

(a) process the information;

(b) collate it;

(c) publish it or reports based on it.

(7) Regulations may provide as to the procedure to be followed in making requirements under this section for information and in providing it.

(8) Where information recorded otherwise than in legible form is required to be provided under this section, it shall be provided in legible form.

(9) For the purposes of this section—

(a) information is "relevant" if it is information as to the operation of this Act; and

(b) a person is under a duty of confidentiality in respect of information although the person could notwithstanding that duty be compelled to give evidence as to that information in proceedings in a court in Scotland.

State hospitals

280   Restriction of Scottish Ministers' power to delegate management of state hospitals

In section 102 of the National Health Service (Scotland) Act 1978 (c.29) (provision and management of state hospitals)—

(a) in subsection (4), paragraph (a) and the word "or" immediately following it; and

(b) subsection (5),

shall cease to have effect.

Communications, security etc.

281   Correspondence of certain persons detained in hospital

(1) A postal packet which is—

(a) addressed to any person by a specified person; and

(b) delivered by the specified person for dispatch,

may, where subsection (2) or (3) below applies, be withheld from the relevant carrier by the managers of the hospital in which the specified person is detained.

(2) This subsection applies if the person in question has requested that communications addressed to such person by the specified person should be withheld.

(3) This subsection applies if—

(a) the postal packet is not addressed to a person mentioned in subsection (5) below; and

(b) the managers of the hospital consider that the postal packet is likely—

(i) to cause distress to the person in question or any other person who is not on the staff of the hospital; or

(ii) to cause danger to any person.

(4) Any request for the purposes of subsection (2) above shall be made in writing to—

(a) the managers of the hospital concerned;

(b) the responsible medical officer; or

(c) the Scottish Ministers.

(5) The persons referred to in subsection (3)(a) above are—

(a) any Minister of the Crown or the Scottish Ministers;

(b) any member of either House of Parliament or member of the Scottish Parliament, National Assembly for Wales or Northern Ireland Assembly;

(c) any member of the European Parliament elected for the United Kingdom;

(d) the Commission or any of its members;

(e) the Parliamentary Commissioner for Administration;

(f) the Scottish Public Services Ombudsman;

(g) a local authority;

(h) any judge or clerk of court;

(i) the Tribunal;

(j) the managers of the hospital in which the specified person is detained;

(k) a Health Board;

(l) a Special Health Board;

(m) a National Health Service trust;

(n) any person who, to the knowledge of the managers of the hospital in which the specified person is detained, is providing independent advocacy services to the specified person under section 259 of this Act;

(o) any legally qualified person instructed by the specified person to act as the specified person's legal adviser;

(p) the European Court of Human Rights; and

(q) such other persons as may be specified in regulations.

(6) A postal packet which—

(a) is addressed to a specified person; and

(b) is not sent by or on behalf of any person mentioned in subsection (5) above,

may be withheld from the specified person by the managers of the hospital in which the specified person is detained if, in their opinion, it is necessary to do so in the interests of the health or safety of the specified person or for the protection of any other person.

(7) The managers of a hospital may inspect and open any postal packet for the purposes of determining—

    (a) whether it is a postal packet to which subsection (1) or (6) above applies; and

    (b) if it is, whether it should be withheld under the subsection in question.

(8) The power to withhold a postal packet under subsection (1) or (6) above includes power to withhold anything contained in such packet.

(9) In this section—

"postal packet" has the meaning given by section 125 of the Postal Services Act 2000 (c.26);

"relevant carrier" means—

    (a) the postal operator (as defined in that section of that Act); or

    (b) the person other than a person mentioned in paragraph (a) above,

who is to receive or collect the postal packet for the purpose of its being conveyed and delivered; and

"specified person" means a person who—

    (a) is detained in a hospital; and

    (b) meets such other conditions, or in relation to whom such other conditions are met, as may be specified in regulations.

282 Correspondence: supplementary

(1) If a postal packet or anything contained in it is withheld under subsection (1) or (6) of section 281 of this Act, the managers of the hospital shall record that fact in writing.

(2) If a postal packet or anything contained in it is withheld under—

    (a) subsection (1) of section 281 of this Act by virtue of subsection (3) of that section; or

    (b) subsection (6) of that section,

the managers of the hospital shall, before the expiry of the period of 7 days beginning with the withholding of the packet or anything contained in it, give notice to the Commission of the matters mentioned in subsection (3) below.

(3) Those matters are—

    (a) the name of the specified person;

    (b) the nature of the postal packet or contents withheld; and

    (c) the reason for withholding the postal packet or contents.

(4) If a postal packet or anything contained in it is withheld under—

    (a) subsection (1) of section 281 of this Act by virtue of subsection (3) of that section; or

    (b) subsection (6) of that section,

the managers of the hospital shall, before the expiry of the period of 7 days beginning with the withholding of the packet or anything contained in it, give notice to the persons mentioned in subsection (5) below of the fact that the postal packet or anything contained in it has been withheld and the effect of section 283 of this Act.

(5)   Those persons are—

     (a)   the specified person; and

     (b)   in a case where the packet is withheld as mentioned in paragraph (b) of subsection (4) above, the person by whom the packet was sent (if known).

(6)   The functions under section 281 of this Act and this section of the managers of a hospital shall be discharged on their behalf by a person on the staff of the hospital appointed by them for that purpose; and different persons may be so appointed to discharge different functions.

(7)   Regulations may—

     (a)   make provision with respect to the exercise of the powers conferred by section 281 of this Act;

     (b)   make provision for that section and this section to apply as if references to postal packets included references to written communications by the means specified in the regulations, with such modifications as may be so specified.

(8)   In this section—

     "postal packet" has the same meaning as in section 281 of this Act; and

     "specified person" has the same meaning as in that section.

283   Review of decision to withhold postal packet

(1)   This section applies where a relevant item is withheld under—

     (a)   subsection (1) of section 281 of this Act by virtue of subsection (3) of that section; or

     (b)   subsection (6) of that section.

(2)   On an application—

     (a)   in the case where a relevant item is withheld as mentioned in paragraph (a) of subsection (1) above, by the specified person; or

     (b)   in the case where a relevant item is withheld as mentioned in paragraph (b) of that subsection, by—

         (i)   the specified person; or

         (ii)   the person by whom the postal packet was sent,

the Commission shall review the decision to withhold the relevant item.

(3)   Any application under subsection (2) above shall be made before the expiry of the period of 6 months beginning with the day on which the person making the application receives notice under section 282(4) of this Act.

(4)   On an application under subsection (2) above the Commission may direct that the relevant item should not be withheld; and the managers of the hospital concerned shall comply with any such direction.

(5) Regulations may make provision with respect to the making of applications under subsection (2) above.

(6) Regulations under subsection (5) above may in particular make provision as to the production to the Commission of relevant items.

(7) In this section—

"postal packet" has the same meaning as in section 281 of this Act;

"relevant item" means a postal packet or anything contained in it; and

"specified person" has the same meaning as in that section.

284 Certain persons detained in hospital: use of telephones

(1) Regulations may make provision for or in connection with regulating the use of telephones by such persons detained in hospital as may be specified in the regulations ("specified persons").

(2) Provision under subsection (1) above may in particular—

    (a) confer rights on specified persons to use telephones;

    (b) make the entitlement to, or exercise of, any such rights subject to conditions imposed by or under regulations;

    (c) restrict, or prohibit, the use of telephones by specified persons;

    (d) authorise the managers of a hospital to intercept, or arrange for the interception of, telephone calls—

        (i) to specified persons; or

        (ii) made by specified persons;

    (e) require the managers of a hospital to make, and maintain, records of such matters as may be specified in the regulations;

    (f) require the managers of a hospital to inform persons specified in the regulations of matters so specified;

    (g) confer power on the Commission to give to the managers of a hospital directions as to matters of any description specified in the regulations;

    (h) require the managers of a hospital to comply with any directions given to them by virtue of paragraph (g) above.

(3) The conditions mentioned in subsection (2)(b) above include in particular conditions as to payment of call charges for calls made by or on behalf of specified persons.

(4) Regulations under this section may not authorise the interception of a telephone call made by a specified person to a person mentioned in subsection (6) below unless—

    (a) the person has requested the interception of telephone calls made by the specified person to the person; or

    (b) the telephone call is or would be unlawful for any reason other than one arising from provision made by virtue of this section.

(5) Regulations under this section may not authorise the interception of a telephone call made to a specified person by a person mentioned in subsection (6) below unless the telephone call is or would be unlawful for any reason other than one arising from provision made by virtue of this section.

(6)   The persons referred to in subsections (4) and (5) above are—

       (a)   any of the persons mentioned in paragraphs (a) to (i), (k) to (n) and (p) of section 281(5) of this Act;

       (b)   the managers of the hospital in which the specified person is detained;

       (c)   a legally qualified person instructed by the specified person to act as the specified person's legal adviser; and

       (d)   such other person as may be specified by the regulations.

(7)   In this section "intercept", in relation to a telephone call, includes—

       (a)   listen to, record or otherwise monitor; and

       (b)   interrupt, cut short, divert or prevent from being connected.

(8)   For the purposes of this section, a telephone call is made when the telephone number of the person being called has been dialled.

285   Directions as to implementation of regulations under section 284(1)

(1)   The Scottish Ministers may give to the managers of a hospital directions as to the implementation by those managers of regulations made under section 284(1) of this Act; and the managers shall comply with any such directions.

(2)   The Scottish Ministers may require the managers of a hospital to provide them with a statement setting out such information as respects the implementation of the regulations by those managers as the Scottish Ministers may specify.

286   Safety and security in hospitals

(1)   Regulations may authorise—

       (a)   the search of such persons detained in hospital by virtue of this Act or the 1995 Act as may be specified in the regulations and of anything they have with them in the hospital in which they are detained;

       (b)   the taking, from external parts of the body of those persons and, by means of swabbing, from the mouth of those persons, of samples of body tissue, blood or other body fluid or other material, the taking hypodermically from those persons of samples of blood and the examination of those samples;

       (c)   the placing of restrictions on the kinds of things which those persons may have with them in the hospitals in which they are detained and the removal from them of articles kept in breach of such restrictions;

       (d)   the placing of prohibitions and restrictions on the entry into and the conduct while in those hospitals of persons ("visitors") visiting those persons or otherwise entering or seeking to enter those hospitals and on the kinds of things which visitors may bring with them into those hospitals;

       (e)   the surveillance, whether directly or otherwise, of those persons and visitors;

       (f)   the search of visitors and of anything they bring with them into those hospitals,

and make that which is authorised subject to conditions specified in the regulations.

(2)   Regulations may require the managers of each hospital of such class as is or classes as are specified to provide—

    (a) the Scottish Ministers, on their request, with a statement describing how regulations made under subsection (1) above—

        (i) have been implemented in that hospital during the period the Ministers specify in their request;

        (ii) are being implemented there at the time of the request;

        (iii) are proposed by those managers to be implemented there after that time;

    (b) the Commission with statements of the incidence and circumstances of the implementation there of regulations under subsection (1) above in such ways as are specified.

(3)   Regulations may confer power on the Commission, by direction—

    (a) to prohibit the implementation of regulations under subsection (1) above in relation to a specified patient in a specified way;

    (b) to require the managers of a hospital in which a specified patient is detained to notify a specified person that such a regulation has been implemented in relation to such a patient in such a way.

(4)   In each of subsections (2) and (3) above, "specified" means specified in the regulations made under that subsection.

(5)   The Scottish Ministers may give to the managers of a hospital directions as to the implementation by those managers of regulations made under subsection (1) above; and the managers shall comply with any such directions.

(6)   Before making regulations under this section the Scottish Ministers shall consult such persons as they consider appropriate.

Information

287   **Scottish Ministers' power to require responsible medical officer to provide certain information**

The Scottish Ministers may, for the purposes of the discharge of their functions under—

    (a) Part 10, 11 or 13 of this Act; or

    (b) section 52F, 52L or 52P of the 1995 Act,

in relation to a patient who has a responsible medical officer, require the patient's responsible medical officer to provide them with such information as they may specify.

Payments for expenses

288   **Payments to persons in hospital to meet personal expenses**

(1)   Where subsections (2) and (3) below apply in relation to a person, the Scottish Ministers may pay to the person such amounts as they consider appropriate in respect of the person's occasional personal expenses.

(2)   This subsection applies where the person—

    (a) has a mental disorder;

    (b) has been admitted to a hospital; and

    (c) is being given treatment there primarily for mental disorder.

(3)   This subsection applies where it appears to the Scottish Ministers that the person would not otherwise have resources to meet the expenses in question.

(4)   For the purposes of the National Health Service (Scotland) Act 1978 (c.29), the making of payments under this section to persons for whom services are provided under that Act shall be treated as included among those services.

(5)   In subsection (2) above, "hospital" means—

   (a) any health service hospital (as defined in section 108(1) of the National Health Service (Scotland) Act 1978 (c.29)); or

   (b) any state hospital.

Cross-border transfer of patients

289   Cross-border transfer: patients subject to requirement other than detention

(1)   Regulations may make provision for or in connection with the removal of a patient subject to a relevant requirement from Scotland to a place outwith Scotland (whether or not a place in the United Kingdom).

(2)   Where that provision is made, the regulations shall—

   (a) require a patient's removal to be authorised by warrant issued by the patient's responsible medical officer;

   (b) provide that a responsible medical officer may give that authority only—

      (i)   where the patient has notified the responsible medical officer of the patient's wish to be so removed; or

      (ii) where, in the case where the patient is not capable of giving that notification, the patient's named person has notified the responsible medical officer that that person considers that it is in the patient's best interests to be so removed;

   (c) provide that the responsible medical officer may give that authority only if satisfied that there are in existence, in the place to which the patient is to go after being so removed, arrangements which will secure for the patient measures, treatment, care or services corresponding or similar to those which the patient is subject to or is receiving by virtue of this Act or, as the case may be, the 1995 Act;

   (d) require a patient's responsible medical officer, before making a decision whether to authorise the removal of the patient, to notify—

      (i)   except where notification referred to in paragraph (b) above has been given by the patient's named person, that person;

      (ii) the mental health officer; and

      (iii) the Commission,

      of the circumstances of the case; and

   (e) authorise a patient's responsible medical officer to give directions in connection with the removal of the patient.

(3)   References in this section to—

(a) a relevant requirement are, as respects a patient, references to a requirement imposed in relation to the patient under section 66(1) of this Act or section 57A(8) of the 1995 Act, not being detention in a hospital;

(b) a patient subject to a relevant requirement include references to a patient in respect of whom section 128(1) (either as enacted or as applied by section 179 of this Act) is in operation.

290   Cross-border transfer: patients subject to detention requirement or otherwise in hospital

(1)   Regulations may make provision for or in connection with—

(a) the removal, of a patient whose detention in hospital is authorised by virtue of this Act or the 1995 Act, from Scotland to a place outwith Scotland (whether or not a place in the United Kingdom);

(b) the removal, of a patient who for the purposes of being given treatment for mental disorder is in hospital otherwise than by virtue of this Act or the 1995 Act, from Scotland to a place outwith the United Kingdom;

(c) the reception in Scotland of a person subject to corresponding measures in England, Wales, Northern Ireland, the Isle of Man or the Channel Islands and removed from there.

(2)   Where provision is made by regulations under paragraph (a) or (b) of subsection (1) above, the regulations shall—

(a) require a patient's removal from Scotland to be authorised by warrant issued by the Scottish Ministers;

(b) require that, among the factors to which the Scottish Ministers have regard in deciding whether to authorise that removal, there are included, as well as the best interests of the patient, the following—

(i) the existence, in the place to which a patient is to go after being removed from Scotland, of arrangements which will secure for the patient measures, treatment, care or services corresponding or similar to those to which the patient is subject or is receiving by virtue of this Act or, as the case may be, the 1995 Act;

(ii) any wish or preference as to the patient's removal from Scotland of which the patient has given notice to the Scottish Ministers; and

(iii) any risk to the safety of any person;

(c) require notice to be given to—

(i) the patient;

(ii) the patient's named person;

(iii) the mental health officer; and

(iv) the Commission,

of any decision that the patient be removed from Scotland under the regulations;

(d) require any such giving of notice to be effected, in a case where removal is to a place in the United Kingdom, at least 7 days before the date proposed for the patient's removal;

(e) require any such giving of notice to be effected, in a case where removal is to a place outwith the United Kingdom, at least 28 days before the date proposed for the patient's removal;

(f) make provision for such a patient to be able to appeal against any such decision; and

(g) provide for such a patient's removal not to take place until proceedings on any such appeal have been concluded.

(3) Where provision is made by regulations under paragraph (a) or (b) of subsection (1) above, the regulations may make provision for exceptions to provisions included in them by virtue of subsection (2)(c), (d), (e) or (g) above.

(4) Where provision is made by regulations under paragraph (c) of subsection (1) above, the regulations shall provide for the reception of patients in Scotland to take place only with the consent of the Scottish Ministers.

(5) Regulations under subsection (1) above may in particular—

(a) make provision for things done under the law of a territory other than Scotland to be treated as things done under provisions of the law of Scotland;

(b) confer powers and immunities on persons engaged in—

(i) escorting persons being moved under the regulations;

(ii) pursuing persons who have absconded while being so moved;

(iii) restraining persons who have absconded, or attempt to abscond, while being so moved;

(c) authorise the Scottish Ministers to arrange for any of their functions under the regulations to be exercised by other persons;

(d) authorise the Scottish Ministers to give directions in connection with removals of persons under the regulations or any particular such removal or removals;

(e) make provision amending provisions of this Act (other than this section) or any other enactment, or providing for any such provision or enactment to have effect with modification.

(6) Subsections (2) to (5) above are without prejudice to the generality of the powers conferred by subsection (1) above.

(7) References in this section to a patient whose detention in hospital is authorised by virtue of this Act or the 1995 Act include references to a patient—

(a) in respect of whom a certificate under section 41(1), 53(1), 127(1) or (3) (either as enacted or as applied by section 179 of this Act), 221(2) or 224(2) of this Act is in operation; or

(b) who has been conditionally discharged under section 193(7) of this Act and not recalled under section 202 of this Act.

(8) For the purposes of paragraph (c) of subsection (1) above, a person is subject to "corresponding measures" in a territory if under the law of that territory the person—

(a) is subject to measures corresponding or similar to detention in hospital authorised by virtue of this Act or the 1995 Act; or

(b) has a status corresponding or similar to that of a patient such as is mentioned in paragraph (b) of that subsection.

Informal patients

291   Application to Tribunal in relation to unlawful detention

(1)   This section applies where, otherwise than by virtue of this Act or the 1995 Act, a person ("the patient")—

    (a) has been admitted to a hospital; and

    (b) is being given treatment there primarily for mental disorder.

(2)   A person mentioned in subsection (4) below may apply to the Tribunal for an order requiring the managers of the hospital to cease to detain the patient.

(3)   On an application under subsection (2) above the Tribunal shall—

    (a) if satisfied that the patient is being unlawfully detained in the hospital, make the order mentioned in subsection (2) above; or

    (b) if not satisfied about the matter mentioned in paragraph (a) above, refuse the application.

(4)   The persons referred to in subsection (2) above are—

    (a) the patient;

    (b) the patient's named person;

    (c) if the patient is a child, any person who has parental responsibilities in relation to the patient;

    (d) a mental health officer;

    (e) the Commission;

    (f) any guardian of the patient;

    (g) any welfare attorney of the patient; and

    (h) any other person having an interest in the welfare of the patient.

(5)   Subsection (2) above is without prejudice to any right that a person has by virtue of any enactment or rule of law.

(6)   In subsection (4)(c) above, "child" and "parental responsibilities" have the same meanings as they have in Part I of the Children (Scotland) Act 1995 (c.36).

PART 19

ENTRY, REMOVAL AND DETENTION POWERS

Entry to premises

292   Warrant to enter premises for purposes of taking patient

(1)   If a sheriff or a justice of the peace is satisfied by an authorised person's evidence on oath as to the matters mentioned in subsection (2) below, the sheriff or, as the case may be, justice of the peace may grant a warrant under this subsection.

(2)   Those matters are—

    (a) that for the purposes for which the authorised person is authorised it is necessary to enter premises; and

    (b) that the authorised person—

       (i)   is unable to obtain entry to those premises; or

       (ii) reasonably apprehends that the authorised person will be unable to obtain entry to those premises.

(3)   A warrant under subsection (1) above is a warrant—

    (a) authorising—

       (i)   the authorised person;

       (ii) any mental health officer appointed by the local authority for the area in which the premises are situated; and

       (iii) any constable of the police force maintained for the area in which the premises are situated,

    to enter the premises specified in the warrant; and

    (b) authorising any constable of the police force for the area in which the premises are situated, for the purpose of exercising the power mentioned in paragraph (a) above, to open lockfast places on premises so specified.

(4)   In the execution of a warrant granted under subsection (1) above, the persons authorised for the purpose of subsection (3)(a) above may be accompanied by—

    (a) a medical practitioner;

    (b) any other authorised person.

(5)   In this section, references to an authorised person are to a person who, in relation to a patient, is authorised by virtue of this Act—

    (a) to take the patient to any place; or

    (b) to take (or retake) into custody the patient where the patient is liable to be taken (or retaken).

Removal to place of safety

293   Removal order

(1)   If, on the application of a relevant mental health officer, a sheriff is satisfied that—

    (a) a person who is aged 16 years or over has a mental disorder;

    (b) any of the circumstances mentioned in subsection (2) below apply in respect of that person; and

    (c) that person is likely to suffer significant harm if not removed to a place of safety,

the sheriff may make an order under this section (any such order being referred to in this Act as a "removal order") in respect of that person.

(2)   The circumstances referred to in subsection (1)(b) above are—

    (a) that the person is subject, or exposed, to—

       (i)   ill-treatment;

       (ii) neglect; or

       (iii) some other deficiency in care or treatment;

    (b) that, because of the mental disorder, the person's property—

        (i).   is suffering loss or damage; or

        (ii)   is at risk of suffering loss or damage; and

    (c)   that the person is—

        (i)   living alone or without care; and

        (ii)   unable to look after himself or his property or financial affairs.

(3)   A removal order is an order—

    (a)   authorising—

        (i)   the mental health officer specified in the order;

        (ii)   any other persons so specified; and

        (iii)   any constable of the police force maintained for the area in which the premises are situated,

    before the expiry of the period of 72 hours beginning with the granting of the order, to enter any premises so specified;

    (b)   authorising any such constable, before the expiry of that period, for the purpose of exercising the power mentioned in paragraph (a) above, to open lockfast places on premises so specified; and

    (c)   authorising—

        (i)   before the expiry of that period, the removal of the person who is the subject of the removal order to a place of safety specified in the order; and

        (ii)   the detention of that person in that place for such period, not exceeding 7 days, as may be specified in the order.

(4)   An application for a removal order shall be made to the sheriff of the sheriffdom in which the premises to which the application relates are situated.

(5)   Before determining an application for a removal order, the sheriff shall, subject to subsection (7) below, afford the persons mentioned in subsection (6) below the opportunity—

    (a)   of making representations (whether orally or in writing); and

    (b)   of leading, or producing, evidence.

(6)   Those persons are—

    (a)   the person who is the subject of the application; and

    (b)   such other persons as may be prescribed by regulations.

(7)   If the sheriff considers that such delay as would result from compliance with the requirements of subsection (5) above would be likely to be prejudicial to the person who is the subject of the application, the sheriff may dispense with the requirements of that subsection.

(8)   In this section "relevant mental health officer" means a mental health officer appointed by the local authority for the area in which the premises to which the application relates are situated.

294   **Removal order: urgent application to justice of the peace**

Where—

   (a)   the making of an application to the sheriff for a removal order is impracticable; and

   (b)   the circumstances are such that any delay in obtaining a removal order is likely to be prejudicial to the person who would be the subject of the application,

the application may be made instead to a justice of the peace for the commission area in which the premises to which the application relates are situated; and subsections (1) to (3) of section 293 of this Act shall apply in relation to an application made by virtue of this section as those subsections apply as respects an application to the sheriff.

295   **Recall or variation of removal order**

  (1)   A person who is the subject of a removal order, or any person claiming an interest in the welfare of that person, may apply to the sheriff for an order under this section—

   (a)   recalling the removal order; or

   (b)   varying that order by—

      (i)   specifying a different place of safety;

      (ii)   authorising, before the expiry of the period mentioned in subsection (2) below, the removal of the person who is the subject of the removal order to that place of safety; and

      (iii)   authorising the detention of the person who is the subject of the removal order in that place of safety for the remainder of such period as may have been specified, by virtue of section 293(3)(c)(ii) of this Act, in the removal order.

  (2)   The period referred to in subsection (1)(b)(ii) above is the period of 72 hours beginning with the granting of the order varying the removal order.

  (3)   An application under section (1) above shall be made to the sheriff of the sheriffdom in which the premises to which the application for a removal order related are situated.

  (4)   Before determining an application under subsection (1) above, the sheriff shall afford the persons mentioned in subsection (5) below the opportunity—

   (a)   of making representations (whether orally or in writing); and

   (b)   of leading, or producing, evidence.

  (5)   Those persons are—

   (a)   the person who is the subject of the removal order to which the application relates; and

   (b)   such persons as may be prescribed by regulations.

  (6)   Where a sheriff makes an order under this section recalling a removal order, the sheriff may, in addition, make such order as the sheriff thinks fit for the person who was the subject of the removal order—

   (a)   to be returned to the premises from which that person was, by virtue of the removal order, removed; or

   (b)   to be taken to some appropriate place chosen by that person.

296   No appeal against decision under section 293 or 295

No appeal shall be competent against—

(a) a decision of a sheriff under—

   (i) section 293(1) of this Act making, or refusing to make, a removal order; or

   (ii) section 295 of this Act making, or refusing to make, an order recalling or varying a removal order; or

(b) a decision of a justice of the peace under section 293(1) of this Act making, or refusing to make, a removal order.

297   Removal from public place

(1) Where—

(a) a constable reasonably suspects—

   (i) that a person (referred to in this section and in section 298 of this Act as a "relevant person") who is in a public place has a mental disorder; and

   (ii) that the relevant person is in immediate need of care or treatment; and

(b) the constable considers that it would be in the interests of the relevant person, or necessary for the protection of any other person, to remove the relevant person to a place of safety,

the constable may remove the relevant person to a place of safety.

(2) A relevant person removed to a place of safety under subsection (1) above may, for the purposes of enabling—

(a) arrangements to be made for a medical practitioner to carry out a medical examination of the relevant person; and

(b) the making of such arrangements as the medical practitioner considers necessary for the relevant person's care or treatment,

be detained there for a period ending not later than 24 hours after the time at which the relevant person is removed from the public place by the constable.

(3) If a relevant person absconds—

(a) while being removed to a place of safety under subsection (1) above; or

(b) from the place of safety,

a constable may, at any time during the period mentioned in subsection (2) above, take the person into custody and remove the person to a place of safety.

(4) In this section, "public place" means a place to which the public, or any section of the public, has, or is permitted to have, access (whether on payment or otherwise); and includes the common parts of a building containing two or more separate dwellings.

(5) If no place of safety is immediately available, a constable may, under subsection (1) or (3) above, remove a relevant person to a police station; and in any such case, any reference in this section and in section 298 of this Act to a place of safety shall be construed as being a reference to a police station.

298   **Removal under section 297: further provision**

(1)   This section applies where a constable removes a relevant person to a place of safety under section 297 of this Act.

(2)   The constable shall—

       (a)   as soon as reasonably practicable after removing a relevant person to a place of safety, ensure—

            (i)   that the local authority in whose area the place of safety is situated are informed of the matters mentioned in subsection (3) below; and

            (ii)   subject to subsection (4) below, that the nearest relative of the relevant person is informed of those matters; and

       (b)   before the expiry of the period of 14 days beginning with the day on which the person is removed to the place of safety, ensure that the Commission is given notice of those matters.

(3)   The matters are—

       (a)   the name and address of the relevant person;

       (b)   the date and time at which the relevant person was removed from the public place;

       (c)   the circumstances giving rise to the removal of the relevant person to the place of safety;

       (d)   the address of the place of safety;

       (e)   if the relevant person is removed to a police station, the reason why the relevant person was removed there; and

       (f)   any other matter prescribed by regulations.

(4)   Where—

       (a)   it is impracticable to ensure that the relevant person's nearest relative is informed of the matters mentioned in subsection (3) above; or

       (b)   the nearest relative is so informed but the nearest relative does not reside with the relevant person,

the constable shall, as soon as reasonably practicable after removing the relevant person to the place of safety, ensure that, where reasonably practicable, a person falling within subsection (5) below is informed of those matters.

(5)   A person falls within this subsection if—

       (a)   the person—

            (i)   resides with the relevant person; or

            (ii)   provides a care service to the relevant person; or

       (b)   the person is an individual who, otherwise than—

            (i)   by virtue of a contract of employment, or other contract, with any person; or

            (ii)   as a volunteer for a voluntary organisation,

         provides care for the relevant person.

(6)   In this section—

"care service" has the meaning given by section 2(1) of the Regulation of Care (Scotland) Act 2001 (asp 8);

"nearest relative" has the meaning given by section 254 of this Act; and

"public place" has the meaning given by section 297 of this Act.

Detention pending medical examination

299   Nurse's power to detain pending medical examination

(1)   This section applies where—

(a)   by virtue of an order under section 228(1) of the 1995 Act which includes—

(i)   by virtue of subsections (1) and (2)(a) of section 230 of that Act, a requirement that the patient submit to treatment as a resident patient in a hospital; or

(ii)   by virtue of subsections (1) and (2)(b) of that section, a requirement that the patient submit to treatment as a non-resident patient at an institution or place specified in the order,

a patient is in hospital and being given medical treatment; or

(b)   otherwise than by virtue of—

(i)   an order such as is mentioned in paragraph (a) above;

(ii)   any other provision of the 1995 Act; or

(iii)   this Act,

a patient is in hospital and being given medical treatment.

(2)   Where—

(a)   a nurse of such class as may be prescribed by regulations considers that it is likely that the conditions mentioned in subsection (3) below are met in respect of the patient; and

(b)   it is not practicable to secure the immediate medical examination of the patient by a medical practitioner,

the patient may, subject to subsection (4) below, be detained in hospital for a period of 2 hours (the "holding period") for the purpose of enabling arrangements to be made for a medical examination of the patient to be carried out.

(3)   The conditions referred to in subsection (2)(a) above are—

(a)   that the patient has a mental disorder;

(b)   that it is necessary for the protection of—

(i)   the health, safety or welfare of the patient; or

(ii)   the safety of any other person,

that the patient be immediately restrained from leaving the hospital; and

(c)   that it is necessary to carry out a medical examination of the patient for the purpose of determining whether the granting of—

(i)   an emergency detention certificate; or

(ii)   a short-term detention certificate,

is warranted.

(4)   If the medical practitioner who first arrives to carry out a medical examination of the patient within the holding period arrives after the expiry of the first hour of the holding period, the period for which the patient may be held shall be the period beginning with the commencement of the patient's detention under subsection (2) above and ending one hour after the arrival of the medical practitioner.

(5)   Where the patient is detained under subsection (2) above the nurse shall, as soon as practicable after the holding period begins, take all reasonable steps to inform a mental health officer of the detention.

(6)   Where the patient is detained under subsection (2) above, the nurse shall, as soon as practicable after the holding period begins, record in writing—

     (a)   the fact that the patient has been detained;

     (b)   the time at which the holding period began; and

     (c)   the nurse's reasons for believing that it is likely that the conditions mentioned in paragraphs (a) to (c) of subsection (3) are met in respect of the patient.

(7)   A record made under subsection (6) above shall, as soon as practicable after it is made, be delivered to the managers of the hospital in which the patient is detained by—

     (a)   the nurse; or

     (b)   a person authorised for the purpose by the nurse.

(8)   Where the managers of a hospital receive a record by virtue of subsection (7) above, they shall, before the expiry of the period of 14 days beginning with the day on which they receive it, send a copy of it to the Commission.

(9)   Any subordinate legislation made under section 25 of the Mental Health (Scotland) Act 1984 (c.36) (detention of patients already in hospital) shall, if in force immediately before the day on which this section comes into force, have effect on and after that day as if made under this section.

Meaning of "place of safety"

300   **Meaning of "place of safety"**

In this Part of this Act, "place of safety" means—

     (a)   a hospital;

     (b)   premises which are used for the purpose of providing a care home service (as defined in section 2(3) of the Regulation of Care (Scotland) Act 2001 (asp 8)); or

     (c)   any other suitable place (other than a police station) the occupier of which is willing temporarily to receive mentally disordered persons.

PART 20

ABSCONDING

Absconding

301   Absconding etc. by patients subject to compulsory treatment order

(1)   A patient who is subject to a compulsory treatment order authorising detention in hospital and who—

    (a)   absconds from—

        (i)   any place where the patient is kept pending removal to hospital under the order; or

        (ii)   the hospital in which, under the order, the patient is being detained; or

    (b)   while being removed to hospital under the order or transferred under section 124 of this Act, absconds,

is liable to be taken into custody and dealt with in accordance with section 303 of this Act.

(2)   A patient who is subject to such an order and in respect of whom—

    (a)   a certificate under section 127(1) of this Act has effect; and

    (b)   a condition under subsection (6) of that section requires—

        (i)   that the patient be kept in the charge of an authorised person or reside continuously or for or at specified times at a specified place; or

        (ii)   that the patient, on being recalled or on the expiry of a specified period or on or after the occurrence of a specified event, return to the hospital in which the patient was detained under the order or go to such other place as may be specified,

and who absconds from the charge of that authorised person or otherwise fails to comply with the condition is liable to be taken into custody and dealt with in accordance with section 303 of this Act.

(3)   A patient who is subject to a compulsory treatment order imposing a requirement that the patient reside at a specified place and who fails to comply with that requirement is liable to be taken into custody and dealt with in accordance with section 303 of this Act.

(4)   A patient who is subject to a compulsory treatment order imposing a requirement that the patient obtain the approval of the mental health officer to any proposed change of address and who changes address without having obtained that approval is liable to be taken into custody and dealt with in accordance with section 303 of this Act.

(5)   A patient who has been taken into custody under this section and who absconds from that custody remains liable to be taken into custody and dealt with in accordance with section 303 of this Act.

302   Absconding etc. by other patients

(1)   Subsection (2) below applies to a patient—

    (a)   who is subject to—

        (i)   an interim compulsory treatment order authorising detention;

        (ii)   a short-term detention certificate; or

        (iii) a certificate under section 114(2) or 115(2) of this Act authorising continued detention;

    (b) who is being detained in pursuance of an extension certificate or under the power conferred by section 68 of this Act;

    (c) to whom an emergency detention certificate applies; or

    (d) who is being detained in hospital under the power conferred by section 113(5) or 299 of this Act.

(2)   A patient to whom this subsection applies and who absconds from—

    (a) any place where the patient is kept pending removal to hospital under the order or certificate; or

    (b) the hospital in which, under the order, certificate or, as the case may be, power, the patient is detained,

is liable to be taken into custody and dealt with in accordance with section 303 of this Act.

(3)   A patient who is subject to an interim compulsory treatment order imposing a requirement that the patient reside continuously or for or at specified times at a specified place and who fails to comply with that requirement is liable to be taken into custody and dealt with in accordance with section 303 of this Act.

(4)   A patient who is subject to an interim compulsory treatment order authorising detention and in respect of whom—

    (a) a certificate under section 127(3) of this Act has effect; and

    (b) a condition under subsection (6) of that section requires—

        (i)   that the patient be kept in the charge of an authorised person or reside continuously or for or at specified times at a specified place; or

        (ii) that the patient, on being recalled or on the expiry of a specified period or on or after the occurrence of a specified event, return to the hospital in which the patient was detained under the order or go to such other place as may be specified,

and who absconds from the charge of that authorised person or otherwise fails to comply with any such condition is liable to be taken into custody and dealt with in accordance with section 303 of this Act.

(5)   A patient who is subject to a short-term detention certificate in respect of whom—

    (a) a certificate under section 53(1) of this Act has effect; and

    (b) a condition under subsection (4) of that section requires—

        (i)   that the patient be kept in the charge of an authorised person or reside continuously or for or at specified times at a specified place; or

        (ii) that the patient, on being recalled or on the expiry of a specified period or on or after the occurrence of a specified event, return to the hospital in which the patient was detained under the certificate or go to such other place as may be specified,

.   and who absconds from the charge of that authorised person or otherwise fails to comply with any such condition is liable to be taken into custody and dealt with in accordance with section 303 of this Act.

(6)   A patient who is subject to an emergency detention certificate in respect of whom—

    (a)   a certificate under section 41(1) of this Act has effect; and

    (b)   a condition under subsection (4) of that section requires—

        (i)   that the patient be kept in the charge of an authorised person or reside continuously or for or at specified times at a specified place; or

        (ii)   that the patient, on being recalled or on the expiry of a specified period or on or after the occurrence of a specified event, return to the hospital in which the patient was detained under the certificate or go to such other place as may be specified,

and who absconds from the charge of that authorised person or otherwise fails to comply with any such condition is liable to be taken into custody and dealt with in accordance with section 303 of this Act.

303   Taking into custody and return of absconding patients

(1)   A person specified in subsection (3)(a) below may, during the period specified in subsection (4) below—

    (a)   take into custody any patient who, under sections 301 or 302 of this Act, is liable to be taken into custody;

    (b)   return the patient to the hospital in which the patient was detained or, as the case may be, take the patient to the hospital in which the patient was to be detained or, if that is not appropriate or practicable, take the patient to any other place considered appropriate by the patient's responsible medical officer;

    (c)   return or take the patient to such other place as the patient absconded from or at which the patient failed to reside or, if that is not appropriate or practicable, take the patient to any other place considered appropriate by the patient's responsible medical officer.

(2)   The person specified in subsection (3)(b) below may, during the period specified in subsection (4) below—

    (a)   take into custody any patient in respect of whom a certificate under section 41(1), 53(1) or 127(1) of this Act has effect and a condition under section 41(4), 53(4) or, as the case may be, 127(6) of this Act requires that the patient be kept in charge of that person and who, under section 301 or 302 of this Act is liable to be taken into custody; and

    (b)   resume the charge of the patient or, if that is not appropriate or practicable, take the patient to any place considered appropriate by the patient's responsible medical officer.

(3)   The—

    (a)   persons referred to in subsection (1) above are—

        (i)   a mental health officer;

        (ii)   a constable;

(iii) a member of staff of any hospital and, where the patient liable to be taken into custody is subject to a compulsory treatment order a condition of which requires the patient to reside in an establishment the address of which is specified in the order, a member of staff of that establishment; and

(iv) any other person authorised for the purposes of that subsection by the patient's responsible medical officer;

(b) person referred to in subsection (2) above is the person who is authorised under section 41(4), 53(4) or, as the case may be, 127(6) of this Act to have charge of the patient.

(4) The period referred to in subsection (1) above is—

(a) in the case of a patient who is subject to a compulsory treatment order, the period of 3 months beginning with the day—

(i) when the patient absconded; or

(ii) when the patient's conduct or failure first gave rise to liability to be taken into custody;

(b) in any other case, the period ending with the expiry of the order, certificate, report or, as the case may be, provision under or in pursuance of which the patient was to be detained.

(5) The expiry, during the period referred to in subsection (1) above, of the authorised period in relation to the compulsory treatment order to which a patient is subject does not affect the powers conferred by this section.

(6) The powers conferred by subsections (1) and (2) above include power to use reasonable force in their exercise.

(7) A patient who is, under section 301 or 302 of this Act, liable to be taken into custody ceases to be so liable—

(a) on returning to the hospital or other place from which the patient absconded or arriving at the hospital in which the patient was to be detained;

(b) on being returned or taken either there or to such other place as is considered appropriate by the patient's responsible medical officer under subsection (1)(b) or (c) or (2)(b) above; or

(c) on being taken into custody under section 113 of this Act.

Effect of unauthorised absence

304   Effect of unauthorised absence

(1) References in this section and sections 305 to 308 of this Act to a patient's unauthorised absence are references to a patient's being liable, under section 301 of this Act, to be taken into custody and dealt with under section 303 of this Act.

(2) Subject to sections 305 to 308 of this Act, a patient's unauthorised absence does not affect the continuity or measurement of any period of time fixed by, under or relative to any provision of this Act or requirement imposed by virtue of it, of which that absence is a breach.

(3) Where, in the case of a patient who is subject to a compulsory treatment order, the patient's unauthorised absence has continued for a period of 3 months, the order shall then cease to have effect.

305 **Effect of long unauthorised absence ending more than 14 days before expiry of compulsory treatment order**

(1) Where the unauthorised absence of a patient who is subject to a compulsory treatment order—

    (a) lasted longer than 28 consecutive days; and

    (b) ceased before the beginning of the period of 14 days ending with the day when the compulsory treatment would, apart from this subsection, cease to authorise the measures specified in it,

the order shall cease to have effect at the expiry of the period of 14 days beginning with the day when the patient's unauthorised absence ceased.

(2) The patient's responsible medical officer shall, during the period of 14 days secondly referred to in subsection (1) above, carry out a review in respect of the compulsory treatment order to which the patient is subject by complying with the requirements set out in section 77(3) of this Act.

(3) Where any part of the period of 14 days referred to in subsection (2) above occurs within the period of 2 months mentioned in subsection (5) of section 77 or subsection (3) of section 78 of this Act, the review which would (apart from this subsection) have been carried out during that period of 2 months under that section shall not be carried out.

(4) The other review provisions (that is to say, section 83(2) and (3) and the subsequent provisions of Chapter 4 of Part 7 of this Act) shall, in accordance with subsections (5) and (6) below, apply in respect and in consequence of a review under this section as they apply in respect and in consequence of the reviews for which that Chapter provides.

(5) Where the compulsory treatment order to which the patient is subject has not been extended as mentioned in section 78(1) of this Act, those of the other review provisions which relate to a first review apply.

(6) Where that order has been so extended, those of the other review provisions which relate to a further review apply.

306 **Effect of unauthorised absence ending simultaneously with or within 14 days before expiry of compulsory treatment order**

(1) Where the unauthorised absence of a patient who is subject to a compulsory treatment order—

    (a) ceases on the day that the order to which the patient is subject would, apart from this subsection, cease to authorise the measures specified in it; or

    (b) ceased within a period of 14 days ending with that day,

the order shall be treated as having continued in effect and, subject to subsection (4) below, as continuing in effect until the end of the period of 14 days beginning with the day on which the patient's unauthorised absence ceased.

(2) The patient's responsible medical officer shall, during the period of 14 days secondly referred to in subsection (1) above, carry out a review in respect of the compulsory treatment order to which the patient is subject by complying with the requirements set out in section 77(3) of this Act.

(3)   Where any part of the period of 14 days referred to in subsection (2) above occurs within the period of 2 months mentioned in subsection (5) of section 77 or subsection (3) of section 78 of this Act, the review which would (apart from this subsection) have been carried out during that period of 2 months under that section shall not be carried out.

(4)   Subsections (4) to (6) of section 305 of this Act apply for the purposes of a review under subsection (2) above as they apply for the purposes of a review under subsection (2) of that section.

(5)   Where—

      (a)   the compulsory treatment order to which a patient is subject is, under this section, treated as continuing in effect; and

      (b)   the patient's unauthorised absence—

          (i)   began at a time when a review of the order was being carried out under section 77 or 78 of this Act; and

          (ii)   lasted for 28 consecutive days or any shorter period,

then anything done by the patient's responsible medical officer for the purposes of that review which (apart from this subsection) would fall to be done for the purposes of a review under this section need not, for those latter purposes, be done.

307   Effect of unauthorised absence ending after expiry of compulsory treatment order

(1)   Where the unauthorised absence of a patient who is subject to a compulsory treatment order ceases—

      (a)   within a period of 3 months beginning with the day on which it began; and

      (b)   after the day when the compulsory treatment order to which the patient was subject would, but for this subsection, have ceased to authorise the measures specified in it,

the order shall be treated as having continued in effect and, subject to subsection (3) below, as continuing in effect until the end of the period of 14 days beginning with the day on which the patient's unauthorised absence ceased.

(2)   The patient's responsible medical officer shall, during the period of 14 days referred to in subsection (1) above, carry out a review of the compulsory treatment order to which the patient is subject by complying with the requirements set out in section 77(3) of this Act.

(3)   Subsections (4) to (6) of section 305 of this Act apply for the purposes of a review under subsection (2) above as they apply for the purposes of a review under subsection (2) of that section.

(4)   Where—

      (a)   the compulsory treatment order to which a patient is subject is, under this section, treated as continuing in effect; and

      (b)   the patient's unauthorised absence—

          (i)   began at a time when a review of the order was being carried out under section 77 or 78 of this Act; and

          (ii)   lasted for 28 consecutive days or any shorter period, then anything done by the patient's responsible medical officer for the purposes of that review which (apart from this subsection) would fall to be done for the purposes of a review under this section need not, for those latter purposes, be done.

308   Effect of unauthorised absence of patient subject to short-term detention certificate or certificate under section 114(2) or 115(2)

Where the unauthorised absence of a patient who is subject to a short-term detention certificate or a certificate under section 114(2) or 115(2) of this Act authorising continued detention ceases within the period of 13 days ending with the day on which the certificate would, but for this section, have ceased to authorise the measures specified in it, the certificate shall continue to authorise those measures until the end of the period of 14 days beginning with the day when the patient's unauthorised absence ceased.

Patients from other jurisdictions

309   Patients from other jurisdictions

(1)   Regulations may make provision applying sections 301 to 303 of this Act to persons in Scotland who are subject to corresponding measures in England, Wales, Northern Ireland, the Isle of Man or the Channel Islands.

(2)   Those regulations may make such modifications of those sections in that application as the Scottish Ministers think fit.

(3)   The reference in subsection (1) above to persons subject to corresponding measures shall be construed in accordance with section 290(8) of this Act.

Absconding by certain other patients

310   Regulations as to absconding by other patients

(1)   Regulations may provide as to—

   (a)   the circumstances in which patients—

      (i)   who are subject to any of the orders or directions mentioned in subsection (3) below; and

      (ii)   who abscond or fail to comply with requirements imposed on them by virtue of the orders or directions to which they are subject or otherwise by virtue of this Act or the 1995 Act,

   are to be liable to be taken into custody by specified persons;

   (b)   the steps which may be taken by those persons upon their taking those patients into custody; and

   (c)   the effect (whether upon the orders or directions to which those patients are subject or otherwise) of such absconding or failure.

(2)   Regulations under subsection (1) above may include provision—

   (a)   requiring patients' responsible medical officers to notify—

      (i)   specified courts;

      (ii)   the Commission;

        (iii) the Scottish Ministers,

of such absconding or failure;

  (b) authorising the use of reasonable force in the exercise of the powers conferred by virtue of subsection (1) above to take patients into custody and to take the steps referred to in that subsection;

  (c) for—

      (i) the review of those orders and directions; and

      (ii) the authorisation of measures additional to or different from those authorised by them,

in consequence of such absconding or failure;

  (d) corresponding to section 309 of this Act and any regulations which may be made under that section.

(3)   The orders referred to in subsection (1) above are—

  (a) assessment orders;

  (b) treatment orders;

  (c) temporary compulsion orders made under section 54(1)(c) of the 1995 Act;

  (d) interim compulsion orders; and

  (e) compulsion orders,

and the directions there referred to are hospital directions and transfer for treatment directions.

(4)   In this section, "specified" means specified in the regulations.

PART 21

OFFENCES

311   Non-consensual sexual acts

(1)   Subject to subsection (5) below, a person who engages in an act mentioned in subsection (2) below with, or towards, a mentally disordered person shall be guilty of an offence if, at the time of the act, the mentally disordered person—

  (a) does not consent to the act; or

  (b) by reason of mental disorder, is incapable of consenting to the act.

(2)   The acts referred to in subsection (1) above are—

  (a) sexual intercourse (whether vaginal or anal); and

  (b) any other sexual act.

(3)   For the purposes of subsection (1)(a) above, a person shall be regarded as not consenting if the person purports to consent as a result of—

  (a) being placed in such a state of fear; or

  (b) being subjected to any such—

      (i) threat;

(ii)   intimidation;

(iii) deceit; or

(iv)   persuasion,

as vitiates that person's consent.

(4)   For the purposes of subsection (1)(b) above, a person is incapable of consenting to an act if the person is unable to—

(a)   understand what the act is;

(b)   form a decision as to whether to engage in the act (or as to whether the act should take place); or

(c)   communicate any such decision.

(5)   Where a person is charged with an offence under subsection (1)(b) above it shall be a defence for such person to prove that, at the time of the sexual intercourse or other sexual act, such person did not know, and could not reasonably have been expected to know, that the other person—

(a)   had a mental disorder; and

(b)   was incapable of consenting to the intercourse or other act.

(6)   A person guilty of an offence under subsection (1) above shall be liable—

(a)   on summary conviction to imprisonment for a term not exceeding 3 months or to a fine not exceeding the statutory maximum or to both;

(b)   on conviction on indictment to imprisonment for life.

(7)   A person guilty of aiding, abetting, counselling, procuring or inciting any other person to commit an offence under subsection (1) above shall be liable—

(a)   on summary conviction to imprisonment for a term not exceeding 3 months or to a fine not exceeding the statutory maximum or to both;

(b)   on conviction on indictment to imprisonment for a term not exceeding 2 years or to a fine or to both.

(8)   In this section "sexual act" means any activity which a reasonable person would, in all the circumstances, regard as sexual.

312   Offences under section 311: extended sentences

In section 210A(10) of the 1995 Act (extended sentences for sex and violent offenders: meaning of certain expressions), in the definition of "sexual offence"—

(a)   the word "and" which occurs immediately after paragraph (xix) shall be omitted; and

(b)   after paragraph (xx) there shall be added "and

(xxi) an offence under section 311(1) of the Mental Health (Care and Treatment) (Scotland) Act 2003 (asp 13) (non-consensual sexual acts).".

313   Persons providing care services: sexual offences

(1)   Subject to subsection (3) below, a person who engages in—

(a)   sexual intercourse (whether vaginal or anal); or

(b) any other sexual act,

with, or towards, a mentally disordered person shall be guilty of an offence if, at the time of the intercourse or other act, the person is one of those specified in subsection (2) below.

(2)   Those persons are—

(a) a person providing care services to the mentally disordered person;

(b) a person who—

(i)   is an individual employed in, or contracted to provide services in or to; or

(ii)   not being the Scottish Ministers, is a manager of,

a hospital in which the mentally disordered person is being given medical treatment.

(3)   Where a person is charged with an offence under subsection (1) above, it shall be a defence for such person to prove that—

(a) at the time of the intercourse or other act—

(i)   such person did not know, and could not reasonably have been expected to know, that the other person was mentally disordered; or

(ii)   the mentally disordered person was the spouse of such person; or

(b) in the case of—

(i)   a person specified in subsection (2)(a) above, immediately before that person began to provide care services to the mentally disordered person; or

(ii)   a person specified in subsection (2)(b) above, immediately before the mentally disordered person was admitted to the hospital referred to in that provision or (where the mentally disordered person has been admitted to that hospital more than once) was last admitted to it,

a sexual relationship existed between them.

(4)   A person guilty of an offence under subsection (1) above shall be liable—

(a) on summary conviction to imprisonment for a term not exceeding 3 months or to a fine not exceeding the statutory maximum or to both;

(b) on conviction on indictment to imprisonment for a term not exceeding 2 years or to a fine or to both.

(5)   References in this section to the provision of care services are references to anything done by way of such services—

(a) by;

(b) by an employee of; or

(c) in the course of a service provided or supplied by,

a care service, whether by virtue of a contract of employment or any other contract or in such other circumstances as may be prescribed by regulations.

(6)   In this section—

"care service" has the meaning given by subsection (1)(a), (b), (e), (g), (h), (k) and (n) as read with subsections (2), (3), (6), (9), (10), (16) and (27) of section 2 of the Regulation of Care (Scotland) Act 2001 (asp 8); and "sexual act" has the meaning given by section 311(8) of this Act.

314   Notification requirements for offenders under sections 311 and 313

In Schedule 1 to the Sex Offenders Act 1997 (c.51) (sexual offences to which Part I applies), in paragraph 2(1), after paragraph (e) there shall be added—

> "(f)   offences under—
>
>> (i)   section 311(1) of the Mental Health (Care and Treatment) (Scotland) Act 2003 (asp 13) (non-consensual sexual acts); and
>>
>> (ii)   section 313(1) of that Act (persons providing care services: sexual offences).".

315   Ill-treatment and wilful neglect of mentally disordered person

(1)   This section applies to a person (a "relevant person") who—

   (a)   is an individual employed in, or contracted to provide services in or to, a hospital;

   (b)   not being the Scottish Ministers, is a manager of a hospital;

   (c)   provides care services; or

   (d)   is an individual who, otherwise than—

      (i)   by virtue of a contract of employment or other contract with any person; or

      (ii)   as a volunteer for a voluntary organisation,

   provides care or treatment.

(2)   A relevant person who—

   (a)   whether under this Act or otherwise—

      (i)   is providing care or treatment; or

      (ii)   purports to provide care or treatment,

   to a patient; and

   (b)   ill-treats, or wilfully neglects, that patient,

shall be guilty of an offence.

(3)   A person guilty of an offence under subsection (2) above shall be liable—

   (a)   on summary conviction to imprisonment for a term not exceeding 6 months or to a fine not exceeding the statutory maximum or to both;

   (b)   on conviction on indictment to imprisonment for a term not exceeding 2 years or to a fine or to both.

(4)   In subsection (1)(c) above, the reference to the provision of care services shall be construed in accordance with section 313(5) of this Act.

316   Inducing and assisting absconding etc.

(1)   A person who knowingly—

(a) induces or assists a patient to do or fail to do anything which results in the patient's being liable under section 301 or 302 of this Act to be taken into custody and dealt with under section 303 of this Act; or

(b) harbours a patient who has, with that result, done or failed to do anything,

shall be guilty of an offence.

(2) Where a person is charged with an offence under subsection (1)(b) above, it shall be a defence for such person to prove that the doing of that with which the person is charged—

(a) did not obstruct the discharge by any person of a function conferred or imposed on that person by virtue of this Act; and

(b) was intended to protect the interests of the patient.

(3) A person guilty of an offence under this section shall be liable—

(a) on summary conviction, to imprisonment for a term not exceeding 6 months or to a fine not exceeding the statutory maximum or both;

(b) on conviction on indictment, to imprisonment for a term not exceeding 2 years or to a fine or both.

(4) The reference in subsection (1) above to sections 301 to 303 of this Act includes a reference to those sections as applied or as applied and modified under section 309 of this Act and to any regulations made under section 310 of this Act which make provision corresponding to sections 301 to 303 of this Act.

317   Obstruction

(1) A person who—

(a) refuses to allow a person authorised by virtue of this Act access to any premises;

(b) refuses to allow access to a mentally disordered person by a person authorised by virtue of this Act to have such access;

(c) refuses to allow the interview or examination of a mentally disordered person by a person authorised by virtue of this Act to interview or examine such person;

(d) persists in being present when requested to withdraw by a person authorised by virtue of this Act to interview or examine, in private, a mentally disordered person;

(e) refuses to produce any document or record to a person authorised by virtue of this Act to require the production of such document or record; or

(f) otherwise obstructs a person in the exercise of any functions conferred on such person by virtue of this Act,

shall be guilty of an offence.

(2) A mentally disordered person shall not be guilty of an offence under subsection (1) above if the person mentioned in that subsection—

(a) who is authorised by virtue of this Act, is so authorised; or

(b) who is exercising functions conferred on that person by virtue of this Act, is exercising those functions,

in relation to that mentally disordered person.

(3) In any proceedings against a person for an offence under subsection (1) above it shall be a defence for the accused to show that the accused had a reasonable excuse for doing that with which the accused is charged.

(4) A person guilty of an offence under subsection (1) above shall be liable on summary conviction to imprisonment for a term not exceeding 3 months or to a fine not exceeding level 3 on the standard scale or to both.

318   False statements

(1) A person who—

    (a) knowingly makes, in a relevant document, an entry or statement which is false in a material particular; or

    (b) with intent to deceive, makes use of any such entry or statement knowing it to be false,

shall be guilty of an offence.

(2) For the purposes of subsection (1) above, a "relevant document"—

    (a) is—

        (i) an application under this Act;

        (ii) a document accompanying any such application; or

        (iii) any other document required or authorised to be granted, prepared, sent or given for any of the purposes of this Act; but

    (b) does not include—

        (i) a nomination of a named person in accordance with section 250(2) of this Act;

        (ii) a declaration made in accordance with section 253(2) of this Act; and

        (iii) an advance statement.

(3) A person guilty of an offence under this section shall be liable—

    (a) on summary conviction, to imprisonment for a term not exceeding 6 months or to a fine not exceeding the statutory maximum or to both;

    (b) on conviction on indictment, to imprisonment for a term not exceeding 2 years or to a fine or to both.

319   Time limit for summary proceedings for offences under sections 311 and 313

Subsections (2) to (4) of section 4 of the Criminal Law (Consolidation) (Scotland) Act 1995 (c.39) (time limits for certain summary proceedings) shall apply to summary proceedings in respect of an offence under section 311 or 313 of this Act as they apply to the summary proceedings to which those subsections relate.

PART 22

APPEALS

320   Appeal to sheriff principal against certain decisions of the Tribunal

(1)   This section applies to the following decisions of the Tribunal—

(a)   a decision under section 50(4) of this Act refusing an application for revocation of a short-term detention certificate;

(b)   a decision under section 64(4)(a) or (b) of this Act making or refusing to make a compulsory treatment order;

(c)   a decision to make an interim compulsory treatment order under section 65(2) of this Act;

(d)   a decision to make an order under section 102(1)(c) or (d) of this Act confirming the determination of a patient's responsible medical officer extending a compulsory treatment order;

(e)   a decision to make an order under section 103(1)(a) or (b) of this Act on an application by the patient's responsible medical officer for an order extending and varying a compulsory treatment order;

(f)   a decision to make an order under section 103(2)(c) or (d) of this Act on an application for revocation of the determination of a patient's responsible medical officer extending a compulsory treatment order;

(g)   a decision to make an order under section 103(3)(b) or (c) of this Act on an application under section 100(2)(a) of this Act to revoke a compulsory treatment order;

(h)   a decision to make an order under section 103(4)(a) of this Act on an application by a patient's responsible medical officer to vary a compulsory treatment order;

(i)   a decision to make an order under section 103(4)(b) of this Act refusing an application under section 100(2)(b) of this Act to vary a compulsory treatment order;

(j)   a decision to make an order under section 104(1)(a) of this Act varying a compulsory treatment order;

(k)   a decision not to revoke under section 120(2) of this Act a certificate granted under section 114(2) or 115(2) of this Act;

(l)   a decision to make or refuse to make an order under section 125(5) or 126(5) of this Act preventing a transfer or requiring that a transferred patient be returned;

(m)   a decision to make an order under section 166(1)(c) or (d) of this Act confirming the determination of a patient's responsible medical officer extending a compulsion order;

(n)   a decision to make an order under section 167(1)(a) of this Act on an application by the patient's responsible medical officer for an order extending a compulsion order;

(o)   a decision to make an order under section 167(2)(a) or (b) of this Act on an application by the patient's responsible medical officer for an order extending and varying a compulsion order;

(p) a decision to make an order under section 167(3)(c) or (d) of this Act on an application for revocation of the determination of a patient's responsible medical officer extending a compulsion order;

(q) a decision to make an order under section 167(4)(b) or (c) of this Act on an application under section 164(2)(a) of this Act;

(r) a decision to make an order under section 167(5)(a) of this Act on an application by a patient's responsible medical officer to vary a compulsion order;

(s) a decision to make an order under section 167(5)(b) of this Act refusing an application under section 164(2)(b) of this Act to vary a compulsion order;

(t) a decision to make or refuse to make an order under section 257(1) of this Act appointing a person to be a patient's named person;

(u) a decision to make or refuse to make an order under section 257(2) of this Act declaring an acting named person not to be a named person or appointing a person to be a patient's named person in place of an acting named person;

(v) a decision to make an order under section 257(3) of this Act;

(w) a decision, in relation to a patient who is not subject to a restriction order, a hospital direction or a transfer for treatment direction—

    (i) to make or refuse to make an order under section 264(2), 265(3) or 266(3) of this Act;

    (ii) under section 267(2) of this Act to recall or refuse to recall an order made under section 264, 265 or 266 of this Act;

    (iii) to make or refuse to make an order under section 268(2), 269(3) or 270(3) of this Act;

    (iv) under section 271(2) of this Act to recall or refuse to recall an order made under section 268, 269 or 270 of this Act; and

(x) a decision granting or refusing an application for an order requiring the managers of the hospital to cease to detain a patient under section 291 of this Act.

(2) A relevant party to proceedings before the Tribunal may appeal to the sheriff principal against a decision to which this section applies.

(3) An appeal to the sheriff principal under subsection (2) above shall be to the sheriff principal—

(a) of the sheriffdom in which the person to whom the decision relates is resident at the time when the appeal is lodged;

(b) where the person to whom the decision relates is detained in a hospital at the time when the appeal is lodged, of the sheriffdom in which the hospital is situated; or

(c) in any other case, of any sheriffdom.

(4) If the sheriff principal to whom an appeal is made considers that the appeal raises an important or difficult question of law that makes it appropriate to remit the appeal to the Court of Session the sheriff principal may—

(a) *ex proprio motu*; or

(b) on the motion of any party to the appeal,

do so.

(5)   Subject to subsections (6) to (9) below, in this section "relevant party" means—

    (a)   the person to whom the decision relates;

    (b)   that person's named person;

    (c)   any guardian of the person;

    (d)   any welfare attorney of the person;

    (e)   the mental health officer; and

    (f)   that person's responsible medical officer.

(6)   Where the person to whom the decision relates is a person to whom subsection (7) below applies, "relevant party" means—

    (a)   the person to whom the decision relates;

    (b)   that person's named person;

    (c)   any guardian of the person;

    (d)   any welfare attorney of the person; and

    (e)   the Scottish Ministers.

(7)   This subsection applies to a patient who is subject to—

    (a)   a compulsion order and a restriction order;

    (b)   a hospital direction; or

    (c)   a transfer for treatment direction.

(8)   Where the appeal is against a decision mentioned in paragraph (w) of subsection (1) above, "relevant party" means—

    (a)   the person to whom the decision relates;

    (b)   that person's named person;

    (c)   any guardian of the person;

    (d)   any welfare attorney of the person;

    (e)   the Commission; and

    (f)   the relevant Health Board (within the meaning of section 273 of this Act).

(9)   Where the appeal is against a decision mentioned in paragraph (x) of subsection (1) above, "relevant party" means—

    (a)   the person to whom the decision relates;

    (b)   that person's named person;

    (c)   any guardian of the person;

    (d)   any welfare attorney of the person;

    (e)   the managers of the hospital; and

    (f)   if the person who applied for the order does not fall within paragraphs (a) to (d) above, the person who applied for the order.

321   Appeal to Court of Session against decisions of sheriff principal

(1)   A relevant party to an appeal to the sheriff principal under section 320(2) of this Act may appeal to the Court of Session against the decision of the sheriff principal allowing or refusing the appeal.

(2)   In subsection (1) above, "relevant party" has the same meaning as in section 320 of this Act.

322   Appeal to Court of Session against certain decisions of the Tribunal

(1)   This section applies to the following decisions of the Tribunal—

    (a)   a decision to make an order revoking a compulsion order under section 193(3) or (4) of this Act;

    (b)   a decision to make an order revoking a restriction order under section 193(5) of this Act;

    (c)   a decision to make an order varying a compulsion order under section 193(6) of this Act;

    (d)   a decision to make an order conditionally discharging a patient under section 193(7) of this Act;

    (e)   a decision, under section 193 of this Act, to make no order under that section;

    (f)   a decision, under section 215(2) of this Act, to make no direction;

    (g)   a decision to make a direction under section 215(3) or (4) of this Act;

    (h)   a decision to make or refuse to make an order under section 219(5) or 220(5) of this Act preventing a transfer or requiring that a transferred patient be returned; and

    (i)   a decision, in relation to a patient who is subject to a restriction order, a hospital direction or a transfer for treatment direction—

        (i)   to make or refuse to make an order under section 264(2), 265(3) or 266(3) of this Act;

        (ii)   under section 267(2) of this Act to recall or refuse to recall an order made under section 264, 265 or 266 of this Act;

        (iii)   to make or refuse to make an order under section 268(2), 269(3) or 270(3) of this Act; or

        (iv)   under section 271(2) of this Act to recall or refuse to recall an order made under section 268, 269 or 270 of this Act.

(2)   A relevant party to proceedings before the Tribunal may appeal to the Court of Session against a decision to which this section applies.

(3)   Subject to subsection (4) below, in this section "relevant party" means—

    (a)   the person to whom the decision relates;

    (b)   that person's named person;

    (c)   any guardian of the person;

    (d)   any welfare attorney of the person; and

    (e)   the Scottish Ministers.

(4)   Where the appeal is against a decision mentioned in paragraph (i) of subsection (1) above, "relevant party" means—

    (a)   the person to whom the decision relates;

    (b)   that person's named person;

    (c)   any guardian of the person;

    (d)   any welfare attorney of the person;

    (e)   the Commission;

    (f)   the relevant Health Board (within the meaning of section 273 of this Act); and

    (g)   the Scottish Ministers.

323   Suspension of decision of Tribunal pending determination of certain appeals

(1)   Where the Scottish Ministers appeal under section 322(2) of this Act against any decision of the Tribunal under section 193 of this Act, or a decision of the Tribunal to make a direction under section 215(3) or (4) of this Act, the Court of Session may, on the motion of the Scottish Ministers, order—

    (a)   that the patient in respect of whom the Tribunal's decision was made shall continue, subject to subsection (2) below, to be detained; and

    (b)   that both the compulsion order and restriction order or, as the case may be, the hospital direction or transfer for treatment direction to which the patient is subject shall continue to have effect accordingly.

(2)   An order under subsection (1) above has the effect of continuing the patient's detention—

    (a)   in a case where no appeal is made to the House of Lords against the decision of the Court of Session under section 322(2) of this Act, until the expiry of the time allowed to so appeal to the House of Lords; or

    (b)   in a case where such an appeal is made, until it is abandoned or finally determined.

324   Appeals: general provisions

(1)   An appeal—

    (a)   to the sheriff principal under section 320(2) of this Act; or

    (b)   to the Court of Session under section 322(2) of this Act,

may be made only on one or more of the grounds mentioned in subsection (2) below.

(2)   The grounds referred to in subsection (1) above are—

    (a)   that the Tribunal's decision was based on an error of law;

    (b)   that there has been a procedural impropriety in the conduct of any hearing by the Tribunal on the application;

    (c)   that the Tribunal has acted unreasonably in the exercise of its discretion;

    (d)   that the Tribunal's decision was not supported by the facts found to be established by the Tribunal.

(3) The Tribunal may be a party to an appeal under section 320(2) or 322(2) and in any appeal from the decision of the sheriff principal under section 321(1).

(4) The court may, where it considers it appropriate, order the Tribunal to be represented at any hearing of an appeal under section 320(2), 321(1) or 322(2).

(5) In allowing an appeal under section 320(2), 321(1) or 322(2) of this Act the court—

    (a) shall set aside the decision of the Tribunal; and

    (b) shall—

        (i) if it considers that it can properly do so on the facts found to be established by the Tribunal, substitute its own decision; or

        (ii) remit the case to the Tribunal for consideration anew.

(6) If the court remits a case under paragraph (b)(ii) of subsection (5) above, the court may—

    (a) direct that the Tribunal be differently constituted from when it made the decision; and

    (b) issue such other directions to the Tribunal about the consideration of the case as it considers appropriate.

(7) Regulations may specify the period within which an appeal under section 320(2), 321(1) or 322(2) of this Act shall be made.

(8) In this section, "the court" means the sheriff principal or the Court of Session as the case may be.

PART 23

GENERAL

325 Power to prescribe forms

Regulations may prescribe—

    (a) the form of any document that is required or authorised to be prepared by virtue of this Act; and

    (b) circumstances in which a form prescribed under paragraph (a) above for a document shall, or may, be used for the document.

326 Orders, regulations and rules

(1) Any power conferred by this Act on the Scottish Ministers to make orders, regulations or rules shall be exercisable by statutory instrument.

(2) Any power conferred by this Act on the Scottish Ministers to make orders, regulations or rules—

    (a) may be exercised so as to make different provision for different cases or descriptions of case or for different purposes; and

    (b) includes power to make such incidental, supplementary, consequential, transitory, transitional or saving provision as the Scottish Ministers consider appropriate.

(3)   A statutory instrument containing an order, regulations or rules made under this Act (other than an order under section 333(2) or (3) of this Act) shall, subject to subsection (4) below, be subject to annulment in pursuance of a resolution of the Scottish Parliament.

(4)   A statutory instrument containing—

    (a) an order under paragraph 3(3) of schedule 1 to this Act;

    (b) an order under section 330(1) of this Act containing provisions adding to, replacing or omitting any part of the text of an Act; or

    (c) regulations under section 21(3), 66(2), 234(2)(b), 237(3)(b), 240(3)(d), 240(5), 244, 268(11) to (14), 281(9), 284, 286, 290, 309, 310 or 313(5) of this Act,

shall not be made unless a draft of the instrument has been laid before, and approved by resolution of, the Scottish Parliament.

327   Directions

(1)   Any power conferred by virtue of this Act to give a direction shall include power to vary or revoke the direction.

(2)   Any direction given by virtue of this Act shall be in writing.

328   Meaning of "mental disorder"

(1)   Subject to subsection (2) below, in this Act "mental disorder" means any—

    (a) mental illness;

    (b) personality disorder; or

    (c) learning disability,

however caused or manifested; and cognate expressions shall be construed accordingly.

(2)   A person is not mentally disordered by reason only of any of the following—

    (a) sexual orientation;

    (b) sexual deviancy;

    (c) transsexualism;

    (d) transvestism;

    (e) dependence on, or use of, alcohol or drugs;

    (f) behaviour that causes, or is likely to cause, harassment, alarm or distress to any other person;

    (g) acting as no prudent person would act.

329   Interpretation

(1)   In this Act, unless the context otherwise requires—

    "the 1995 Act" means the Criminal Procedure (Scotland) Act 1995 (c.46);

    "advance statement" has the meaning given by section 275 of this Act;

    "approved medical practitioner" has the meaning given by section 22(4) of this Act;

"assessment order" means an order made under section 52D(2) of the 1995 Act;

"care plan", in relation to a patient, means a plan prepared under subsection (1)(a) of section 76 of this Act; and includes a reference to a care plan amended by virtue of subsection (3) or (4)(a) of that section;

"carer", in relation to a person, means an individual who, otherwise than—

(a)   by virtue of a contract of employment or other contract with any person; or

(b)   as a volunteer for a voluntary organisation,

provides, on a regular basis, a substantial amount of care for, and support to, the person; and includes, in the case where the person is in hospital, an individual who, before the person was admitted to hospital, provided, on a regular basis, a substantial amount of care for, and support to, the person;

"the Commission" means the Mental Welfare Commission for Scotland;

"community care services" has the meaning given by section 5A(4) of the Social Work (Scotland) Act 1968 (c.49);

"compulsion order" means an order made under section 57A(2) of the 1995 Act;

"compulsory treatment order" means an order made under section 64(4)(a) of this Act;

"designated medical practitioner" has the meaning given by section 233(2) of this Act;

"emergency detention certificate" means a certificate granted under section 36(1) of this Act;

"extension certificate" means a certificate granted under section 47(1) of this Act;

"guardian" means a person appointed as a guardian under the Adults with Incapacity (Scotland) Act 2000 (asp 4) who has power by virtue of section 64(1)(a) or (b) of that Act in relation to the personal welfare of a person;

"Health Board" means a board constituted by order under section 2(1)(a) of the National Health Service (Scotland) Act 1978 (c.29);

"hospital" means—

(a)   any health service hospital (as defined in section 108(1) of the National Health Service (Scotland) Act 1978 (c.29));

(b)   any independent health care service; or

(c)   any state hospital;

"hospital direction" means a direction made under section 59A of the 1995 Act;

"independent health care service" has the meaning given by section 2(5) of the Regulation of Care (Scotland) Act 2001 (asp 8);

"interim compulsion order" means an order made under section 53(2) of the 1995 Act;

"interim compulsory treatment order" means an order made under section 65(2) of this Act;

"local authority" means a council constituted under section 2 of the Local Government etc. (Scotland) Act 1994 (c.39);

"managers", in relation to a hospital, means—

(a) in the case of a hospital vested in the Scottish Ministers for the purposes of their functions under the National Health Service (Scotland) Act 1978 (c.29), the Health Board or Special Health Board responsible for the administration of the hospital;

(b) in the case of a hospital vested in a National Health Service trust, the directors of the trust;

(c) in the case of an independent health care service which is registered under Part 1 of the Regulation of Care (Scotland) Act 2001 (asp 8), the person providing the service; and

(d) in the case of a state hospital—

(i) where the Scottish Ministers have delegated the management of the hospital to a Health Board, Special Health Board, National Health Service trust or the Common Services Agency for the Scottish Health Service, that Board, trust or Agency;

(ii) where the management of the hospital has not been so delegated, the Scottish Ministers;

"medical practitioner" means registered medical practitioner;

"medical records" has the meaning given by section 77(1) of the Regulation of Care (Scotland) Act 2001 (asp 8);

"medical treatment" means treatment for mental disorder; and for this purpose "treatment" includes—

(a) nursing;

(b) care;

(c) psychological intervention;

(d) habilitation (including education, and training in work, social and independent living skills); and

(e) rehabilitation (read in accordance with paragraph (d) above);

"mental health officer" means a person appointed (or deemed to be appointed) under section 32(1) of this Act, and "the mental health officer", in relation to a patient, means a mental health officer having responsibility for the patient's case;

"mental health report" has the meaning given by section 57(4) of this Act;

"named person" means the person who is, in relation to another person, that other person's named person by virtue of any of sections 250 to 254 and 257 of this Act;

"National Health Service trust" means a body established by order under section 12A(1) of the National Health Service (Scotland) Act 1978 (c.29);

"notice" means notice in writing;

"patient" means a person who has, or appears to have, a mental disorder;

"primary", in relation to a carer, means the individual who provides all, or most, of the care for, and support for, the person;

"prison" includes any prison other than a naval, military or air force prison;

"recorded matter" has the meaning given by section 64(4)(a)(ii) of this Act;

"regulations" means regulations made by the Scottish Ministers;

"relevant services" has the meaning given by section 19(2) of the Children (Scotland) Act 1995 (c.36);

"restriction order" means an order made under section 59 of the 1995 Act;

"short-term detention certificate" means a certificate granted under section 44(1) of this Act;

"Special Health Board" means a board constituted by order under section 2(1)(b) of the National Health Service (Scotland) Act 1978 (c.29);

"state hospital" means a hospital provided under section 102(1) of the National Health Service (Scotland) Act 1978 (c.29);

"transfer for treatment direction" has the meaning given by section 136 of this Act;

"treatment order" means an order made under section 52M of the 1995 Act;

"the Tribunal" means the Mental Health Tribunal for Scotland;

"voluntary organisation" means a body, other than a public or local authority, the activities of which are not carried on for profit;

"welfare attorney" means an individual authorised, by a welfare power of attorney granted under section 16 of the Adults with Incapacity (Scotland) Act 2000 (asp 4) and registered under section 19 of that Act, to act as such; and

"young offenders institution" has the same meaning as in the Prisons (Scotland) Act 1989 (c.45).

(2) In this Act, unless the context otherwise requires, a reference to the Tribunal is, where the power conferred by paragraph 7(1) of schedule 2 is exercised, to be construed as a reference to the tribunal concerned.

(3) References in this Act to the giving of medical treatment to a person include references to medical treatment being performed on a person.

(4) References in this Act to a patient's responsible medical officer appointed by the managers of a hospital under any provision of this Act include references to any approved medical practitioner authorised by the managers to act in place of the responsible medical officer under section 230(3)(b) of this Act.

330   Supplementary provisions etc.

(1) The Scottish Ministers may by order make such supplementary, incidental or consequential provision as they consider appropriate for the purposes of, in consequence of, or for giving full effect to, any provision of this Act.

(2) An order under subsection (1) above may modify any enactment (including this Act).

331   Minor and consequential amendments, repeals and revocations

(1) Schedule 4 to this Act, which contains minor amendments and amendments consequential on the provisions of this Act, shall have effect.

(2)   The enactments mentioned in Part 1 of schedule 5 to this Act (which include provisions that are spent) are hereby repealed to the extent specified in the second column of that schedule.

(3)   The enactments mentioned in Part 2 of schedule 5 to this Act (which include provisions that are spent) are hereby revoked to the extent specified in the second column of that schedule.

332   Transitional provisions etc.

(1)   Schedule 6 to this Act (which contains certain transitory amendments of the Mental Health (Scotland) Act 1984) shall have effect.

(2)   The Scottish Ministers may by order make such other provision as they consider necessary or expedient for transitory, transitional or saving purposes in connection with the coming into force of any provision of this Act.

333   Short title and commencement

(1)   This Act may be cited as the Mental Health (Care and Treatment) (Scotland) Act 2003.

(2)   Chapter 3 of Part 17 of this Act shall come into force on 1st May 2006 or such earlier day as the Scottish Ministers may by order appoint.

(3)   The remaining provisions of this Act, other than this section and sections 325, 326, 330 and 332, shall come into force on such day as the Scottish Ministers may by order appoint.

(4)   Different days may be appointed under subsection (2) or (3) above for different purposes.

Mental Health (Care and Treatment) (Scotland) Act 2003 (asp 13)
Schedule 1—The Mental Welfare Commission for Scotland
Part 1—Membership, proceedings etc.

245

SCHEDULE 1

(*introduced by section 4*)

THE MENTAL WELFARE COMMISSION FOR SCOTLAND

PART 1

MEMBERSHIP, PROCEEDINGS ETC.

Status

1   The Commission shall not be regarded as the servant or agent of the Crown, or as having any status, immunity or privilege of the Crown, nor shall its members or employees be regarded as civil servants, nor its property as property of, or held on behalf of, the Crown.

General powers

2   The Commission may do anything which appears to it to be necessary or expedient for the purposes of, or in connection with, the exercise of its functions; and without prejudice to that generality the Commission may in particular—

   (a) acquire and dispose of land and other property; and

   (b) enter into contracts.

Membership

3 (1) The Commission shall consist of the following members appointed by Her Majesty on the recommendation of the Scottish Ministers—

   (a) a member appointed to serve as convener;

   (b) a minimum of three members, who have such qualifications, training and experience as may be prescribed by regulations, appointed to serve as medical commissioners; and

   (c) other members who meet such other requirements as may be so prescribed.

   (2) The person who holds the post of chief officer of the Commission shall—

   (a) be a member *ex officio* of the Commission; and

   (b) cease automatically to hold office as such member on ceasing to hold that post.

   (3) The Scottish Ministers may, after consulting such persons, or groups of persons, as they consider appropriate, by order—

   (a) amend sub-paragraph (1) above by—

      (i)   adding to that sub-paragraph categories of members; or

      (ii) removing from it a category which is for the time being set out there;

   (b) specify the number (including a minimum or maximum number) of—

      (i)   the members of the Commission; or

      (ii) any category of member,

      that may be appointed under sub-paragraph (1) above;

246   *Mental Health (Care and Treatment) (Scotland) Act 2003 (asp 13)*
Schedule 1—The Mental Welfare Commission for Scotland
Part 1—Membership, proceedings etc.

(c) specify the maximum term of appointment (including any reappointment) of a member appointed under that sub-paragraph; or

(d) amend sub-paragraph (2) above by adding to it further posts, the holders of which shall—

  (i) be members *ex officio* of the Commission; and

  (ii) cease to be such members on ceasing to hold such posts.

Terms of office etc.

4 (1) The provisions of this paragraph apply as respects a person appointed as member under paragraph 3(1) above.

  (2) Subject to the provisions of this schedule, the appointment shall be on such terms and conditions as the Scottish Ministers may determine.

  (3) Subject to section 23 of the Ethical Standards in Public Life etc. (Scotland) Act 2000 (asp 7), a person holds and vacates office as member in accordance with the terms of appointment of that person.

  (4) A person may resign office as member at any time by notice to the Scottish Ministers.

Eligibility for reappointment

5 Subject to paragraph 3(3)(c) above, a person who ceases, otherwise than by virtue of section 23 of the Ethical Standards in Public Life etc. (Scotland) Act 2000 (asp 7), to be a member of the Commission is eligible for reappointment.

Remuneration, pensions, allowances etc.

6 The Commission shall pay—

  (a) to its members (and to the members of its committees and sub-committees who are not members of the Commission) such remuneration and allowances—

    (i) on such terms; and

    (ii) subject to such conditions,

  as the Scottish Ministers may determine;

  (b) to, or in respect of, persons who have been a member of it (or such members of committees and sub-committees as are mentioned in paragraph (a) above) such pensions, allowances and gratuities—

    (i) on such terms; and

    (ii) subject to such conditions,

  as the Scottish Ministers may determine; or

  (c) to any person who ceases, other than on the expiry of a term of office, to be a member of it, such compensation as the Scottish Ministers may determine.

Appointment etc. of chief officer and other staff

7 (1) Subject to sub-paragraphs (2) and (3) below, the Commission—

Mental Health (Care and Treatment) (Scotland) Act 2003 (asp 13)
Schedule 1—The Mental Welfare Commission for Scotland
Part 1—Membership, proceedings etc.

247

(a) shall appoint a chief officer; and

(b) may appoint such other staff as it considers appropriate,

on such terms and conditions as it may, with the approval of the Scottish Ministers, determine.

(2) A member of the Commission may not be appointed as a member of its staff.

(3) The Commission shall obtain the approval of the Scottish Ministers before appointing a chief officer.

(4) The Commission may pay to the members of its staff, including its chief officer, (referred to in this paragraph collectively as "employees") such remuneration and allowances as the Scottish Ministers may determine.

(5) The Commission may—

(a) pay, or make arrangements for the payment of;

(b) make payments towards the provision of; and

(c) provide and maintain schemes (whether contributory or not) for the payment of,

such pensions, allowances and gratuities to or in respect of such of its employees, or former employees, as the Scottish Ministers may determine.

(6) The reference in sub-paragraph (5) above to pensions, allowances and gratuities includes a reference to pensions, allowances and gratuities by way of compensation for loss of employment or reduction in remuneration.

(7) A determination under sub-paragraph (4) or (5) above may make different provision for different cases or descriptions of case.

Regulations as to proceedings and delegation of functions

8 (1) Subject to sub-paragraph (2) below, regulations may make provision as to—

(a) the appointment of and composition of committees and sub-committees of the Commission (including committees and sub-committees which consist of or include persons who are not members of the Commission);

(b) the procedure of the Commission and of any of its committees or sub-committees (including the constitution of a quorum and the validation of proceedings in the event of vacancies or of defects in appointment);

(c) the exercise of functions by any such committee or sub-committee;

(d) the delegation by the Commission of any of its functions to any of its committees, sub-committees, members or staff; and

(e) what functions the Commission shall not so delegate.

(2) Before making regulations under sub-paragraph (1) above, the Scottish Ministers shall consult such persons, or groups of persons, as they consider appropriate.

Accounts

9 The following provisions of the National Health Service (Scotland) Act 1978 (c.29) shall continue to apply to the Commission as they apply to a Special Health Board—

(a) section 85 (which makes provision for payment of funds by the Scottish Ministers towards expenditure attributable to performance of functions by the Board);

(b) section 85A(1) and (3) (which imposes corresponding financial duties on the Board); and

(c) section 86 (which provides for the keeping, transmission to Scottish Ministers and auditing, of accounts).

PART 2

TRANSITIONAL PROVISION

10 (1)   The Mental Health (Scotland) Act 1984 (c.36) shall be amended as follows.

(2)   In section 2 (membership etc. of the Mental Welfare Commission)—

     (a) in subsection (2), after "commissioners", where it first occurs, insert "appointed under subsection (4) of this section";

     (b) in subsection (4), at the beginning, insert "Subject to subsection (5A) of this section,";

     (c) after subsection (5), insert—

     "(5A) The person who holds the post of chief officer of the Mental Welfare Commission shall—

         (a) be a member *ex officio* of the Commission; and

         (b) cease automatically to hold office as such member on ceasing to hold that post."; and

     (d) in subsection (7), for "the said commissioners", in both places where it occurs, substitute "commissioners appointed under subsection (4) of this section".

(3)   In section 6 (appointment and payment etc. of officers and staff)—

     (a) at the beginning, insert—

     "(1)   The Mental Welfare Commission shall appoint a chief officer on such terms and conditions as the Scottish Ministers may determine.

     (2)   Before appointing a chief officer under subsection (1) above, the Commission shall obtain the approval of the Scottish Ministers.

     (3)"; and

     (b) in subsection (3) (being the existing wording of the section)—

         (i) in paragraph (a), after "appoint", insert "other"; and

         (ii) in paragraph (b)(ii), after "of", insert "its chief officer or in respect of".

Mental Health (Care and Treatment) (Scotland) Act 2003 (asp 13) 249
Schedule 2—The Mental Health Tribunal for Scotland
Part 1—Members of the Tribunal etc.

SCHEDULE 2

(introduced by section 21)

THE MENTAL HEALTH TRIBUNAL FOR SCOTLAND

PART 1

MEMBERS OF THE TRIBUNAL ETC.

Members

1 (1)   The Scottish Ministers shall appoint as members of the Tribunal—

    (a)   a panel of persons who have such legal—

        (i)   qualifications;

        (ii)   training; and

        (iii)   experience,

    as may be prescribed in regulations for the purposes of serving as legal members of the Tribunal;

    (b)   a panel of persons who have such qualifications, training and experience—

        (i)   in medicine; and

        (ii)   in the diagnosis and treatment of mental disorder,

    as may be prescribed in regulations for the purposes of serving as medical members of the Tribunal; and

    (c)   a panel of persons who have—

        (i)   such qualifications, training, skills and experience in caring for, or providing services to, persons having a mental disorder; or

        (ii)   experience of such description,

    as may be prescribed in regulations for the purposes of serving as general members of the Tribunal.

  (2)   A person is disqualified from appointment as, and being, a member of the Tribunal if the person—

    (a)   is a member of the Scottish Parliament;

    (b)   is a member of the Scottish Executive or a junior Scottish Minister; or

    (c)   is of such other description as may be prescribed in regulations.

Shrieval panel

2   There shall be a panel consisting of each person who for the time being holds the office of—

    (a)   sheriff principal;

    (b)   sheriff; or

    (c)   part-time sheriff,

for the purposes of serving as sheriff conveners of the Tribunal.

250   *Mental Health (Care and Treatment) (Scotland) Act 2003 (asp 13)*
Schedule 2—The Mental Health Tribunal for Scotland
Part 1—Members of the Tribunal etc.

The President

3   (1)   The Scottish Ministers shall appoint a person to be known as the President of the Mental Health Tribunal for Scotland (the "President").

    (2)   The President—

       (a)   shall preside over the discharge of the Tribunal's functions; and

       (b)   may serve as a convener of the Tribunal.

    (3)   The Scottish Ministers may not appoint a person to be the President unless that person has such—

       (a)   qualifications;

       (b)   training; and

       (c)   experience,

as may be prescribed by regulations.

    (4)   The following provisions of this schedule apply (with the necessary modifications) to the President as they apply to a member of the Tribunal—

       (a)   paragraph 1(2);

       (b)   paragraph 4;

       (c)   paragraph 5; and

       (d)   paragraph 6.

    (5)   The functions of the President may, if the President is absent or otherwise unable to act, be discharged by one of the members of the panel mentioned in paragraph 1(1)(a) above appointed for that purpose by the Scottish Ministers.

    (6)   Regulations may make provision as to the delegation by the President of any of the President's functions to any of the members of the Tribunal or its staff.

    (7)   Regulations made under sub-paragraph (6) above may include provision for different functions to be delegated to different persons for different areas.

Terms of office etc.

4   (1)   Subject to this paragraph and paragraph 5 below, each member of the Tribunal shall hold office in accordance with the terms of such member's instrument of appointment.

    (2)   An appointment as a member of the Tribunal shall, subject to sub-paragraphs (3) and (4) below, last for 5 years.

    (3)   A member of the Tribunal—

       (a)   may at any time resign office by notice to the Scottish Ministers;

       (b)   shall vacate office on the day on which such member attains the age of 70; and

       (c)   shall vacate office on becoming disqualified from being a member of the Tribunal by virtue of paragraph 1(2) above.

    (4)   A member of the Tribunal's appointment shall come to an end upon the member's being removed from office under paragraph 5(1) below.

Mental Health (Care and Treatment) (Scotland) Act 2003 (asp 13) 251
Schedule 2—The Mental Health Tribunal for Scotland
Part 1—Members of the Tribunal etc.

(5) A member of the Tribunal whose appointment comes to an end by operation of sub-paragraph (2) above may be reappointed and, except in the circumstances set out in sub-paragraph (6) below, shall be reappointed.

(6) The circumstances referred to in sub-paragraph (5) above are that—

    (a) the member of the Tribunal has declined that reappointment;

    (b) the member of the Tribunal is aged 69 or over;

    (c) the President has made a recommendation to the Scottish Ministers against the reappointment;

    (d) there has, since the member of the Tribunal was last appointed, been a reduction in the number of members of the panel to which the member belongs required by the Tribunal to discharge its functions;

    (e) since the member of the Tribunal was last appointed, the member has, without reasonable excuse, failed to comply with the terms of the member's appointment; or

    (f) the member of the Tribunal does not have such qualifications, training, skills or experience as are for the time being prescribed under paragraph 1(1) above for appointment to the panel to which the member of the Tribunal belongs.

5 (1) A member of the Tribunal may be removed from office only by order of the disciplinary committee constituted under sub-paragraph (3) below.

(2) The disciplinary committee may order the removal from office of a member of the Tribunal only if, after investigation carried out at the request of the Scottish Ministers, it finds that the member is unfit for office by reason of inability, neglect of duty or misbehaviour.

(3) The disciplinary committee shall consist of—

    (a) a Senator of the College of Justice or a sheriff principal (who shall preside);

    (b) a person who is a solicitor or an advocate of at least ten years' standing; and

    (c) one other person,

all appointed by the Lord President of the Court of Session.

(4) Regulations—

    (a) may make provision—

        (i) enabling the disciplinary committee, at any time during an investigation, to suspend a member of the Tribunal from office; and

        (ii) as to the effect and duration of such suspension; and

    (b) shall make such further provision as respects the disciplinary committee (including in particular provision for the procedure of the committee) as the Scottish Ministers consider necessary or expedient.

Remuneration and pensions etc.

6 (1) The Scottish Ministers may pay, or make provision for paying, to, or in respect of, each member of the Tribunal such remuneration, expenses, pensions, allowances and

252   *Mental Health (Care and Treatment) (Scotland) Act 2003 (asp 13)*
Schedule 2—The Mental Health Tribunal for Scotland
Part 2—Organisation and administration of the Tribunal

gratuities (including by way of compensation for loss of office) as the Scottish Ministers may determine.

(2)   Sub-paragraph (1) above, so far as relating to pensions, allowances and gratuities, shall not have effect in relation to persons to whom Part I of the Judicial Pensions and Retirement Act 1993 (c.8) applies, except to the extent provided by virtue of that Act.

Part 2

Organisation and administration of the Tribunal

Organisation and administration of the functions of the Tribunal

7 (1)   The functions of the Tribunal shall be discharged by such number of tribunals as may be determined from time to time by the President.

(2)   The Tribunal shall sit at such times and in such places as the President may determine.

(3)   Subject to sub-paragraph (4) below, and to any rules made under paragraph 10(1) below, a tribunal constituted under sub-paragraph (1) above shall consist of—

    (a) a convener who shall be—

        (i)   the President; or

        (ii) a member selected by the President from the panel mentioned in paragraph 1(1)(a) above; and

    (b) a member selected by the President from each of the panels mentioned in paragraph 1(1)(b) and (c) above.

(4)   In relation to an application to the Tribunal under section 191 or 192 of this Act, the convener shall be—

    (a) the President; or

    (b) a person selected by the President from the panel mentioned in paragraph 2 above.

(5)   Subject to the provisions of this Act, regulations made under section 21 of this Act and rules made under paragraph 10 below, the President shall secure that the functions of the Tribunal are discharged efficiently and effectively.

(6)   The President may—

    (a) give such directions; and

    (b) issue such guidance,

about the administration of the Tribunal as appear to the President to be necessary or expedient for the purpose of securing that the functions of the Tribunal are discharged efficiently and effectively.

Staff and accommodation

8 (1)   The Scottish Ministers may appoint such staff and provide such accommodation for the Tribunal as they may determine.

(2)   The Scottish Ministers may pay, or make provision for paying, to, or in respect of, the Tribunal's staff, such remuneration, expenses, pensions, allowances and gratuities (including by way of compensation for loss of employment) as the Scottish Ministers may determine.

(3)   The persons mentioned in sub-paragraph (4) below shall, in so far as it is reasonably practicable to do so, provide, in response to a request by the President, accommodation for the holding of hearings by the Tribunal.

(4)   The persons referred to in sub-paragraph (3) above are—

    (a) a Health Board;

    (b) the State Hospitals Board for Scotland;

    (c) a local authority.

Finance

9   Such expenses of the Tribunal as the Scottish Ministers may determine shall be defrayed by the Scottish Ministers.

PART 3

TRIBUNAL PROCEDURE

Rules

10 (1)   The Scottish Ministers may make rules as to the practice and procedure of the Tribunal.

(2)   Such rules may, without prejudice to the generality of sub-paragraph (1) above, include provision for or in connection with—

    (a) the composition of the Tribunal for the purposes of its discharge of particular functions;

    (b) where the functions of the Tribunal are being discharged by more than one tribunal—

        (i) determining by which tribunal any proceedings are to be dealt with; and

        (ii) transferring proceedings from one tribunal to another;

    (c) the form of applications to the Tribunal;

    (d) the recovery and inspection of documents;

    (e) the persons who may appear on behalf of the parties;

    (f) enabling specified persons other than the parties to appear or be represented in specified circumstances;

    (g) requiring specified persons to give notice to other specified persons of specified matters in such form and by such method as may be specified;

    (h) as to the time within which any notice by virtue of sub-paragraph (g) above shall be given;

    (i) enabling any matters that are preliminary or incidental to the determination of proceedings to be determined by the convener alone or with such other members of the Tribunal as may be specified;

(j)   enabling hearings to be held in private;

(k)   enabling the Tribunal (or the convener, with such other members of the Tribunal as may be specified, as the case may be) to exclude the person to whom the proceedings relate from attending all or part of hearings;

(l)   enabling specified proceedings or specified matters that are preliminary or incidental to the determination of proceedings to be determined in specified circumstances without the holding of a hearing;

(m)   enabling the Tribunal to hear and determine concurrently two or more sets of proceedings relating to the same person;

(n)   the recording, publication and enforcement of decisions and orders of the Tribunal;

(o)   the admissibility of evidence to the Tribunal;

(p)   enabling matters to be referred to the Commission;

(q)   enabling the Tribunal to commission medical and other reports in specified circumstances;

(r)   requiring specified proceedings, or specified matters that are preliminary or incidental to the determination of proceedings, to be determined, or other specified actions to be taken, within specified periods;

(s)   the circumstances in which a *curator ad litem* may be appointed.

(3)   In sub-paragraph (2) above, "specified" means specified in the rules.

Practice directions

11   Subject to rules made under paragraph 10 above the President may give directions as to the practice and procedure to be followed by the Tribunal in relation to any matter.

Evidence

12 (1)   The Tribunal may by citation require any person to attend, at such time and place as is specified in the citation, for the purpose of—

(a)   giving evidence; or

(b)   producing any document in the custody, or under the control, of such person which the Tribunal considers it necessary to examine.

(2)   In relation to persons giving evidence the Tribunal may administer oaths and take affirmations.

(3)   A person who is cited to attend the Tribunal and—

(a)   refuses or fails—

(i)   to attend; or

(ii)   to give evidence; or

(b)   alters, conceals or destroys, or refuses to produce, a document which such person may be required to produce for the purposes of proceedings before the Tribunal,

shall, subject to sub-paragraph (4) below, be guilty of an offence.

Mental Health (Care and Treatment) (Scotland) Act 2003 (asp 13)
Schedule 2—The Mental Health Tribunal for Scotland
Part 4—Reports, information etc.

255

(4)   A person need not give evidence or produce any document if, were it evidence which might be given or a document that might be produced in any court in Scotland, the person having that evidence or document could not be compelled to give or produce it in such proceedings.

(5)   It shall be a defence for a person charged with contravening sub-paragraph (3) above to show that the person has a reasonable excuse for such contravention.

(6)   A person guilty of an offence under sub-paragraph (3)(a) above shall be liable on summary conviction to a fine not exceeding level 5 on the standard scale.

(7)   A person guilty of an offence under sub-paragraph (3)(b) above shall be liable—

(a) on summary conviction to a fine not exceeding the statutory maximum;

(b) on conviction on indictment to imprisonment for a term not exceeding 2 years or a fine or both.

Decisions of the Tribunal

13 (1)   Subject to sub-paragraph (2) below, where a decision is to be made by more than one member of the Tribunal, the decision of the Tribunal shall be made by majority.

(2)   If there is a tie, the convener shall have a second vote as a casting vote.

(3)   A decision of the Tribunal shall be recorded in a document which contains a full statement of the facts found by the Tribunal and the reasons for the decision.

(4)   The Tribunal shall—

(a) inform each party of its decision; and

(b) as soon as practicable after being requested to do so by one of the parties, send a copy of the document mentioned in sub-paragraph (3) above to each party.

PART 4

REPORTS, INFORMATION ETC.

Annual report

14 (1)   The President shall, in respect of each period of 12 months beginning on 1st April, prepare a written report as to the Tribunal's discharge of its functions during that period.

(2)   The President shall submit each report prepared under sub-paragraph (1) above, as soon as practicable after the period to which it relates, to the Scottish Ministers.

(3)   The Scottish Ministers shall lay before the Scottish Parliament a copy of each report submitted to them under sub-paragraph (2) above.

Disclosure of information

15   The President shall, at such times and in respect of such periods as the Scottish Ministers may specify, provide to—

(a) the Scottish Ministers;

(b) such persons as the Scottish Ministers may specify,

such information relating to the discharge of the Tribunal's functions as the Scottish Ministers may direct.

Allowances etc. for attendance at hearings of the Tribunal and preparation of reports

16 (1)   The Tribunal may pay to any person (other than a member of the Tribunal or a member of the staff of the Tribunal) such allowances and expenses as the President shall determine for the purposes of, or in connection with, the person's attendance at hearings of the Tribunal.

(2)   The Tribunal may pay to any person (other than a member of the Tribunal or a member of the staff of the Tribunal) such amounts as the President shall determine in connection with any report prepared by the person in accordance with rules made under paragraph 10(2)(q) above.

SCHEDULE 3

(introduced by section 71)

APPLICATION OF CHAPTER 1 OF PART 7 TO CERTAIN PATIENTS

1   Section 57(3) of this Act shall have effect as if, for paragraph (e), there were substituted the following—

"(e)   that it will be necessary, immediately after the hospital direction or, as the case may be, transfer for treatment direction to which the patient is subject ceases to have effect, for the patient to be subject to a compulsory treatment order.".

2 (1)   Section 64(4)(a)(i) of this Act shall have effect subject to the following—

(a)   where a compulsory treatment order is made in respect of a patient who is subject to—

(i)   a hospital direction; or

(ii)   a transfer for treatment direction,

that order shall authorise the measures specified in it only if the direction to which the patient is subject ceases, by virtue of section 217(2) of this Act, to have effect before the expiry of the period of 28 days beginning with the day on which the order is made; and

(b)   where—

(i)   a compulsory treatment order is made in respect of such a patient; and

(ii)   the direction to which the patient is subject ceases, by virtue of section 217(2) of this Act, to have effect before the expiry of the period of 28 days mentioned in sub-sub-paragraph (a) above,

the compulsory treatment order shall authorise the measures specified in it for the period of 6 months beginning with the day on which that direction ceases to have effect.

(2)   Section 64(5) shall have effect as if, for paragraph (e), there were substituted—

   "(e) that it will be necessary, immediately after the hospital direction or, as the case may be, transfer for treatment direction to which the patient is subject ceases to have effect, for the patient to be subject to a compulsory treatment order.".

3   Section 65 of this Act shall not have effect.

SCHEDULE 4
(introduced by section 331(1))

MINOR AND CONSEQUENTIAL AMENDMENTS

The Social Work (Scotland) Act 1968 (c.49)

1 (1)   The Social Work (Scotland) Act 1968 shall be amended as follows.

  (2)   In section 4 (assistance by voluntary organisations in performance of functions), for the words from "section 7" to "1984" substitute "section 25 (provision of care and support services for persons who have or have had a mental disorder), 26 (provision of services designed to promote well-being and social development of such persons) or 27 (assistance with travel in connection with such services) of the Mental Health (Care and Treatment) (Scotland) Act 2003 (asp 13)".

  (3)   In section 5(1B) (compliance by local authorities with directions by Scottish Ministers in exercise of functions under certain Acts), for paragraph (k) substitute—

      "(k) the Mental Health (Care and Treatment) (Scotland) Act 2003 (asp 13);".

  (4)   In section 5A(4) (local authority plans for community care services), in the definition of "community care services", for the words from "section 7" to "1984" substitute "section 25 (provision of care and support services for persons who have or have had a mental disorder), 26 (provision of services designed to promote well-being and social development of such persons) or 27 (assistance with travel in connection with such services) of the Mental Health (Care and Treatment) (Scotland) Act 2003 (asp 13)".

  (5)   In section 6—

    (a) in subsection (1)—

      (i) for the words from "section 7" to "1984", where they first occur, substitute "section 25 (provision of care and support services for persons who have or have had a mental disorder) or 26 (provision of services designed to promote well-being and social development of such persons) of the Mental Health (Care and Treatment) (Scotland) Act 2003 (asp 13)"; and

      (ii) in paragraph (a), for the words from "section 7" to "1984" substitute "section 25 or 26 of the Mental Health (Care and Treatment) (Scotland) Act 2003"; and

    (b) in subsection (2), for the words from "section 7" to "1984" substitute "section 25 or 26 of the Mental Health (Care and Treatment) (Scotland) Act 2003".

  (6)   In section 59(1) (provision by local authorities of residential and other establishments etc.), for the words "section 13A" substitute "sections 12 and 13A".

  (7)   In section 86(1) (recovery of expenditure on provision of services for person ordinarily resident in the area of another local authority), for paragraph (e) substitute—

"(e) in the provision, for persons ordinarily so resident, of services under section 25 (care and support services for persons who have or who have had a mental disorder), 26 (services designed to promote well-being and social development of such persons) or 27 (assistance with travel in connection with such services) of the Mental Health (Care and Treatment) (Scotland) Act 2003 (asp 13);".

(8)   In section 94(1) (interpretation), for the definition of "mental health officer" substitute—

""mental health officer" means a person appointed under subsection (1) of section 32 of the Mental Health (Care and Treatment) (Scotland) Act 2003 (asp 13); and includes a person deemed, by virtue of subsection (3) of that section, to be so appointed;".

The Local Government (Scotland) Act 1973 (c.65)

2   In section 64(5) of the Local Government (Scotland) Act 1973 (enactments concerning appointment of officers continuing to have effect), for paragraph (bb) substitute—

"(bb) section 32 of the Mental Health (Care and Treatment) (Scotland) Act 2003 (asp 13);".

The National Health Service (Scotland) Act 1978 (c.29)

3   In section 102(1) of the National Health Service (Scotland) Act 1978 (duty of Scottish Ministers to provide state hospitals)—

(a)   after the word "under" insert "the Criminal Procedure (Scotland) Act 1995 (c.46) or"; and

(b)   for the words "Mental Health (Scotland) Act 1984" substitute "Mental Health (Care and Treatment) (Scotland) Act 2003 (asp 13)".

The Disabled Persons (Services, Consultation and Representation) Act 1986 (c.33)

4 (1)   The Disabled Persons (Services, Consultation and Representation) Act 1986 shall be amended as follows.

(2)   In section 2(5)(b) (right of authorised representative to visit disabled person in accommodation provided by virtue of certain enactments), for the words "section 7 of the 1984 Act" substitute "section 25 of the 2003 Act".

(3)   In section 16(1) (interpretation)—

(a)   for the definition of "the 1984 Act" substitute—

""the 2003 Act" means the Mental Health (Care and Treatment) (Scotland) Act 2003 (asp 13);" and

(b)   in paragraph (b) of the definition of "the welfare enactments", for the words "sections 7 and 8 of the 1984 Act" substitute "sections 25 and 26 of the 2003 Act".

The Tribunals and Inquiries Act 1992 (c.53)

5   In Part II of Schedule 1 to the Tribunals and Inquiries Act 1992 (tribunals under the supervision of the Scottish Committee of the Council on Tribunals), after paragraph 54 insert—

"Mental health	54A. The Mental Health Tribunal for Scotland constituted under section 21 of the Mental Health (Care and Treatment) (Scotland) Act 2003 (asp 13).".

The Prisoners and Criminal Proceedings (Scotland) Act 1993 (c.9)

6   In section 4(1) of the Prisoners and Criminal Proceedings (Scotland) Act 1993 (persons detained under the Mental Health (Scotland) Act 1984 (c.36) by virtue of transfer direction and restriction direction), for the words from first "direction" to "given", substitute "for treatment direction under section 136(2) of the Mental Health (Care and Treatment) (Scotland) Act 2003 (asp 13) is made".

The Children (Scotland) Act 1995 (c.36)

7   In section 23(2) of the Children (Scotland) Act 1995 (children affected by disability), for the words from "suffers" to the end substitute "has a mental disorder (as defined in section 328(1) of the Mental Health (Care and Treatment) (Scotland) Act 2003 (asp 13))".

The Criminal Procedure (Scotland) Act 1995 (c.46)

8 (1)   The Criminal Procedure (Scotland) Act 1995 shall be amended as follows.

   (2)   In section 54 (insanity in bar of trial)—

        (a) in paragraph (c) of subsection (1)—

             (i)   in sub-paragraph (i), for the words from "he" to "1984" substitute "the conditions mentioned in subsection (2A) below are met in respect of the person";

             (ii) for the words "temporary hospital order" there shall be substituted "temporary compulsion order";

             (iii) for the words "committing him to that hospital" substitute "authorising the measures mentioned in subsection (2B) below in respect of the person";

        (b) after subsection (2) insert—

        "(2A) The conditions referred to in subsection (1)(c)(i) above are—

             (a) that the person has a mental disorder;

             (b) that medical treatment which would be likely to—

                  (i)   prevent the mental disorder worsening; or

                  (ii) alleviate any of the symptoms, or effects, of the disorder,

                  is available for the person; and

             (c) that if the person were not provided with such medical treatment there would be a significant risk—

    (a)   to the health, safety or welfare of the person; or

    (b)   to the safety of any other person.

(2B)   The measures referred to in subsection (1)(c)(i) above are—

    (a)   in the case of a person who, when the temporary compulsion order is made, has not been admitted to the specified hospital, the removal, before the expiry of the period of 7 days beginning with the day on which the order is made of the person to the specified hospital by—

        (i)   a constable;

        (ii)   a person employed in, or contracted to provide services in or to, the specified hospital who is authorised by the managers of that hospital to remove persons to hospital for the purposes of this section; or

        (iii)   a specified person;

    (b)   the detention of the person in the specified hospital; and

    (c)   the giving to the person, in accordance with Part 16 of the Mental Health (Care and Treatment) (Scotland) Act 2003 (asp 13), of medical treatment.";

(c)   in subsection (4), for the word "hospital" there shall be substituted "compulsion"; and

(d)   in subsection (8), after "section" insert—

    ""medical treatment" has the same meaning as in section 52D of this Act;

    "specified" means specified in the temporary compulsion order; and".

(3)   In section 57 (disposals in cases where accused found to be insane)—

    (a)   in subsection (2)—

        (i)   in paragraph (a), for the words from "make" to the end substitute "subject to subsection (4) below, make a compulsion order authorising the detention of the person in a hospital";

        (ii)   in paragraph (b), for the words from first "an" to the end substitute "such a compulsion order, subject to subsection (4A) below, make a restriction order in respect of the person";

        (iii)   for paragraph (bb), substitute—

            "(bb)   subject to subsections (3A) and (4B) below, make an interim compulsion order in respect of the person;";

        (iv)   in paragraph (c), for the words from "make" to the end substitute "subject to subsections (4C) and (6) below, make a guardianship order in respect of the person";

        (v)   in paragraph (d)—

            (A)   at the beginning insert "subject to subsection (5) below,"; and

            (B)   after "Act)" insert "in respect of the person";

    (b)   in subsection (3), for the word "hospital" substitute "compulsion";

    (c)   after subsection (3) insert—

"(3A) The court may make an interim compulsion order under paragraph (bb) of subsection (2) above in respect of a person only where it has not previously made such an order in respect of the person under that paragraph."; and

(d) for subsection (4) substitute—

"(4) For the purposes of subsection (2)(a) above—

(a) subsections (2) to (16) of section 57A of this Act shall apply as they apply for the purposes of subsection (1) of that section, subject to the following modifications—

    (i) references to the offender shall be construed as references to the person to whom this section applies; and

    (ii) in subsection (4)(b)(i), the reference to the offence of which the offender was convicted shall be construed as a reference to the offence with which the person to whom this section applies was charged;

(b) section 57B of this Act shall have effect subject to the modification that references to the offender shall be construed as references to the person to whom this section applies;

(c) section 57C of this Act shall have effect subject to the following modifications—

    (i) references to the offender shall be construed as references to the person to whom this section applies; and

    (ii) references to section 57A of this Act shall be construed as references to subsection (2)(a) above; and

(d) section 57D of this Act shall have effect subject to the modification that references to the offender shall be construed as references to the person to whom this section applies.

(4A) For the purposes of subsection (2)(b) above, section 59 of this Act shall have effect.

(4B) For the purposes of subsection (2)(bb) above—

(a) subsections (2) to (13) of section 53 of this Act shall apply as they apply for the purposes of subsection (1) of that section, subject to the following modifications—

    (i) references to the offender shall be construed as references to the person to whom this section applies;

    (ii) in subsection (3)(a)(ii), the reference to one of the disposals mentioned in subsection (6) of that section shall be construed as a reference to the disposal mentioned in subsection (6)(a) of that section;

    (iii) in subsection (4)(a), the reference to the offence of which the offender is convicted shall be construed as a reference to the offence with which the person to whom this section applies is charged; and

    (iv) subsection (6)(b) shall not apply;

(b)   section 53A of this Act shall have effect subject to the modification that references to the offender shall be construed as references to the person to whom this section applies;

(c)   section 53B of this Act shall have effect subject to the following modifications—

    (i)   references to the offender shall be construed as references to the person to whom this section applies; and

    (ii) for paragraphs (a) and (b) of subsection (8) there shall be substituted ", revoke the interim compulsion order and—

      (a)   make an order in respect of the person under paragraph (a), (b), (c) or (d) of subsection (2) of section 57 of this Act; or

      (b)   decide, under paragraph (e) of that subsection, to make no order in respect of the person.";

(d)   section 53C of this Act shall have effect subject to the following modifications—

    (i)   references to the offender shall be construed as references to the person to whom this section applies; and

    (ii) for paragraphs (a) to (c) of subsection (1) there shall be substituted—

      "(a) makes an order in respect of the person under paragraph (a), (b), (c) or (d) of subsection (2) of section 57 of this Act; or

      (b)   decides, under paragraph (e) of that subsection, to make no order in respect of the person."; and

(e)   section 53D of this Act shall have effect subject to the modification that the reference to the offender shall be construed as a reference to the person to whom this section applies.

(4C) For the purposes of subsection (2)(c) above, subsections (1A), (6) to (8) and (11) of section 58 of this Act shall apply, subject to the modifications that the reference to a person convicted and any references to the offender shall be construed as references to the person to whom this section applies.".

(4)   In section 58 (orders for hospital admission or guardianship)—

(a)   in subsection (1A), for the words "as mentioned in subsection (1) above" there shall be substituted "in the High Court or the sheriff court of an offence, other than an offence the sentence for which is fixed by law, punishable by that court with imprisonment,"; and

(b)   in subsection (7)—

    (i)   for the words from first "the" to first "suffering" substitute "(by reference to the appropriate paragraph (or paragraphs) of the definition of "mental disorder" in section 328(1) of the Mental Health (Care and Treatment) (Scotland) Act 2003 (asp 13)) the type (or types) of mental disorder that the offender has"; and

> (ii) for the words from "unless" to third "form" substitute "the descriptions of the offender's mental disorder by each of the medical practitioners, whose evidence is taken into account under subsection (1A)(a) above, specifies at least one type of mental disorder that is also specified by the other".

(5) In section 59 (hospital orders: restrictions on discharge)—

  (a) in subsection (1)—

> (i) for the words "hospital order" there shall be substituted "compulsion order authorising the detention of a person in a hospital by virtue of paragraph (a) of section 57A(8) of this Act"; and

> (ii) for the words "section 62(1) of the Mental Health (Scotland) Act 1984" there shall be substituted "Part 10 of the Mental Health (Care and Treatment) (Scotland) Act 2003 (asp 13)";

  (b) in subsection (2)—

> (i) for the words "medical practitioner approved by the Health Board for the purposes of section 20 of the Mental Health (Scotland) Act 1984" there shall be substituted "approved medical practitioner"; and

> (ii) for the words "section 58(1)(a)" there shall be substituted "section 57A(2)(a)"; and

  (c) after subsection (2) insert—

"(2A) The court may, in the case of a person in respect of whom it did not, before making the compulsion order, make an interim compulsion order, make a restriction order in respect of the person only if satisfied that, in all the circumstances, it was not appropriate to make an interim compulsion order in respect of the person.".

(6) For section 59A (hospital directions) substitute—

"Hospital directions

59A   Hospital direction

(1) This section applies where a person, not being a child, (in this section and in sections 59B and 59C of this Act referred to as the "offender") is convicted on indictment in—

  (a) the High Court; or

  (b) the sheriff court,

of an offence punishable by imprisonment.

(2) If the court is satisfied—

  (a) on the written or oral evidence of two medical practitioners—

> (i) that the conditions mentioned in subsection (3) below are met in respect of the offender; and

> (ii) as to the matters mentioned in subsection (4) below; and

  (b) that, having regard to the matters mentioned in subsection (5) below, it is appropriate, the court may, in addition to any sentence of imprisonment which it has the power or the duty to impose, make, subject to subsection (6) below, a direction (in this Act referred to as a "hospital direction") authorising the measures mentioned in subsection (7) below.

(3)   The conditions referred to in subsection (2)(a)(i) above are—

    (a) that the offender has a mental disorder;

    (b) that medical treatment which would be likely to—

        (i)   prevent the mental disorder worsening; or

        (ii) alleviate any of the symptoms, or effects, of the disorder,

    is available for the offender;

    (c) that if the offender were not provided with such medical treatment there would be a significant risk—

        (i)   to the health, safety or welfare of the offender; or

        (ii) to the safety of any other person; and

    (d) that the making of a hospital direction in respect of the offender is necessary.

(4)   The matters referred to in subsection (2)(a)(ii) above are—

    (a) that the hospital proposed by the two medical practitioners mentioned in subsection (2)(a) above is suitable for the purpose of giving the medical treatment mentioned in paragraph (b) of subsection (3) above to the offender; and

    (b) that, were a hospital direction made, the offender could be admitted to such hospital before the expiry of the period of 7 days beginning with the day on which the direction is made.

(5)   The matters referred to in subsection (2)(b) above are—

    (a) the mental health officer's report, prepared in accordance with section 59B of this Act, in respect of the offender;

    (b) all the circumstances, including—

        (i)   the nature of the offence of which the offender was convicted; and

        (ii) the antecedents of the offender; and

    (c) any alternative means of dealing with the offender.

(6)   A hospital direction may authorise detention in a state hospital only if, on the written or oral evidence of the two medical practitioners mentioned in subsection (2)(a) above, it appears to the court—

    (a) that the offender requires to be detained in a state hospital under conditions of special security; and

    (b) that such conditions of special security can be provided only in a state hospital.

(7)   The measures mentioned in subsection (2) above are—

      (a) in the case of an offender who, when the hospital direction is made, has not been admitted to the specified hospital, the removal, before the expiry of the period of 7 days beginning with the day on which the direction is made, of the offender to the specified hospital by—

         (i) a constable;

         (ii) a person employed in, or contracted to provide services in or to, the specified hospital who is authorised by the managers of that hospital to remove persons to hospital for the purposes of this section; or

         (iii) a specified person;

      (b) the detention of the offender in the specified hospital; and

      (c) the giving to the offender, in accordance with Part 16 of the Mental Health (Care and Treatment) (Scotland) Act 2003 (asp 13), of medical treatment.

(8)   The court shall be satisfied as to the condition mentioned in subsection (3)(a) above only if the description of the offender's mental disorder by each of the medical practitioners mentioned in subsection (2)(a) above specifies, by reference to the appropriate paragraph (or paragraphs) of the definition of "mental disorder" in section 328(1) of the Mental Health (Care and Treatment) (Scotland) Act 2003 (asp 13), at least one type of mental disorder that the offender has that is also specified by the other.

(9)   A hospital direction—

      (a) shall specify, by reference to the appropriate paragraph (or paragraphs) of the definition of "mental disorder" in section 328(1) of the Mental Health (Care and Treatment) (Scotland) Act 2003 (asp 13), the type (or types) of mental disorder that each of the medical practitioners mentioned in subsection (2)(a) above specifies that is also specified by the other; and

      (b) may include such directions as the court thinks fit for the removal of the offender to, and the detention of the offender in, a place of safety pending the offender's admission to the specified hospital.

(10) In this section—

        "medical treatment" has the same meaning as in section 52D of this Act; and

        "specified" means specified in the hospital direction.

59B   Hospital direction: mental health officer's report

(1)   This section applies where the court is considering making a hospital direction in relation to an offender under section 59A of this Act.

(2)   If directed to do so by the court, the mental health officer shall—

      (a) subject to subsection (3) below, interview the offender; and

      (b) prepare a report in relation to the offender in accordance with subsection (4) below.

(3)   If it is impracticable for the mental health officer to comply with the requirement in subsection (2)(a) above, the mental health officer need not do so.

(4)   The report shall state—

    (a) the name and address of the offender;

    (b) if known by the mental health officer, the name and address of the offender's primary carer;

    (c) in so far as relevant for the purposes of section 59A of this Act, details of the personal circumstances of the offender; and

    (d) any other information that the mental health officer considers relevant for the purposes of that section.

(5)   In this section, "carer", "primary", in relation to a carer, and "mental health officer" have the same meanings as in section 57C of this Act.

59C   Hospital direction: supplementary

(1)   If, before the expiry of the period of 7 days beginning with the day on which a hospital direction is made, it appears to the court, or, as the case may be, the Scottish Ministers, that, by reason of emergency or other special circumstances, it is not reasonably practicable for the offender to be admitted to the hospital specified in the hospital direction, the court, or, as the case may be, the Scottish Ministers, may direct that the offender be admitted to such other hospital as is specified.

(2)   Where—

    (a) the court makes a direction under subsection (1) above, it shall inform the person having custody of the offender; and

    (b) the Scottish Ministers make such a direction, they shall inform—

        (i)   the court; and

        (ii) the person having custody of the offender.

(3)   Where a direction is made under subsection (1) above, the hospital direction shall have effect as if the hospital specified in the hospital direction were the hospital specified by the court, or, as the case may be, the Scottish Ministers, under subsection (1) above.

(4)   In this section, "court" means the court which made the hospital direction.".

(7) In section 60 (appeals against hospital orders)—

    (a) for the word "hospital" where it first, second and fourth occurs there shall be substituted "compulsion"; and

    (b) for the word "renewal" there shall be substituted "extension".

(8) In section 60A (appeal by prosecutor against hospital orders etc.), in subsection (1), for paragraphs (a) and (b) substitute—

    "(a) a compulsion order;

    (b) a restriction order;

    (c) a guardianship order;

(d) a decision under section 57(2)(e) of this Act to make no order; or

(e) a hospital direction.".

(9) In section 60B (intervention orders), for the word "hospital" there shall be substituted "compulsion".

(10) In section 61 (requirements as to medical evidence)—

(a) in subsection (1), for the words from second "a" to "disorder" substitute "an approved medical practitioner";

(b) in subsection (1A)—

(i) for "53(1)" substitute "52M(2)(a), 53(2)(a)"; and

(ii) for "58(1)(a)(i)" substitute "57A(2)(a)";

(c) in subsection (2), after first "of" insert "section 52D(2)(a) or";

(d) in subsection (3), after "section" insert "52D(2)(a) or";

(e) in subsection (6), for "53(1), 54(1)(c), 58(1)(a) and 59A(3)(a) and (b)" substitute "52M(2)(a), 53(2)(a), 54(1)(c), 57A(2)(a), 58(1A)(a), 59A(2)(a) and 60C(2)(a)"; and

(f) after subsection (6) insert—

"(7) In this section, "approved medical practitioner" has the meaning given by section 22 of the Mental Health (Care and Treatment) (Scotland) Act 2003 (asp 13).".

(11) In section 118 (disposal of appeals), in subsection (6), for the words "(3) and (4)" substitute "(3) to (6)".

(12) In section 190 (disposal of appeal where appellant insane), in subsection (2), for the words "Subsection (4)" substitute "Subsections (3) to (6)".

(13) In section 200 (remand for inquiry into physical or mental conditions)—

(a) in subsection (2), for paragraph (b)(ii) there shall be substituted—

"(ii) that the accused could be admitted to a hospital that is suitable for his detention,"; and

(b) in subsection (3)(a), for the words "a suitable hospital is available" there shall be substituted "he could be admitted to a hospital that is suitable".

(14) In section 210 (consideration of time spent in custody), in subsection (1)—

(a) in paragraph (a), after "virtue" insert "of an assessment order, a treatment order or an interim compulsion order or by virtue"; and

(b) in paragraph (c)(iii), after "virtue" insert "of an assessment order, a treatment order or an interim compulsion order or by virtue".

(15) In section 230 (probation orders requiring treatment for mental disorder)—

(a) in subsection (1)—

(i) for the words "a registered medical practitioner approved under section 20 of the Mental Health (Scotland) Act 1984" there shall be substituted "an approved medical practitioner"; and

(ii) for the words "hospital order under Part V of that Act, or under this Act," there shall be substituted "compulsory treatment order under section 64 of the Mental Health (Care and Treatment) (Scotland) Act 2003 (asp 13) or a compulsion order"; and

(b) in subsection (2), in paragraph (a), for "1984" there shall be substituted "2003".

(16) In section 307 (interpretation), in subsection (1)—

(a) after the definition of "appropriate court" there shall be inserted—

""assessment order" has the meaning given by section 52D of this Act;";

(b) after the definition of "complaint" there shall be inserted—

""compulsion order" has the meaning given by section 57A of this Act;";

(c) after the definition of "indictment" there shall be inserted—

""interim compulsion order" has the meaning given by section 53 of this Act;";

(d) after the definition of "Lord Commissioner of Justiciary" there shall be inserted—

""mental disorder" has the meaning given by section 328(1) of the Mental Health (Care and Treatment) (Scotland) Act 2003 (asp 13);

"Mental Welfare Commission" means the Mental Welfare Commission for Scotland;"; and

(e) after the definition of "training school order" there shall be inserted—

""treatment order" has the meaning given by section 52M of this Act;".

The Adults with Incapacity (Scotland) Act 2000 (asp 4)

9 (1) The Adults with Incapacity (Scotland) Act 2000 shall be amended as follows.

(2) In section 35(5) (definitions of certain expressions for the purposes of Part 4 of Act), for the words "who is liable to be detained there under the 1984 Act" substitute "whose detention there is authorised by virtue of the Criminal Procedure (Scotland) Act 1995 (c.46) or the 2003 Act".

(3) In section 47(2) (authority in relation to medical treatment of incapable adult), after "section" insert "and sections 234, 237, 240, 242, 243 and 244 of the 2003 Act".

(4) In section 57 (application for guardianship order)—

(a) in subsection (3)(a), for "a" where it second occurs substitute "an approved"; and

(b) after subsection (6) insert—

"(7) In subsection (3)(a), "approved medical practitioner" has the meaning given by section 22 of the 2003 Act.".

(5) In section 87(1) (interpretation)—

(a) in the definition of "mental disorder", for the words from "means" to the end substitute "has the meaning given by section 328 of the 2003 Act";

(b) after the definition of "mental disorder" insert—

""mental health officer" has the meaning given by section 329 of the 2003 Act;";

(c) in the definition of "Mental Welfare Commission", for the words "section 2 of the 1984 Act" substitute "section 4 of the 2003 Act";

(d) in the definition of "nearest relative", for the words from "means" to the end substitute "has the meaning given by section 254 of the 2003 Act"; and

(e) after the definition of "the 1984 Act" insert—

""the 2003 Act" means the Mental Health (Care and Treatment) (Scotland) Act 2003 (asp 13).".

The Regulation of Care (Scotland) Act 2001 (asp 8)

10   In section 77(1) of the Regulation of Care (Scotland) Act 2001 (interpretation)—

(a) in the definition of "independent hospital", for the words from "is" to the end substitute ", subject to subsection (2) below, is not a health service hospital"; and

(b) in the definition of "mental disorder", for "Mental Health (Scotland) Act 1984 (c.36)" substitute "Mental Health (Care and Treatment) (Scotland) Act 2003 (asp 13)".

The Housing (Scotland) Act 2001 (asp 10)

11   In paragraph 4(6) of schedule 7 to the Housing (Scotland) Act 2001 (power of Scottish Ministers to remove director, trustee, etc. of a registered social landlord), for the words "Mental Health (Scotland) Act 1984 (c.36)" substitute "Mental Health (Care and Treatment) (Scotland) Act 2003 (asp 13)".

The Community Care and Health (Scotland) Act 2002 (asp 5)

12 (1) The Community Care and Health (Scotland) Act 2002 shall be amended as follows.

(2)   In section 4(1) (payment towards cost of accommodation more expensive than local authority would expect usually to provide), for the words from "section 7" to "authorities)" substitute "section 25 of the 2003 Act (provision of care and support services for persons who have or have had a mental disorder)".

(3)   In section 6(1)(a) (deferred payment of accommodation costs) for the words from "section 7" to "authorities)" substitute "section 25 of the 2003 Act (provision of care and support services for persons who have or have had a mental disorder)".

The Scottish Public Services Ombudsman Act 2002 (asp 11)

13   In schedule 3 to the Scottish Public Services Ombudsman Act 2002 (which specifies tribunals for the purpose of making the administrative actions of certain administrative staff of those tribunals liable to investigation under that Act), after paragraph 4 insert—

"4A   The Mental Health Tribunal for Scotland.".

270   *Mental Health (Care and Treatment) (Scotland) Act 2003 (asp 13)*
Schedule 5—Repeals and revocations
Part 1—Repeals

SCHEDULE 5

(introduced by section 331(2) and (3))

REPEALS AND REVOCATIONS

PART 1

REPEALS

Enactment	*Extent of repeal*
The National Health Service (Scotland) Act 1978 (c.29)	In section 102, paragraph (a) of subsection (4), the word "or" immediately following that paragraph and subsection (5).
The Mental Health (Scotland) Act 1984 (c.36)	The whole Act.
The Law Reform (Miscellaneous Provisions) (Scotland) Act 1985 (c.73)	Section 51(2)(b).
The Disabled Persons (Services, Consultation and Representation) Act 1986 (c.33)	In section 7(9), in paragraph (c) of the definition of "the managers", the words from "a State Hospital Management Committee" to "constituted)".
The Children Act 1989 (c.41)	In Schedule 13, paragraph 50.
The National Health Service and Community Care Act 1990 (c.19)	In Schedule 5, paragraph 13. In Schedule 9, paragraph 28.
The Access to Health Records Act 1990 (c.23)	In section 11, in the definition of "health service body", paragraph (c).
The Mental Health (Detention) (Scotland) Act 1991 (c.47)	The whole Act.
The Further and Higher Education (Scotland) Act 1992 (c.37)	In Schedule 9, paragraph 9.
The Prisoners and Criminal Proceedings (Scotland) Act 1993 (c.9)	Section 4(2) and (3). In Schedule 5, paragraph 2.
The State Hospitals (Scotland) Act 1994 (c.16)	Section 2(4) and (5).
The Children (Scotland) Act 1995 (c.36)	In Schedule 4, paragraph 33.

Mental Health (Care and Treatment) (Scotland) Act 2003 (asp 13) 271
Schedule 5—Repeals and revocations
Part 1—Repeals

Enactment	Extent of repeal
The Criminal Law (Consolidation) (Scotland) Act 1995 (c.39)	Section 13(3).
The Criminal Procedure (Consequential Provisions) (Scotland) Act 1995 (c.40)	In Schedule 4, paragraph 50.
The Criminal Procedure (Scotland) Act 1995 (c.46)	In section 52, subsections (2) to (7).
	In section 58, subsection (1); in subsections (2) and (3), the words "(1) or"; subsections (4) and (5); in subsection (7), the words "hospital order or" and "paragraph (a) of subsection (1)"; subsection (9); subsection (10); in subsection (11), the words "subsection (1) of".
	Section 59(3).
	In section 200(9), the words "within 24 hours of his remand or, as the case may be, committal,".
	In section 210(1), in paragraphs (a) and (c)(iii), the words "52, 53 or".
	In section 230(1), the words ", not extending beyond 12 months from the date of the requirement,".
	In section 307(1), the definitions of "hospital order", "residential establishment" and "responsible medical officer".
The Mental Health (Patients in the Community) Act 1995 (c.52)	Sections 4 to 6.

Schedule 2. |
| The Crime (Sentences) Act 1997 (c.43) | In schedule 3, paragraphs 6 to 10. |
| The Crime and Punishment (Scotland) Act 1997 (c.48) | Sections 7 and 8.

In Schedule 1, paragraph 9. |
| The Crime and Disorder Act 1998 (c.37) | In Schedule 8, paragraph 55. |
| The Health Act 1999 (c.8) | In Schedule 4, paragraph 70. |

272   *Mental Health (Care and Treatment) (Scotland) Act 2003 (asp 13)*
Schedule 5—Repeals and revocations
Part 1—Repeals

Enactment	Extent of repeal
The Mental Health (Public Safety and Appeals) (Scotland) Act 1999 (asp 1)	The whole Act.
The Mental Health (Amendment) (Scotland) Act 1999 (c.32)	The whole Act.
The Immigration and Asylum Act 1999 (c.33)	Section 120(4) and (5).
	In Schedule 15, paragraph 10.
The Adults with Incapacity (Scotland) Act 2000 (asp 4)	In section 9(1), the words "Without prejudice to their functions under the 1984 Act," and paragraphs (a), (b), (e) and (f).
	In section 12(1)(b), the words "or (e)".
	In section 35(1)(b), the words "or private psychiatric hospital".
	Section 38(4).
	In section 47(2), the words "and to".
	Section 48(1).
	In section 57(3)(a), the words from "approved" to the end.
	Section 87(2) and (3).
	In schedule 1, paragraph 1(c)(ii) and the word "or" immediately following it.
	In schedule 5, paragraph 17(3) to (24).
The Regulation of Care (Scotland) Act 2001 (asp 8)	Section 2(5)(b).
	In section 77, in subsection (1), the definition of "private psychiatric hospital" and, in subsection (2), the words "(not being a private psychiatric hospital)".
	In schedule 3, paragraph 11(2) to (7).
The International Criminal Court (Scotland) Act 2001 (asp 13)	Section 25.
The Scottish Public Services Ombudsman Act 2002 (asp 11)	In schedule 6, paragraph 6.

PART 2

REVOCATIONS

Enactment	Extent of revocation
The Scotland Act 1998 (Consequential Modifications) (No.2) Order 1999 (S.I. 1999/1820)	In Schedule 2, paragraph 74.
The Postal Services Act 2000 (Consequential Modifications No.1) Order 2001 (S.I. 2001/1149)	In Schedule 1, paragraph 60.

SCHEDULE 6
(introduced by section 332(1))

TRANSITORY AMENDMENTS OF THE MENTAL HEALTH (SCOTLAND) ACT 1984

1   Sections 33, 64 and 66 of the Mental Health (Scotland) Act 1984 (c.36) shall, until their repeal by this Act, have effect as follows.

2   In section 33 (discharge of patients from hospital), in subsection (4)—

     (a)   after "is", where secondly occurring, insert "not"; and

     (b)   in each of paragraphs (a) and (b) omit "not".

3   In section 64 (appeal by patient subject to restriction order)—

     (a)   in subsection (1)—

         (i)   after "shall" insert ", subject to subsection (2) of this section,";

         (ii)   after "is", where first occurring, insert "not";

         (iii)   in each of paragraphs (a) and (b) omit "not";

         (iv)   omit "and (in either case)" and paragraph (c);

     (b)   in subsection (2)—

         (i)   for "(1)" substitute "(A1)";

         (ii)   after "is", where secondly occurring, insert "not";

         (iii)   for the words from "not" to "subsection", where thirdly occurring, substitute "is satisfied that it is appropriate for the patient to remain liable to be recalled to hospital for further treatment".

4   In section 66 (further consideration of case of conditionally discharged patient) in subsection (3) after "is", where first, secondly and thirdly occurring, insert "not".

Printed in the UK by The Stationery Office Limited
under the authority and superintendence of Carol Tullo, the Queen's Printer for Scotland